BELIEVE

OLIVIA & RAF OCAÑA

First published by 5th Dimension Earth 2019.

Written by Olivia & Raf Ocaña.

Cover and illustrations formatted by Helen Poole.

To find out more about The Law of Attraction and Abraham-Hicks, © by Jerry & Esther Hicks please visit www.AbrahamHicks.com

ISBN 978-1-916402-92-8

CONTENTS

INTRODUCTION

Believe in more that you are, more than you know, more than you can see and hear and feel and taste and touch. Believe that there is eternalness, that you have access to broader perspective, to wider knowledge, to All That Is.

Now take this belief and bring with it your faith, faith that we are with you, that we will help and guide you to understand and know us better. Faith that you will experience the wonder as you open your hearts and minds to Non Physical energy. Faith that you will come to understand more than your current lifetime's experience would allow. We have chosen Raf and Olivia to be our Physical teachers. To transpose and translate our broadest perspective to you, so that you are able to understand all that is shared here with you. For it is with the most open mind and heart that you will be able to feel and understand all that is offered within this book and with it, offering you a connection that you have been longing for, yearning for.

We translate this book into a series of philosophical understanding topics, ones that we are able to share with you Universal insight and information in order for you to truly understand the meaning and the truth. We also have practical exercises for you to engage in so that you may be able to cement your understanding and move from learned information to true knowledge.

Much of this book is also inclusive of Olivia and Raf's own experience as we wish for them to share with you some of their Journey. This will help with the practical exercise application, for these to be something not only achievable for you but with the Physical context of experience. Read closely and allow yourself to Believe. Believe in you. We Believe in you.

We love you always.

Abraham and Jesus

I

WHO ARE WE?

WHO AM I – JESUS

I am the ascended soul of Jesus Christ. I am all that he is and so much more. For I, Jesus, am the head of The Christ Collective Consciousness. We are a Collective of almost a million other souls with many Collectives also within it.

The beautiful, precious soul of Jesus Christ still exists and always will. My Soul, Jesus, which ascended from that of Christ in a unique way, exists as a separate entity and a separate Soul. My role as the head of the Christ Collective Consciousness has so many wondrous functions here in Non Physical. My closeness to God and to Abraham is what has brought us together in this way and at this time, this very special time.

My message is for all, regardless of religious belief, and my message is of love. For love conquers all, as the saying goes, and little do you realise just how true this is. Ask Raf and

Olivia just how much love has freed them, fed them, guided them and shown them how to live the most wonderful lives.

All of you will meet me when you eventually transition to Non Physical for it is one of my many roles to greet all those that have died here on Earth and welcome them back to their friends here in heaven. Friends, Guides, loved ones will all eventually be reunited with you when you transition but just before this happens we spend some precious time together. For at this moment comes a time for us to reflect, to learn what you have learnt, to understand what you haven't and to rejoice in your growth for the time that you spent on Earth. This moment is one of the greatest love for you and a moment of nothing but joy at what you have understood, regardless of your experiences.

Take time to read this book, to feel every word, every sentiment, every piece of guidance and knowledge. Know that this is only the beginning for Abraham and Jesus. Know that together we aspire to share our love, our wisdom and our divine and infinite insight with all that seek it from us. Know that Raf and Olivia are here on Earth to share with you all that they are and all that we are. For through them this Universe opens up to you, through them love calls you and through them comes all that you ever wish to be.

Know this to be true, feel it, allow it and then share it. For through you our message can also be given. See yourself as this person. Desire to be the best that you can possibly be, to live a life without fear and instead live with utter freedom. And in doing so not only will you receive and share our message, you will become our message, you will become us.

We love you.

Jesus

2

WHO AM I – ABRAHAM

I, we, Abraham is accessible to all at all times. The energy that forms the Abraham Collective Consciousness is vast, expansive, Multiversal. This means that we, Abraham, is available to all, and I, Abraham, am available to all. For I am also a Soul, independent of the Collective, so close to God, so close to Jesus. Close to you all.

I am a Non Physical entity that has never been and never will be incarnate on Earth. I am an entity that expands this Universe as well as all others in the Multiverse. My role across all Universes differs but know that I am a Being of the greatest love for you and all others. It is through Olivia and Raf that something very special is happening now. Something so special that only time and evidence will truly allow you to connect to the reality of what can be made possible. Know too that this reality can be yours, the impossible made

7

possible for you, so keep this in mind as you read the words in this book.

The Collective of Abraham is not ever something to fear, feel is too big, feel is out of reach nor to hold yourself apart from. There are layers of Abraham energy through various Dimensions and with this you can almost imagine streams of Consciousness flowing through the Universes in various ways and therefore reaching individuals in order to assist, to help and to aid in greater understanding. For one of the Abraham Collectives reason for being is to share love, share understanding, share clarity and insight to all on all things here in this Physical experience and also through other Dimensions.

As you will learn about Collectives in this book, there is the ultimate energy that is the 'holder' of the collective and this ultimate energy is the Abraham energy that is channelled in this book, channelled through Olivia primarily but also through Raf and also who has channelled through Esther and Jerry Hicks. We offer now expansive new insight and information but know that all that has come before is where the broader Abraham energy can be 'tapped into' by all at all times through your Higher Self.

So, Ask. Ask Abraham for guidance. Allow that insight in should you so desire it.

Abraham

WHO AM I – OLIVIA OCAÑA

I am a child of God, as we all are. This doesn't feel strange to write, but here in my Physical body I am the child of Susan and Robin, the sister of Michael, the wife of Raf, the mother of Alex, Josh and Lily. I don't go to church. I don't come from a religious family. This knowing of who I am, this transcends all of that. For who am I eternally? I am the daughter of God. I am love. I am light. I am immense energy. I am hope. I am Truth. I am Balance. I am Desire. I am eternal. I am all that I am and all I have ever been before but I am new, here in this Physical experience, remembering who I am and expanding who I am.

And why am I doing this? And how do I know?

I BELIEVE. I believe to the utter core of all that I am that this is the truth. I feel utterly, without doubt that this is who I am. I trust. I trust in all that I receive for this could not EVER be made up and the love, the guidance, the insight that I have been given, this has come only from a place of love and for this I am truly and utterly grateful.

Have I always felt this way? No. In my life's experience I have endured, conquered, overcome, sacrificed, emerged, understood, suffered, loved, gained, lost and GROWN. For those who are closest to me, and there is no one closer to me now than Raf, what would he say? He would say I am Titanium. He would say I am Love. And what would I say about this life? I say, it was all worth it. I can say that already, and I haven't transitioned yet. So now my focus is not on what has happened but what is happening.

For I am Hope. I know I have said this, but what does that mean? That means that I see for our incredible world great, enormous, unquantifiable Change. I see bodies healing from the unhealable. I see Emotionally crippled beings being freed. I see abundance in all that is good being given and received. I feel energy like no other emerging through the decay, the sadness, the stress, the loneliness that is evident. I see a shift from looking at evidence and instead, feeling into what is possible. I see and FEEL immense connection. I see HOPE for each and every one of you reading this, feeling this, connecting to this, connecting to you, remembering who you are.

Who am I? I've remembered. I want to help you to remember too.

Olivia

WHO AM I - RAF OCAÑA

A proud father a loving son and brother, a devoted husband, a great friend? Yes.

Have I always been this? Yes.

Have I always felt this? No.

Have I always shown this? No.

So have I failed myself and others? No.

Were the failures in my life my fault and the fault of others? No.

So who's fault were they? God asks to take that blame for allowing my Journey.

Have I made the most of my life? At times I have but not fully until now.

Why did I not feel this way until now? It was all meant to be that way.

What about my successes were they mine or God's? Both.

Do I take credit for my successes only and ignore my influence on failures? I have influenced them both but the failures are not my fault and I accept both failures and successes with love for myself.

Do I think I've had it easy because the failures are not my fault? No, I have suffered greatly.

Do I take my failures lightly? Definitely not.

So do I take any responsibility over my failures? Oh yes. I take responsibility to heal to learn and to grow from them. This is all that God asks of me. This is all that God asks of all of us.

Connect to this right now. Allow this, feel the Truth of this and I promise that you will be led to all that you truly are.

So have I Changed? Oh yes, and for the better.

So who am I now? I am love, I am hope, I am truth, I am strength, I am trust. I have always been love but I have never felt love like I feel it now. I have never felt love for myself like I feel it now for myself. I have never allowed love like I allow it now for myself. I have never given love like I give it now to others. I have always been hope. Even in my darkest moments the light of hope has shone within me, guiding me, lifting me, building me. I have always been truth. So powerful in me is truth and the need for the truth and the need to be truthful. This is why when I was not truthful or not told the truth it created such a conflict in me. I do not fear the truth now, nor shall I ever again. And strength. Oh how strength has held me in, held me back, held me up, held me down. But now my strength drives me in a wondrous way, a powerful way. And then trust. How I have spent my life desperately seeking to trust and be trusted, and now at last I have found that place. And most of all in this place is trust of myself. My unique energy signature is Power (Strength + Love), and within this Power lies something so strong in me. Desire. Desire to inspire and be inspired.

What do love, hope, truth, strength and trust give me? They give me faith, in myself. They give me a connection to God. They make me like God. Not in a power-crazy egotistical way but in a way that Aligns me to all that he is, every single thing that he is. Connect to who you truly are and faith will do this for you too, eternally.

Am I eternal? Yes. I have lived many lives, not as Raf, there is only one Raf. Special Raf. The lives that I have lived are through my Higher Self. For all that he is and all that he has learned, all that he has ever felt and known, is within me. I feel this so strongly. I connect to all that I am because I connect to him. Precious him. Him who is always with me, him who always feels my pain and always feels my joy. Him who always knows my thoughts and always knows my fears, and him who always has the answer to all of my questions, even those that I dare not ask myself. Your Higher Self is with you right now in this way too and is just as accessible to you. You simply have to feel, to allow and to connect to the knowing that your Higher Self sees you as the perfect Human Being, no matter what you have done, no matter who you have hurt, no matter what you have said, no matter what you have thought.

Connect to this right now. Allow this, feel the Truth of this and I promise that you will be led to all that you truly are.

Is my Journey complete? No. It's only just warming up in this life. Today, right now and for eternity my Journey continues. My Journey as Raf started before the point of my conception on this Earth and as I entered the Physical world my Soul did so fully knowing the suffering that awaited me, but did so with courage and with the absolute belief that I could heal, that I would grow and that I would find a path of wonder and light. For this is my reason for being on this wonderful planet. Not just to find growth from the past, my painful past. Oh no, I am here to grow from love and joy and enlightenment. This was my mission set out in my Soul Contract. This is your mission should you choose to remember that you have already accepted it.

Connect to this right now. Allow this, feel the Truth of this and I promise that you will be led to all that you truly are.

What do I offer you? Freedom. Freedom to be, just be. Be anything, be everything, be nothing, just be.

Am I free? Yes.

Was it easy to achieve? No.

How did I do it? Love. A love for myself and those that I care for so dearly. Love is entwined into every part of my life now and therefore into every single word I have written in this book. Love from me, love from Olivia, love from Jesus, love from Abraham, love from my Higher Self, love from my other Guides, and love from God. In these written words of love you will find clarity. Clarity borne from the guidance that we have received from God, Jesus, Abraham and our Higher Selves. Words that have been wonderful, loving, trying, testing. Words that I have followed and acted upon, words that I have been inspired by, words that I have been so desperately hurt and angered by and words that have lifted me to freedom. For the words written in this book, based on the unwavering support provided so lovingly by our Guides, and accepted by Olivia and me with equal love, have literally held my hand through my Awakening and led me to you. Amazing you, angry you, fearful you, vulnerable you, loving you. Yes you ARE loving and you ARE love.

Connect to this right now. Allow this, feel the Truth of this and I promise that you will be led to all that you truly are.

So what do I desire the most now? Balance. Balance brings me peace and I so desire peace for myself. Peace within, peace without, peace with all and peace for all, all in my reality here on Earth. Peace brings me together, peace brings us all together, perfectly in Balance. For Balance in me and in all of us means Alignment. Alignment to the Self, and Alignment to the Self brings me Alignment to all that this Multiverse has to offer. So Balance is what I have always longed for and Balance is what is calling out to you in this book.

Connect to this right now. Allow this, feel the Truth of this and I promise that you will be led to all that you truly are.

Raf

WHO ARE WE – THE ABRAHAM AND JESUS COLLECTIVE

We are a newly created Collective made up of current Physical Souls as well as Non Physical Souls. We are Raf Ocaña, Olivia Ocaña, Jesus, Abraham, Adam, Ophelia and God.

Who are Adam and Ophelia? They are Archangels, unknown to many and they are the Higher Selves of Raf and Olivia. They are the very first Souls ever created by God billions of years ago. They are the Higher Selves of the very first human Souls and are the Higher Selves of many other notorious, magnificent and famous Souls on Earth. They are Love, Desire, Balance, Truth and almighty Strength, and through Raf and Olivia they plan to help take things on this planet to a place it has never been thought possible before. And trust us they are more than capable of this.

Trust that this Collective will succeed in bringing Earth to 5th Dimension living. Trust this Earth will achieve a perspective where all that live on it will live in harmony with themselves and each other. Trust this Earth will be abundant and safe and Balanced. Trust this Earth will offer freedom and hope and love and so much more. And why will it do this?

Because we have God on our side, on your side. Because God has decided that the time is now. God has recognised that the world needs him now more than ever and he has answered your call. God knows that there are so many of you out there right now leading your own drive for 5th Dimension Earth and he is here to help you and ask for your help too.

For the Abraham and Jesus Collective is not an exclusive club. Oh no. We need you to come on board, to shift your Vibration to that of Non Physical and then be ready. Be ready to take this planet by storm and spread the goodness to everyone else so that they can join this Collective too.

You see we can't do this alone. We need you and this is why the time has come for an intervention. An intervention of love so strong you won't be able to avoid it. You may be able to disallow it and this is your choice but our greatest Desire is that not only do you allow it but that you also give it back to you, to others, to everyone and when you're done giving love, allow yourself to sit and accept some more for you.

Love is everything that this Collective shares with you in this book. Read it feel it love it. Yes that's right, love love, and love yourself in the process.

We love you.

God, Ophelia, Adam, Abraham, Jesus, Olivia and Raf

II

WONDROUS INSIGHT

AWAKENING

Just take a moment to ask yourself what the word 'Awakening' really means to you. Perhaps you envisage a Journey of wonder and hope, full of discovery and enlightenment. As two people that have been through this we can certainly say that you would be right to say this. But we also say, that Awakening comes at a price.

For in order for you to truly release yourself from the past, to break free from those limiting beliefs, negative thought patterns and the Emotional pain that can so imprison you, you need to be prepared to give your all, and we mean ALL.

This means complete and utter honesty with yourself and those that you love, personal sacrifice in order to at times run through Emotional walls of pain and hurt, and the sheer will to carry on when there is no end in sight. All of this takes courage, it takes hope, faith and trust in those around you and in particular those in Non Physical that love you so.

For at times know that despite the love that they have for you, all that you will see and feel towards them is anger, frustration and at times disbelief that they are putting you through an experience that is supposed to be taking you to a better place.

We often hear the term 'asleep' used for those that are yet to Awaken but for some the word 'comatose' would perhaps be more appropriate. For being in a coma is a more descriptive of how distant some people can be from themselves, how they really feel and who they truly are. And for this reason we prefer to use the term 'disconnected' for those that are yet to fully Awaken.

Still want to Awaken?

Pain is not something that appeals to us humans and in particular Emotional pain, and it is this which we would like to focus on as it has formed such a huge part of both of our Journeys. It's not until you start to release yourself from some of these Emotions that you realise just how much they blight your life, impact your Vibration and in doing so stop you from being the best that you can be.

At our first ever event in London for The 25 Messages from Heaven, Jesus eluded to the fact that we (Raf and Olivia) are infinitely linked through our Higher Selves and that their Soul incarnations when on Earth at the same time, are always together as husband and wife. What we have since discovered is that in this life our Emotional experiences are also linked, in fact completely comparable and something that was amazing to understand.

For we have both suffered in our lives, something that is particular to all the previous lives on Earth of our Higher Selves when they have visited this planet. Of course we are not alone in this and many of you reading this book will have suffered Physically, mentally and Emotionally through your own lives. But for us it was fascinating to discover through our Awakening Journey that traumas in our personal situations and family's lives, although not exactly the same, lead to the same Emotional impacts and therefore the holding of similar limiting beliefs and fears.

So why after 20 years of being together could we not recognise this! Well that's simple, we didn't talk about it. And this point should not be lost on you, in fact it's probably the most important point to understand in all that we say in this chapter. As humans, even with those that we love the most, our fears often control key parts of our thinking and our actions. So a couple so much in love with each other, as we are, will often hide their deepest fears for many reasons.

It could be to protect those that we love, or not wanting to be seen as weak or not good enough, or often it is because we actually just don't recognise the fears as what they are. For we can spend years, often from an early age, hiding and covering up what we are afraid of, and so by the time we reach adulthood those fears have morphed into something completely unrecognisable even to yourself. And so the practiced behaviours or spiralling thoughts that become part of your everyday life are so well hidden that you yourself won't realise it, let alone those closest to you.

So what has this got to do with Awakening? Well everything.

For it is in the understanding of this that you can recognise why it is your whole life has been the way it has. And the deeper and more painful these Emotions are, the further disconnected you become from who you truly are and the harder it is for you to lead a happy life. You can become so far removed from yourself that literally nothing can take away the pain that blights your life like a dull ache pulling at you, influencing you and literally destroying you.

So it is only in the recognition of your disconnection to your Self that the Awakening can begin. In our particular experience our Higher Selves and Guides, Jesus and Abraham, played a huge role in this, and in the beginning this was hard for us both. For what they did was highlight for us some of those Low Vibrational Emotions that we still held in us, leaving us at times with feelings of utter despair, loss of hope, isolation, fear of everything, even fear of the good.

During our Awakening we were Physically impacted, taken through extreme symptoms of fever, pain and for long periods left with a feeling of being so drained of life and even the energy and enthusiasm to get out of bed. These were challenging times, especially when our Guides made the decision that would have hurt them so, of stepping back from all of this in order for us to find a way through some this with very little guidance. Not because they wished for us to suffer but because in going through some the Journey alone so much more was seen, felt and learnt. And in going through a section of this Journey alone we were ultimately mirroring the lives of many of those that we work with and thereby so much more able to give guidance on how they too could find a way out of the difficulties that they face, no matter how large or small the issues.

So what does disconnection from the Self actually mean? It's a disconnection from being the best that you can possibly be. It's also a disconnection from your Higher Self, a Non Physical entity full of love for you and most important of all, a Being whose perception of you is that you are absolutely perfect, and literally nothing anyone (including you) can say or do will ever Change the way your Higher Self sees it. Your Higher Self is your safe haven, your absolute protector and giver of total unconditional love, for you. So when we as humans go about our lives questioning ourselves at work or in relationships, full of anger for what happened to us as children or in the more recent past, or feeling fear because of judgement from those that we love the most, all that this is doing is making the perception that we have of ourselves completely the opposite of what our Higher Self sees. And herein forms the disconnection from the Self, from who you truly are, from the energy of your Inner Being that is so tied to your Higher Self.

And so full of these deeply held Emotions our lives can manifest themselves into a world of self-sabotaging thoughts and Low Vibrational feelings which depending on the depth of pain and length of time held can lead to a life of Physical ailments or mental health issues which at times can be so difficult to deal with, that life becomes wrapped in a continual cloak of despair. And for those of you that are reading this and thinking this is extreme and therefore you must be fine and not disconnected from who you are, think again. For we doubt if there are too many of us that doesn't hold a fear, or apprehension, or a negative view of themselves or isn't holding something within that they wouldn't dare tell anyone, or have found it difficult to share, this list no doubt could go on. And so all of these examples no matter if extreme, or considered relatively mild in comparison, can be classed as indicators of your own disconnection from your Self and Higher Self.

So what's the harm in being a little disconnected you say? And we say, so much harm. For over time self-sabotaging thoughts can become more common, literally every minute. Your Vibration and love for life can be so sapped potentially leading you to dark places, lonely places, frightening places. And as humans when trapped in a corner we tend to lash out to defend ourselves and whilst we may not be facing a hungry lion in this Emotionally debilitating corner, our instincts are the same and this leads us at times to do things that are far removed from who we really are just to be able to escape the Emotional battering. And so we carry out activities as part of the escape plan out of this Emotional corner, it could be a spending spree, a drinking binge or perhaps a lot worse and whilst a temporary reprieve can often be obtained, very soon after, the pain, the guilt, the shame, the anger, the despair will return.

Still want to Awaken?

If any of the above applies to you then the answer should be an absolute YES!

And so how, when potentially faced with such debilitating circumstances, do we move beyond all of this? Well, the answer is simple, love. It's about making a personal choice that at times will be so difficult to make. Those times when you are in Physical pain and think there's never going to be a day when you don't feel it. The mornings when you can't get out of bed and you're feeling so low that you just want to curl under the cover and stay there. When you are so spiralling with Emotional thoughts and feelings of hurt, anger, betrayal, disbelief, despair that you literally want to end it, these are the times when you make that choice. A choice that is so powerful it can literally mean the difference between life and death, a good day or a dark day, a moment of utter appreciation or total depreciation. A conscious choice to choose love, but not just any old love, this is total and unconditional love for YOU.

For in doing this you connect to that part of you that you may have long since been disconnected from; this is your Inner Being, the Self. Your Inner Being that together with your Higher Self makes you Whole and that can lead you to your strength, your power, to the pure positive energy that is you, that is love. And in doing so put you onto those tracks of that perfect circle that allows you to feel love for you and then for others and then receive it back. This Journey of Awakening can lead you to memories of those that have hurt you so much in the past but in connecting to their story and to their own pain you further understand and find love and compassion for them. From this place you allow yourself to move on, not to forgive but to forget and to let go and in doing so you continue on giving to yourself yet more love and carry on that circle of love.

On the subject of moving on we will talk about this in another chapter but we want to bring you back to the choice, the choice of love. This choice is not an easy one to make, it takes willpower and so much more. So difficult this choice, in particular if you are embroiled in the mental, Emotional or Physical prisons that we can find ourselves in. And this is why love for you is key, not only key but the only way. A love for you that says you deserve better, that you can have a great life, that you have suffered enough. A love that sees only light, happiness and appreciation for all that you are and all that is in your life. This starts small, catching those fearful thoughts and trying to turn to them into feelings of appreciation.

It could be the family photo on the fireplace, the happy face of the dog, a kind deed from a stranger in a shop, anything that connects you to that circle of love. And in doing so not only will you feel better and perhaps more motivated, but you will also be manifesting more love for you. For it is in those moments when you just don't feel like doing anything positive, when the world is such a harsh place to live in that you just don't have the energy to make the effort, or that it's not worth the effort, it is in these moments that you need to know that making that choice will lead you to something better, and better and better.

And maintaining this approach takes dedication and a belief that you can get better, that enough is enough with the negativity. It means no longer yearning for love where it isn't forthcoming and instead connecting to the love of those friends or family that you truly feel it from. Connecting to the love that you feel within and telling yourself that you do deserve this. The connection to these things is what brings the feelings of safety and security that truly allows you to actually believe these words. And so this takes practice and it's not just about connecting to positive thoughts, experiences and feelings but making sure that you also don't reach for those negative thoughts that you are so used to directing yourself to and that you have undertaken habitually in the past almost like an addiction.

Don't undertake this task alone, try to relive and share a moment with a friend about something you did together last week, send them a message of love or a great story via email, the support of those around you is essential. Be kind to yourself when searching for these positive feelings. Squeezing yourself to the back of the lift to allow one more person in is a great thing to do, so appreciate that you are the sort of person that does these things. Appreciate the interruptions in your busy life no matter how inconvenient, the kids, the phone, the man to read the electric meter. Looking to rush through these moments so you can get back to what you were doing will not help your Vibration so take the chance to do something different for a minute or two.

Don't overthink or berate yourself and remember that you are human and can make mistakes or do things that your parents said were wrong or behave in ways that don't exactly match with what society or the media or your communities say. It's all too easy to see the negative in these situations whether it be in your own thoughts or in the answers or reactions you receive from the people that you interact with. So stop 'mind reading' them or pre-paving the negative responses from them and start connecting to LOVE.

Prioritising you is essential so remember it's ok to say no to people. Don't connect to the guilt of this, connect to the strength and freedom of it. And of course, life will get in the way, so try to do all of this from a place of some ease and feeling good. For some this will simply mean going for a walk or meditating, others will need to work much harder at it over a period of time and will need to think about what external factors there are that they may need to control to effect this; medication, alcohol, too much time on phones and laptops etc.

We know this may all sound too difficult or time consuming for some and having gone through our own Awakening experience we completely understand this. For others you will feel very motivated by this but perhaps will have a nagging doubt that you may not be able to see it through or have the courage to unturn those stones that you have been ignoring but that drive your Low Vibration. Know that for all of you, hope is the key and know that hope truly does exist for you if you search for it, because it is within each and every one of you, in fact hope beyond measure.

When you perhaps have heard words like this before they may have seemed unobtainable to you but they are not. Hope is one of the truest Emotions that you can connect to that can lead you on your path to Awakening. Hope is eternal, that flame of what could be. Hope is an Awakening point, where no matter what you think or feel in the moment there is somewhere or something inside of you that hopes for better. Hope is a trigger, hope is a reminder to you of what Awakening really means.

So what does it mean?

Awakening is remembering. Remembering who you really are and what you really know. It means connection not only to the Self, your Inner Being, but to the broadest perspective of you and your connection to the Universe through your connection to your Higher Self and all that is beyond that, for those of you that want to extend it that far. And through this connection to your Higher Self you will become more Aligned to the truth of who you are and truly happy because of it.

You will feel a sense of freedom, a sense of Wholeness, with very little reliance on others, which is so key for it's with this understanding and ability that nothing can steer you off your path. Instead you will have a great reliance on your own feelings of connection and to your Inner Being and by doing so you will notice quickly when things are a little out of kilter.

You will feel strength within and a Physical Balance. Not big diving peaks and troughs of Emotion but stillness within, the boat that barely rocks. You will be able to enjoy the small things, to experience contrast but swiftly be able to adjust back to Balance. Awakening means living in truth, the truth of you and your Change, and because of this no other opinion will alter that, the boat will not be rocked, only you will do the rocking and this is one the greatest gifts your Awakening will give you. By living your life in truth, you do not hide who you are, what you think or feel, because you can't. Because in doing so it takes you away from the Self and that makes you feel strange or worse still you feel extremely ill at ease and disconnected from all that you have just learnt, so you just don't let that happen.

31

So how do you know that you are Awakening?

You will feel it, there is no escaping it. The call for Change will hit you both Physically and Emotionally and your Higher Self will be at the centre of it. We have travelled on this path together side by side, but we have not been constant mirrors in this Awakening. We know from our Guides that this was meant to be this way. There were different aspects and understandings that were critical for us to unfold individually and together, to understand so that we can help those that we work with. At times we have been a catalyst for the other, at times the safe haven, the one that supported the other and then at times the challenger for the other. For it takes contrast always in life, in order to expand and this completely Aligns to our Awakening.

Your Awakening will not be one dawn of a new day. It takes time and in fact in our experience we would like to reference a term instead which is a 'rebirth' which took us over a year. This doesn't mean that the after a year passed it was all complete, ta-dah! No, this means that over that period we were being strongly stretched, challenged, enlightened, connected, trained, filled with wonder and experience and led to understand the depths of all that we are. But this continues, we carry on learning, we carry on being challenged and this is how it will always be for this is the role of those that truly Awaken. And so it is with trust, belief, faith and hope that we continue.

Also know that what we have spoken of briefly here will not represent everyone's Journey for every single person is unique. You are on a continual quest for expansion. This is the whole purpose of your Being. What your Awakening, this rebirth, can signify is the start of expansion, expansion here on Earth. Take this Journey that is given even when not understood, learn from it, love it and allow it, no matter how difficult for the rewards are wondrous. And we implore you to seek support from others should you accept this challenge. You will attract them by being true, by feeling your way to who you can connect with during this experience.

Remember to undertake all of this with great love for yourself. Follow the impulse, the inspiration, perhaps seemingly out of nowhere but totally Aligned to you, it will just feel right. Then just keep following, stepping and allowing, and when this happens be open to it, trusting, focused. At a deep level, understand that no matter what is happening to you it comes with the greatest love from those in Non Physical and with understanding and acceptance that you will start to gain the clarity and an unfolding to the knowing of all that you are.

It is this connection to the understanding of your Journey, to the love that surrounds it from Non Physical that truly brings the acceptance and therefore, importantly with this comes the desire. It is that desire that will pull you through what could be a very difficult Journey and it is desire that will see you over that line. For have no doubts that there will be times when you look at all that you have learnt and all that you have felt and yet you will still feel like there is no end in sight, scarred by the challenges of what you have conquered, it is the finishing line that will stare you in the face and fill you with the most fear.

Fear that you will never be who you feel inside you are, fear and that you will not even be able to return to those positive parts of you that existed before your Awakening began. For know that this Journey will Change you, not beyond recognition, but sufficiently for you to perhaps not know how to live in this new skin and in this enhanced soul and way of living, and so in this moment turn to desire. Desire to allow you to dare that this is going to happen, that your life is going to Change forever and that you will be everything that you can be and wish it to be.

The finish line is nearing at this point. You will feel strong and in control. You will know instinctively what to do or what your Higher Self is leading you to and if you listen carefully you will get over that finishing line. It takes bravery and trust to complete this stage in your Journey but know that all that you have learnt will allow you to do this. Go with what you feel, always, and forget that the finishing line is there. Focus on what's important, on what matters to you, what drives your desires, it could be your relationship, your family or your career. Just try and remember why you're on this Journey and take your conscious thoughts away from ticking the boxes of the final tasks that you see need to be completed. The jigsaw WILL complete itself.

And with the completion of this jigsaw know that your Awakening is just a feeling away. Be conscious of your habitual thoughts and behaviours and the old yearnings to connect to pain, for these may make you feel something that does not exist, a disconnection or a fear for something that has already been dealt with. The Subconscious Mind has been the master of many of us for many years and so it takes dedication, determination and so much love in puncturing its control in order to allow you to live your new truth.

And what is that truth?

That truth is something simply quite amazing, astounding and astonishing to those that will never have felt this feeling before. This feeling that you are totally and utterly in full Alignment to the Universe, and with that everything that it has to offer and all that you have ever desired. Wow, what a feeling this is and know that when you get there you will have truly Awakened. And with this Awakening will come the understanding that what you have learned is just the beginning. The beginning of the next chapter in your eternal existence, a chapter that will still hold tough challenges for you but that will be full of wonder, opportunity and excitement.

And so finally we bring this back to a choice. Will you have the strength to consistently and in your most difficult moments choose you, choose love? This is the question only you can answer but know that if you can do this you will Awaken, you will be free, you will truly live a life of love and hope and peace and enlightenment and in doing so connect to your eternal Self and follow the path that you were so desperate to walk on before you came to this beautiful planet.

Olivia and Raf

WHO IS MORE HUMAN, THEM OR US?

What an awesome specimen the Human Being is. Physically capable, Emotionally powerful and yet vulnerable at the same time, intelligence that seems to know no bounds and is forever evolving.

We speak of course of those Human Beings that live here on Earth, but also in every part of our Universe as well as the Multiverse.

The Non Physical Human.

The Non Physical Humans that link to their Higher Selves, and who have themselves incarnated potentially thousands of different Souls here on Earth as a Physical Human.

The Non Physical Human that prior to the existence of Physical Human life on Earth perhaps was also part of the Earth's creation, as well as that of many other of the planets in the Multiverse.

The Non Physical Human, full of passion, determination, a deep deep love for themselves and others. Hope beyond what they can understand and perhaps ever will understand, and with a thirst to allow their faith to lead them beyond the boundaries of their current existence and knowledge.

A connection to God so strong and permanently on.

An energy that when properly harnessed connects them to all that the Multiverse has to offer, but most importantly to all that they are.

And what are they?

They are you and you are them.

You, being the Physical Human.

The Physical Human, full of passion, determination, a deep deep love for themselves and others. Hope beyond what they can understand and perhaps ever will understand, and with a thirst to allow their faith to lead them beyond the boundaries of their current existence and knowledge.

A connection to God so strong and permanently on.

An energy that when properly harnessed connects them to all that the Multiverse has to offer, but most importantly to all that they are.

And what are they?

They are you and you are them.

You, being the Non Physical Human.

Yes, the Non Physical Human. They too will be reading this

book and they too will have a view on it just like the Physical Humans that will read it. The one difference to be guaranteed between the Non Physical Humans and the Physical Humans that read this book is that every single one of the Non Physical Humans, without fail will believe.

Believe in every single word that is written.

Believe in themselves.

Believe in God.

Believe in you.

If you are a Physical Human reading this book ask yourself will you believe.

Believe in yourself.

Believe in God.

Believe in them.

Tick all three of these points and you have a chance of freedom. Freedom to be whatever it is you want to be, see whatever it is you wish to see and feel like whatever it is you wish to feel like.

Non Physical Humans all have freedom.

Not because they live in heaven, glorious beautiful heaven. Not because they are close to God and his love is all around them. They have freedom because they tick all three points.

Physical Humans do not all have freedom.

Not because they live in the real world. Not because their

lives are full of difficulty and suffering. They don't all have freedom because they CHOOSE not to tick all three points.

All Humans, Physical and Non Physical, were created by God to be free. To live an eternal life of wonder and enlightenment. At times along that eternal path may come challenges, opportunities for growth, God would say. But if you tick all three points....

....if you tick all three points, God would say....

....well what would God say?

Why don't you ask him yourself. If you tick all three points he will answer.

No? Feels silly? Can't see, feel or hear God so not sure if he's real? You're not religious so he can't be real?

That's fine. No problem at all in fact. Probably best if you just close this book and make it another one of those that you'll eventually get around to finishing.

But know this. God is with you right now. God is in every part of you right now. Because God is in every part of every Human Being, Physical and Non Physical.

Those that tick all three points know this. Those that tick all three points are lucky, not just because they believe, but because they allow.

They allow themselves to be immersed into everything that a Human Being truly is. They allow themselves to be led by what they don't see, by what they can't find, and that which they can only FEEL.

Feel your way through this book and you will find yourself in a place that ticks all three points.

And what is this place? Paradise? Infinite love?

It's much simpler than that. You will find yourself at Humanness. A place that only those that believe and allow can find. Freedom is what you will find, for freedom is what Humanness is.

So who is more Human, them or us?

In answering this question do not look to split Physical and Non Physical for they have equal rights to Humanness. It is those that display the attributes of Humanness the most that are most human.

Those that are most connected to all that they are because they believe.

Believe in you, believe in me, believe in them.

Olivia and Raf, Abraham and Jesus, God

8

WHAT IS GOD?

God is love.

And God is anger. God is hope. God is despair. God is me. God is you. God is your dog. God is the trees and the mountains and the seas. God is the stars, suns, moons and the Earth. God is faith. God is joy. God is all that is good. God is all that is bad. God is strength. God is power. God is light. God is dark. God is creator and creation. God is destruction. God is enlightenment. God is wonder. God is healing. God is suffering. God is here. God is there. God is now. God is then. God is family. God is enemy. God is laughter. God is tears. God understands. God listens. God acts. God gives. God takes. God hurts. God is truth. God is courage. God is trust. God is Balance. God is desire. God is in me. God is in you. God is me. God is you. God is perfect. God is imperfect. God is Consciousness. God has a Consciousness. God is everything. God is REAL.

God is literally in the fabric of all that is life. Every Universe every star every planet every mountain every stone. Every human every animal every tree every plant every seed. Every sea every river every lake every pond every puddle. Every wind every gust every breeze. Every storm every downpour every shower. Everything that you cannot see but that is within you; feelings, Emotions, thoughts, light, they are all God.

God is free will and yet is not part of free will and yet is within free will.

God is love.

God is love, love is God. And so love is within everything, everything, everything, absolutely everything. Everything you see feel taste smell hear touch. Everything you cannot see feel taste smell hear touch. Everything is love.

But wait this is about God not love?

God is love, love is God. And so love is within everything, everything, everything, absolutely everything. Physical energy and Non Physical energy. ALL contains God, ALL contains love.

Your partner is love your children is love your cat is love your garden is love your car is love your washing machine is love. All of these are love because all of these contain the energy of God, and God is love.

God IS love.

And because of this, love is powerful love is freeing love is reconciling love is moving love is painful love is needed, no, love is essential. Essential to life essential to you essential to me essential to God.

God is good therefore love is good.

God is true therefore love is true.

God lifts you therefore love lifts you.

But you said God hurts and God takes and so love hurts and love takes right?

God heals therefore love heals.

So my washing machine is love? Or does that depend on the make and model?

Your washing machine IS love. You ARE love.

I'm capable of love but I am not love.

You ARE love. You ARE. We ARE love, all of us, every one of us. Every one of them, whoever and whatever 'them' is. Your washing machine IS love, regardless of the make and model.

Why is my washing machine love?

Allow yourself to believe this to connect to this. Allow yourself to feel the flow of this. Allow yourself to be soothed by this. Allow yourself to be excited by this. Allow yourself to trust this.

What the washing machine?

We talk of God and love. They are the same. They feel the same they do the same thing. They create they bond they cement people, nature, things, together. They deliver wonder they deliver life they deliver hope. They challenge you, continually challenge you. They bring you clarity they bring assurance they bring loss but then they bring peace. They bring cleansing and vibrancy, turbulence and fear. Belief, laughter and so, so much more they both bring.

Yes but what about the washing machine? How is this love? How is this God?

Well, what is God if he isn't love, if he isn't everything that there is. Is he some almighty power that sits upon a throne somewhere up there in the clouds? You will be disappointed if you think this is who he is. God is not just in the clouds but in every single thing, alive or dead, created naturally or man made. And so the washing machine being man made holds his energy, and is therefore still love.

But how is God in man made things?

Because God is energy and is in the fabric of all energy, and everything in this Universe whether it be man made or not, is energy. Therefore God is in the washing machine...as is love.

Allow yourself to believe this to connect to this. Allow yourself to feel the flow of this. Allow yourself to be soothed by this. Allow yourself to be excited by this. Allow yourself to trust this.

Allow God in.

But I'm not sure if I believe in God.

Allow love in then.

Allow love and also give love, to you. Be free with your love to YOU, always. Fall in love with love. Be inspired by love, give in to love, lead the way with love, run directly to love and never stop running to it. Never grow tired of love. Believe in your connection to love. And then, when you think you have had all the love you can get ask for a little bit more love, and a little bit more from love.

God IS love.

God is good.

Love is good.

You are good. We are good. They are good. Everything is good.

Because. You are God. We are God. They are God. Everything is God.

God IS love.

God is patience. God is Balance. God lets go. God moves on. God forgets. But God never forgets you.

Never forget love.

Never forget God....is love.

Olivia and Raf, Abraham and Jesus, God

9

DON'T FEAR THE JOURNEY

This Journey of yours will hopefully be a long one and so we ask that you don't fear it.

Don't fear the losses the judgement the confusion the paranoia the hurt the anger and the fear itself. Don't fear the people the places the sounds the smells the thoughts the sights the being seen.

Do fear getting to the end of your Journey having only been to the same old place with the same old faces and eaten the same old food and walking the same old routes with the dog. Do fear not loving or being loved, hating yourself and others and being hated by them, not trusting yourself or anybody else. Do fear going without hope love trust strength truth and faith.

This Journey of yours will come to an end soon enough and then you will be out of your misery and you can go back to being Non Physical and getting excited about coming back to Earth again as your Higher Self incarnates as new Soul so you can get your fun pack of fears going again.

Wake up! Wake up and become all that you truly are. Get cracking with those desires, not too many for now, one will be enough as long as it's strongly felt and you let nothing get in your way of it. And when we say nothing we mean nothing, not you, not them, not anybody.

Have a go at something new right now. Get up now! We're not talking about taking that same old walk again so you can say you've had a bit of fresh air we mean DO SOMETHING.

Don't complain to the other half or the neighbour or the work colleague about 'this and that' and how it's stopping you from doing 'this and that'. Stop being a 'this and that' expert and become an expert on you. Anything about you will do just find out something about yourself that you didn't know before and then put it to good use.

We're not talking about making millions or climbing a mountain or saving the world. Just connect to something that's good about you, no, something that's amazing about you and then harness it. Harness it so it makes 'you' feel better, make others feel better make us all feel better we don't mind, just get on with it.

We know you've had it hard but come on, break free from this. See that this was all part of what YOU asked for and now act like you care and shift yourself. Shift your body shift your mind shift your Emotions shift your luck, your outlook, your outcomes.

Don't fear the Journey, drive the Journey, mould the Journey, pour stardust onto that Journey and have a go! HAVE A GO!!

We all have our own Journey.

Our Journey in life takes us on many different challenges along the way. Some of it is predetermined in our Soul Contract and therefore there is nothing we can do to Change what happens, and neither for that matter can anybody else.

And this is an extremely important point as often the challenges that we encounter are because of someone else. Soul Contracts are tied and Aligned to the generation of our grandparents and often Souls are created many years before they incarnate in order for agreements to take place between them all as to what may or may not occur and be acceptable to those Souls.

We have come across so many people that have been hurt by a close parent or grandparent in life and at times they have not just been hurt but terribly abused by that family member. In Non Physical this is such a difficult time for the Higher Selves of these Souls as they will have usually had eternal relationships through Soul Groups with each other and so to see a Soul being hurt by another Soul Group member is hard. In particular as they would have also had many wonderful lives in previous incarnations as different Souls, and of course not to mention the deeply loving relationship that they hold with each other eternally in Non Physical as Higher Selves.

In The Releasing Process that we teach with regards to letting go of the past experiences to raise your Vibration there is always a difficult situation that needs to be addressed with someone that a person loves or is related to, which requires a new understanding of that past experience in order for that person to, with love, let it go.

This is where the understanding of both your own Journey as well the Journey of others is so important. The quicker that you can connect to the fact that everything that as happened to you is not your fault, the easier it will be for you to let go the past.

Vibrational mastery comes with being able to look at someone that has done such terrible things to you and let them go. Not to forgive, for we never forgive as this would be leaving something behind, something unresolved and not truly released. Because the nature of forgiveness is conceding and therefore this would not stop the generation of Low Vibration within you.

If by forgiveness you mean showing love for yourself and for the suffering you have endured, and then finding true love and compassion for the person that inflicted this on you because you have understood why they did it, and accept it's not their fault, and you can create a new Truth for this experience, then that is fine. But if it's just a case that you just want to move on and forgiveness just seems like the kindest thing for you to do for yourself then think again. As this will not be kind on you if the Low Vibration continues to be created in you, potentially daily because you are constantly being triggered by stealth as the Subconscious Mind Aligns the relevant past memories that you seek to forgive, to your every day experiences in the most subtle of ways.

Forget is the word we use because by forgetting you show love for you in the first instance and you also ensure that you have control of that situation in terms of how it makes you feel. That's mastery of your Vibration, and we are going to teach you how to do this.

Your Higher Self plays such a key role in the process of letting go the past and often brings through the insight needed to remind you of specific details of an experience that you may have forgotten, and in particular the Emotions that you will have felt. But they also allow the connection to information about the other person in order to bring through something that you perhaps could not have known. This is the wonder of the Higher Self relationship with regards to The Releasing Process.

But for all the wonder that this brings, if you cannot bring yourself to accept that those others that have caused you such distress were on their own Journey, it will be impossible for you to truly let go. A parent that abused you Physically may have been themselves abused sexually and perhaps without you knowing this fact. The disconnection that this would have generated from themselves and the Self would have caused them to continually generate any number of different Emotions, and at the centre of these for this example would be fear, anger, lack of love and lust. And this disconnection from the Self would have given them little or no chance of being able to create a truly loving relationship with themselves and therefore very little chance of creating one with you. So whether as a result of this disconnection they abused you or perhaps they just couldn't bring themselves to show you the love that a child should expect, the net result is disconnection from you and of course a disconnection from your own Self by you.

Allow yourself some time to think through what it is another has gone through that you may not be aware of and how this could make them so disconnected from themselves that they impart on you pain and suffering, at times of the greatest proportions. If this person is no longer alive then the Higher Self will be able to share with you something that may bring you enough comfort to find compassion for that person.

Know that the Soul of the person that has died will be desperate to help you move on from whatever it is that they did to you whilst they were on Earth with you. Know that those that have hurt you that are still alive may also be just as desperate to make amends but are just too disconnected and too fearful of upsetting you to try. Understanding that we all have our own Journeys that interlink at times in a way that were supposed to impact us both positively and negatively will help you to let go.

And it's letting go that is important for you now. Don't let the past hold you any longer and don't let the past influence everything that you do on this Journey of yours. Let go the fear of the past, let go the fear of the present and the future. Let go the fear of your Journey.

We love you.

Olivia and Raf, Abraham and Jesus

10

IT'S NOT YOUR FAULT BUT IT IS YOUR RESPONSIBILITY

Your Soul Contract is your agreement with God and Your Higher Self. It is your pre-life manifestation and what you accepted that this Physical experience was going to teach you. This agreement and contract is all about growth.

Growth for you, for your Higher Self, the Collective you are a part of, for God and ultimately the Multiverse. This all intertwines and all links together with your real life Physical and Emotional experiences that form your Soul's Journey through this Physical life. Your Soul Contract outlines the expectation of your growth, the Emotions that will stretch you, the suffering and wonder that will impact you, but not the actions and day to day decisions taken from those growth experiences.

There are many, many Emotions that are created and generated through your life experiences and sequences of events that make you choose and take action in the moment. The actions that you choose, past and present, good or bad, they are not your fault but they are your responsibility.

For consider a Soul Contract that defines great suffering during childhood leading to disconnection but then with a later return to a connected state which then triggers the evolution of your Journey to abundance and great joy. The Soul Contract will not state the 'how'. So for example there may be a reference to a loss when you were a child, of a parent or a disconnection from a family member or partner.

Within this statement, free will then determines the 'how' and this could result in your parent being lost to a terminal illness or you experiencing abuse, betrayal or other actions that lead you to suffer at the hands of your relative or partner.

The Soul Contract also does not stipulate the next outcomes of the experiences that occur. In other words whether you have suffered or had a joyous moment, your reactions are also your own free will. These reactions are of course the choices that occur along your path. For every individual who has suffered great loss, they have had before them options, choices, chances.

Some as a result of their suffering choose addictions. Some choose love. Some choose anger and volatility. Some choose violence. Some choose abuse. Some choose illness. Some choose sadness. Some choose connection. Some choose hope and faith and belief. Some choose to let go, understand and forget. Some choose one way and then another later. Some choose light and some choose dark. Rarely, but it is possible to, some choose both at the same time.

Many, many choices. Many paths weave before you in so many moments. This is Free Will. This is why God does not choose. This is why God does not interfere. This is why Universal Entities do not step in and say "Halt! Do not pass, for once you step on this path your life will Change for the worse". This is why your Ancestral Guides do not say, "Please don't drink that, please, we love you, put the drink down".

For in doing this, in changing the course you are setting, it stops you being you and it robs you of the opportunity to take a different step, to choose a different fork in the road a little while down the path. For if you are to 'just be told' you do not ever truly learn and grow. You are dictated to. You don't even really understand it, it is acquired intelligence, not actual wisdom. It isn't growth.

We say again, all of these choices are not your fault, but they are your responsibility.

Your responsibility to heal. Your responsibility to enable growth, to not stay static and in situ, but to grow through your experiences, no matter what they are. Your responsibility is to understand, truly understand yourself, your own Journey, who you are, who you are becoming and who you want to be. To learn to move from being in a disconnected state back to being in a connected state. To learn to return to Self. To let go of the suffering by understanding it.

When you have been the receiver of pain, where your life experiences have been manoeuvred by the Journey of others onto your path and you then have been impacted by their own problems, and perhaps trusted and been let down by them, this too has been part of your request to God, and often, part of your pre-manifested Soul Contract.

Even when in pain, your responsibility is to know that it isn't your fault. Your responsibility is to act accordingly and that action is to allow yourself growth and to choose love. If you go into combat with pain as well as the person who is causing it and try to fight it with all of your might, then the suffering only grows. This fight generates resistance and attracts more suffering, for this is The Law of Attraction working in all the ways that it does.

When you have hurt others, your responsibility for the pain that you have caused them through the actions that you took, is to heal and truly learn from this. To allow true Change of yourself and to choose differently moving forwards each and every time.

Choose love. It is your responsibility to always choose love. It is your responsibility to be really honest. Honest with yourself. Honest with others. Honest about what you want, what you need, who you were and who you want to be. Let go the fault and self-blame and the blame of others. Instead be responsible for all that you are now.

Choose Love we say! Love for yourself. Love for others.

Choose Understanding. Understanding of what your Journey is and learn to understand others on their own Journey.

Choose your path consciously, actively and without fear. Learn to let go. Stop berating yourself, stop the self-sabotage.

IT'S NOT YOUR FAULT.

Learn to feel good again, to trust yourself and to love yourself. You can do no more than this but must do no less than this. This is your responsibility.

Olivia and Raf, Abraham and Jesus

CONNECTION TO YOUR HIGHER SELF

Know that your Higher Self is so connected to you. They will be either male or female and therefore any Soul lives that they have incarnated will always match their own gender.

In other words if you are male then your Higher Self is male and all of his incarnated Souls will also have been male, and if you are female that means that your Higher Self is female and all of her incarnated Souls will also have been female. The Higher Self never incarnates mixed gender Souls over different lives and this is an important point to understand as there has been much confusion over this in the past.

Likewise, a misconception that there is gender-free energy only in Non Physical, that Non Physical do not Align themselves to either male or female energy, this too is a misconception and one to fully clarify. Male and female energies exist in Non Physical, and not only do they exist but they are importantly differentiated in this way. A Collective

Energy will have both male and female energies within, therefore this will absolutely be a blend of both but a Collective is full of singular entities. Singular Entities Align to either male or female and as you come to understand more of this whilst reading this book, you will further understand the 'singular' Entity is always present, even in a Collective. Just for clarity, your Higher Self is a singular Entity.

Connection to your Higher Self does not require you to have a special gift or the ability to talk with Non Physical, as would be required should you be wanting to connect with Non Physical Guides from other dimensions. Your Higher Self is with you always and therefore 'allowing' him or her in is as complex as it gets. The chapter on 'Feelsets' at the end of this book provides some simple steps for connecting to your Higher Self.

The process is very simple and it can be a wonderful way to start your day each day. Achieving this close connection to your Higher Self in this way will open up all sorts of possibilities for you as you go about your life. Expect to receive subtle messages and guidance to help you on your way and as your relationship develops the information you receive becomes more specific and often linked to your Journey and Soul Contract.

The messages that you receive could be in the form of songs or downloaded thoughts or perhaps signs such as a tap on the hand to draw your attention to something. Once you get to the more advanced level of connection with your Higher Self things take on a whole new perspective. A walk with the dog could see you having a full conversation with them as they draw your attention to wonderful things along the route, or perhaps tell you a story about your life that they want to bring to your attention. This can be a truly incredible experience as passing insects, cars, other people, places, literally anything, form part of the story that is being told and all of it happening naturally and in perfect timing as if it had all been pre-planned.

This is the awesome ability of your Higher Self and the true wonder of the connection with them. For when you have this connection strongly made everything opens up for you and access to divine insight is literally available on tap. Think about how powerful your work presentation would be with potentially billions of years of divine energy along side you. Or how much more innovation and creation you will be able to drive with the influence of your Higher Self guiding you and suggesting ideas for you. Spiritual connection in this way is essentially limitless for you in terms of providing you support in your daily life.

We would suggest that you make connection to your Higher Self mandatory for you as part of your ongoing daily life whether it be at work or play. Do not think of connection to the Higher Self in the same way as connection to other higher dimensional Non Physical entities, such as Guides and Ancestral Guides, where you receive messages or guidance on the past present or future and where you have to follow a specific process of connection and protection. The connection to your Higher Self can be likened to constantly being with your very best friend, a friend that loves you no matter what you think, do, act or say, or don't think, do, act or say. You can literally ask your Higher Self for guidance on anything without fear of judgement and often those questions that we are too afraid to ask even ourselves are the ones that your Higher Self would be able to answer for you with clarity and love and safety.

The more advanced connection with the Higher Self can also bring Physical healing for you. Anything from soothing a bump or bruise or a headache, to much more complex conditions. Depending on how ascended your Higher Self is and also how Vibrationally high you are in order to receive the healing from them, you will find that what they can offer you holds no boundaries.

For those of you that are working with your Higher Self as part of releasing Low Vibration from past experiences you will find that their insight is extraordinary, both in recovering past forgotten memories as well as revealing relevant information about other people that may have been part of those hurtful experiences. This information from them could give you a different perspective on that past experience and therefore allow you to perhaps view a situation with love and compassion and thus creating a new Truth for you that ultimately allows you to let go and move on. Often Olivia and Raf through their own Awakening found that the information received from their Higher Selves was so valuable, and at times allowed them to let go of something in a day that perhaps through a more traditional approach would have taken months of analysis or perhaps even longer.

The connection to the Higher Self is something to be cherished but also very much respected, as is connection to all Non Physical. Whilst connection to other Non Physical entities must be done at the highest Vibration possible for you, the connection to your Higher Self needs no protection and can be undertaken in whatever state of Vibration you are in and whenever it is that you feel that you need them.

Allow this wonderful relationship to flourish today, right now if you can. It will be one of the greatest decisions you will have ever made in your life and the benefits to you and those that you care for will be immense.

Your Higher Self loves you.

Olivia and Raf, Abraham and Jesus

LET GO THE PAST, LET GO THE NOW

Let go the need to scratch that itch from the past. An itch that tempts you back over and over and each time you scratch you disrupt, unsettle or completely reopen the sore. A sore that just won't seem to heal no matter how hard you try to make it better. Until over time, somehow you manage to allow yourself to leave it alone long enough for the bleeding to stop and for the wound to heal, leaving nothing but a scar.

A scar that will forever be a reminder of what happened, of what you did or another did to you. We talk now of the Emotional scar, and this scar unlike the Physical one, is a lot more painful and a lot more damaging to your here and now and perhaps to your every moment, sending you on a spiral of self-sabotage and conflict with yourself and others.

How do we find a way beyond this Emotional pain? Many try for years to escape it looking to bury it deep within. Others may dig it up to analyse it and relive it, and yet somehow at times neither approach seems to shake them from the clutches of what is their Emotional prison that blights their very existence. For this is the strength of the past and the price we must pay for not letting it go.

How can I let this go? You have no idea how painful this is, how horrific it was, how much I have been hurt, how much I have hurt another. You expect me to just forgive them or myself and move on, is that what you ask?

And we say no, not ever. As we have stated, never ever forgive for forgiveness does not solve the problem. Forgiveness is a compromise, and a compromise will only set forth a different spiral of Emotions to hurt you. Forget. Forget is what we say. Understand, love, move on, forget.

That's easy for you to say it didn't happen to you.

We understand it's a tough ask. Have you asked what happened to those that have hurt you? What led them to do the things that caused you such pain. What was their Journey and what horrors or hardship did they endure to disconnect themselves from who they are so badly that they inflicted all that they did on you? Do not misunderstand what we say here for whatever they did, as we have also said before, they must take full responsibility for and you have every right to be angry, sad, hurt, shocked and so much more. But do not linger on this feeling because in the end you only hurt yourself.

Instead learn to master those experiences from the past as well as the Emotions and influences that they still create for you in the now. For know that the past will be creating pain for you in circumstances that you would never link back to that original experience, in the smallest of ways, creating new doubts and new fears. Know that all the Low Vibrational Emotion that was created from the original experience is still within you. Taking a greater foothold on you and your Subconscious Mind and in doing so, day by day the Subconscious Mind will be strengthening its protection of you and therefore it's negative influence on your current thoughts and feelings.

So master all that suffering and connect to love, and in this choice you disconnect from the pain. Connect to the love for yourself, make that choice and if needed, be angry for anger is love, love for you. For in the anger you recognise your suffering rather than bury it. You recognise that you have suffered enough and that you deserve better. This is choosing love for YOU. Then, and only then, can you look to those that have caused you pain and seek to find compassion for them. For in this moment you feel stronger, safer, more in control and from this place comes the ability to look at others and understand their own Journey.

Do not over analyse but do enough only to understand. Do not reconnect to the original pain and stress but do enough to recognise that you did suffer. And then in doing all of this, also recognise that they too suffered and had become so disconnected, so unworthy, so in need of love themselves that they would literally do anything to take away their own pain. And it is in this connection to their pain that you are able to understand why they did what they did to you, no matter how despicable, and you will be able to find clarity, and in this clarity comes the understanding that we speak of, and with this then comes love.

Love for you and your Journey, love for them and their Journey.

A Journey that may have been manifested before they even came to this life. A Journey where everything is their responsibility but not their fault. (Heard these words before?)

And if it is you that has inflicted suffering on another and now suffer yourself from guilt or shame, know that the advice given is no different. Recognise that you too have suffered and that you too have become disconnected sufficiently enough to carry out acts that hurt others and yourself. Understanding your own pain, not just how you feel now, but that pain which lead you to cause suffering for others in the past, is the only way for you too to move on.

And so in this moment you have truly started to master that experience inflicted on you by others or by yourself, and in this moment you have found a way to move on and let go.

And what does this bring? FREEDOM.

Freedom in this very moment. Freedom in every other moment enabled by a control of your current Emotions, of your thoughts, of your ego, and a true connection to the Self. For it is this that you must strive for and it is this connection which will set you free.

We urge you to disconnect from your suffering and connect to love. Choose love for you and others, always, in every moment no matter how small. Know that the past and all that it has brought you is a gift from God to be cherished and learnt from.

Growth is your gift, growth is your saviour from the past, and growth is your doorway to escaping all the pain that you feel right now.

Olivia and Raf, Abraham and Jesus

13

GET HAPPY

The name of this chapter is an important one for you to notice for we are not asking you to 'be happy'. Instead we are wanting to explain at a high level how you can become happy.

This chapter isn't going to list out a bunch of inspiring words or activities that will have you skipping down the road in no time. Instead we wish to detail for you something that has never been understood before about your Vibration, how to manage it and how to increase your Stored Vibration percentage and also how to improve your Transitional Vibration percentage.

Essentially in this chapter we look to encompass briefly for you The Releasing Process that is central to what we teach those looking to become predominantly High Vibrational. The more detailed Releasing Process is specified in The Feelset Tools chapter at the end of this book. As are detailed explanations about Stored and Transitional Vibration in the Chapter 'Understanding Low Vibration and the Cellular Impact'.

Getting happy is such a simple process but not easy to do. Roaring like a tiger or force feeding yourself joy won't do it. Mindset is driven by your Subconscious and Conscious Minds so if there's any kind of Low Vibration held within you your Emotional Bodies will reflect this back to your Subconscious Mind, and therefore it won't be fooled for long, no matter how loud you roar. This too is explained further in Your Bodies Chapters.

Getting happy needs to come from a place of Truth and achieving this can be painful depending on the experiences you have had, and the Emotions that you are subsequently holding.

The process of turning over those Emotional stones often requires so much love and support from those around you and this can be difficult given that their Emotions may have also have been negatively affected by you, as well as in return caused you a level of pain.

But The Releasing Process is simple if you have the courage to follow it. And know that you are not alone for at the core of this is your Higher Self. The uniqueness of this process is not the steps that you take but how those steps are deployed by your Higher Self.

We ask that in the first instance you connect to some core experiences, also called by us Level 1 Experiences, that have driven Low Vibration into your Stored Vibration and that still continue to drip feed these into your Transitional Vibration (your in the moment Vibration). Your Higher Self feeds you these past experiences that you need to focus on and in addition connects you to the Emotions that you felt with these experiences.

From this point you receive further downloads from your Higher Self which gives you an insight into those past events that you may have even forgotten some of, or that your Subconscious Mind has locked memories for. This 'experience led' releasing, also gives you access to relevant information that you will never have received before because the people involved are either no longer alive or because they may not have shared vital information with you. Again this is all provided by your Higher Self.

The importance of this insight should not be underestimated because it can be the difference between being forced to move on from the past without properly letting go (and therefore still generating Low Vibration for it), or being able to be totally free from all the hurt that an experience has created within you throughout your life. A parent, a sibling, a grandparent or perhaps a friend that has been at the centre of your suffering can often be the one that we find it the hardest to set ourselves free from, if they have caused us Emotional or Physical pain.

But imagine if you now knew something that they hadn't shared with you before. Perhaps that they were abused as a child, or maybe that they had strong fears borne out of a childhood condition or perhaps that they had lost a love early in their life. All experiences which could have made them completely disconnected from themselves, from love and therefore from you. The list of possibilities here is endless for types of human suffering but know that through your Higher Self these unknown circumstances could be made clear to you if relevant to your own suffering and could be enough to give you a different perspective on things, and therefore it could just be the information that you need to let go of something that has hounded you for years. Please note that your Higher Self will only bring through information on another that is relevant to you and this will only be at a high level, to detail the understanding needed by you.

The releasing of your Low Vibration occurs when the energy attached to the memories of an experience Changes. So if you held anger for an experience but through a new understanding you now feel love for that same scenario the Vibrational frequency that was anger for that experience also Changes to the Vibrational frequency of love. And in accordance with the Physical Laws of energy the love energy then disconnects from the anger energy, as it no longer attracts, and so it leaves your Physical body. This is a very simplified explanation but is sufficient for the purposes of understanding how you can start to raise your Stored and Transitional Vibration using The Releasing Process.

Once you have been through and understood these core or Level 1 past experiences of yours and let them go it is at this point that you will have generated a series of Truths. These Truths which are about these new understandings of the past will eventually start to build Truths that form part of broader 'Journey level' Truths and those Journey Level experiences are termed Level 2. Statements such as 'it's not my fault', 'it's not their fault', 'I trust myself', 'I trust others', 'I allow love' the list is huge but these types of Truths can only be truly felt, and thus created within The Law of Truth, if you have gone through sufficient understanding and letting go of your key and core past experiences that your Higher Self leads you to.

At the point that your Journey level Truths are strong and varied enough you can then begin 'Emotion led' releasing. With this phase of The Releasing Process there is no need to go into the specifics about an experience and instead you can broadly connect to a topic and the set of related Emotions that you will have gone through many times in the past, for many scenarios, and through your Higher Self apply your new Truths to the memories held in your Subconscious Mind.

The example could be when you have been judged for doing something wrong. Your Subconscious Mind will literally hold hundreds of thousands of memories of this scenario of you with friends, relatives, at work etc. And those memories that are held will not only refer to when the actual experiences happened but also the times that you spent thinking about them over and over again. And so each thought is a memory in the Subconscious Mind which is also linked to Low Vibration . By applying your new Truths the memories can be 'relabelled' and the Low Vibration released immediately. This is a truly magical process and one that can only be delivered in partnership with your Higher Self.

Again, the Low Vibration is released because there has been a new understanding around those experiences, only this time you haven't had to analyse them you have simply applied your Journey Truths through your Higher Self and the Subconscious Mind has relabelled the memories to represent your new perspective.

This new perspective then triggers the Change in the Vibrational frequency of the linked Emotions and once again they disconnect and release from the energies that they are no longer similar to e.g. the Vibration was fear but is now love so it detaches from the other fear Emotions held in your Physical body.

The target with the Emotion led releasing is to Change all of your past experiences to be recorded in your Subconscious Mind as memories that you now feel love for. This process can take a few weeks but tackles literally tens of millions of memories and is something you simply could not address on your own or through other counselling methods over a whole lifetime. The way your Higher Self is able to dovetail with the intricate workings of your Subconscious Mind to apply your Journey level Truths is a truly unique and miraculous process and can literally stop the generation of ALL Low Vibration linked to past events and in doing so shift your overall Vibration to be predominately high, and probably higher than most people on the planet.

This is not a process to be feared by the way, just ask Raf and Olivia who have been freed by it, as well as their clients who also have achieved their own freedom from the past. Know that once your relationship with your Higher Self is sufficiently tuned to be able to receive the downloads from them nothing else is technically needed to get you through this process.

Of course you will need a fair helping of courage, determination and self-love to get you to where you need to be, and to shift yourself away from the past. But in undertaking The Releasing Process you will find a new level of Vibrational mastery.

We love you so much.

Olivia and Raf, Abraham and Jesus

14

ALIGNMENT – YOUR LIFE'S WORK

Yes it really is your life's work.

Our Awakening took us to a point in a very rapid timeframe and so much was understood, learned and healed as part of this Journey. And yet there is still so much to evolve to and we are desperate to take advantage of every minute of this lifetime in order to evolve to what we could become.

And we are going to give it a damn good go and attempt to become people on this Earth that we ourselves have not even imagined we could be. We have talked of teleportation, working with the Science, Technology and Engineering Communities to create new capability to underpin all that we are sharing, Soul level travel to distant planets, instant healing for millions at the same time. We're literally reaching for the stars with what we hope to achieve.

So how do we in tend to do this? It's actually really simple.

Alignment.

Alignment to the Self and Higher Self and therefore everything that the Universe has at its disposal. Every Law, every Non Physical entity, including God, especially God, and every other Physical human on this planet that wants to join us to make it happen. And when we say to make it happen we don't just mean for us but for everyone.

Maintaining Alignment is paramount to these aspirations and therefore from our perspective we are determined to stay High Vibrational, always, forever, literally for life. Read the contents of this book and you'll get an idea of how we plan to achieve this but we also know that there's so much more to learn that will be given to us to share in terms of how we evolve to a status of Non Physical Vibration whilst living a Physical life here on Earth.

But staying High Vibrational doesn't mean that we will be skipping out of bed every day, pouring ourselves a healthy smoothie and then spending the rest of the day in a state of Zen (although we will be trying to). In reality we know, and embrace the fact, that contrast will come our way. And it's this contrast that will in fact drive us towards evolving towards the future aspirations that we hold. But not only that, it's this contrast that means that if we wish to stay Aligned we literally will be working on it our whole life....awesome!

And by Alignment we don't mean in a constant state of euphoria either. No, Alignment isn't this. Alignment is peace within, it's Balance, it's no severe Emotional swings from high to low. It's a life without fear and yet it's a life that experiences fear but without fear of it.

Those that we work with are taught many skills and techniques on how to move their Vibration from Low to predominately High. But they are also shown how to keep it there and this is key. Effecting Change is relatively simple if you are willing. Change can happen in an instant but acting on that Change to ensure that it lasts is all together a different kettle of fish.

Your in the moment Transitional Vibration, which we talk in more detail on in later chapters, can be constantly being tested by Low Vibrational experiences or self-sabotaging thoughts which trigger Low Vibration. So, the trick is to be aware that it's happening and manage it in the moment or at least at some point soon after in that same day, to ensure that the Emotional energy doesn't stay long enough to become part of your Stored Vibration, in other words held in your cells. Long term held Low Vibration as we have seen with the people that we work with, can influence the Physical body dramatically for ailments ranging from a sore back and muscles, to more serious nerve conditions, cancer, heart conditions, multiple sclerosis, in fact there's no condition out there that cannot be influenced or triggered by a storage of Low Vibrational energy in your cells.

A key part of what we teach and are guided on by Abraham and Jesus are the 'Feelset Tools' that enable the management of both the Transitional and Stored Vibration. At the centre of these Feelset Tools is the connection to your Higher Self.

Your Higher Self will have lived many lives before you as

different Souls but all that has been learnt in those lives is within the energy of your Inner Being. They have also felt everything that you have felt in every part of your life and they know what you are thinking right in this very moment. Your Higher Self is not a coloured cloud somewhere in the sky, they are sitting next to you right now, loving you and protecting you and guiding you (even if you don't realise it). The connection to your Higher Self brings a greater connection to your Self and with this comes a stronger connection to Universal love.

So the key to maintaining Balance and a consistently High Vibration is therefore keeping Aligned to your Higher Self. A morning meditation is not enough, for you can quickly and easily slip out of whatever it is you have achieved the minute Low Vibration or contrast takes hold, even if just for a moment.

Maintaining this connection requires a more solid type of engagement and intention agreed on by both parties. It requires you to let go of your old ways of thinking which see you only allowing them in when you remember or need them, or just feel like it. A connection to your Higher Self once truly cemented needs to be held onto at all times. This doesn't mean you always have your head in the clouds and are never quite engaged here on Earth. In fact it's quite the contrary, for in fact you need to be even more human for your Higher Self connection to be at its strongest.

Allowing. It's this simple. Allowing yourself to be accessible to their love is all that it takes. No special routines or meditations just an intention to receive them with love, to accept all that they give you with love and to give your love back to them in return. At times this won't be easy in particular at the beginning of your relationship where you may find yourself being challenged in the most difficult of ways, as they do all that they can to get you to where you want to be. But as long as you can find a way to not turn your anger, your fears and your doubts back onto them, that channel will be maintained and with this comes your opportunity to remain Consciously Whole.

For it is those that remain Consciously Whole for the most consistent of times that give themselves the best opportunity of also maintaining a consistent Vibration, maintaining their Alignment to the Self and their Higher Self, and therefore Alignment to all that this wish to achieve during their life.

Olivia and Raf, Abraham and Jesus

BE THE MASTER OF YOUR EXPERIENCE

We wish to say to you, here and now, words that we want you to feel to your very core. Words that you can use and that become even a mantra to you.

You are the Master of Your Experience.

Feel this, know this to be true. Feel the power of this. Oh we know this is not simple to implement necessarily, we know that your ego may well flare up, and your Subconscious Mind go into panic at the mere mention of it but just for a second let the power of this knowing fill you up.

You are the Master of Your Experience.

That means that if something doesn't quite go the way you are expecting, don't let the dark cloud of doom fester over your head and lower your Vibration and everyone else's around you. If someone says something that hurts you or feels inappropriate or derogatory, don't let this be the thing that rises in you so you are desperate to put things right and add more and more fuel to the Low Vibrational furnace.

Choose.

Choose in that moment, Master that moment in time. Do not let anything, anything alter you feeling good. Feel what you want, whatever experience you want and make that happen for you. For as you now know you are the Master of Your Experience so be that Master. Own that title and live up to that job description.

It doesn't matter what is going on, no example cannot have a Mastery option. If you feel lonely and cannot be with the ones that you love because of Physical distance, work, Change or life in general, then think of them, love them as if you were. Reach out to them with that incredible Vibration and just pick up the phone, have a video call, whatever you can do but start and end with love. Leave the hurt, the sadness, the lack behind and fill yourself up with all the love that you can and let it pour out from you because it feels good to you. Master the spiralling whirlwind of mind thoughts and subsequent feelings that start small and sneak up on you. Put feeling good first and choose, and choose again and again and allow your thoughts and feelings to be more nourishing than you have ever, ever had before.

Wow, stirring words. Have you even managed to get out of bed? No? Well, you see then, all of these words we have just given are just that.

Words.

And words won't get you anywhere unless you follow them

with action. Oh please, we hear you say, let's not go down the inspirational speech route.

Ok, how about this then? Words are no good without feeling. Feeling able, feeling up for it, feeling good, just feeling something.

How you feel in every given moment will dictate that action that backs up those words. Feel love in every moment and whatever that person says or has said won't be an issue. Now that's Vibrational Mastery right there. But we don't mean the pretence that it won't be an issue, the puffing of the chest or the suppressing of the feelings that you really hold at the time. We mean actually acting like it isn't an issue because it truly isn't an issue. This kind of Mastery takes practice and dedication and time.

This kind of Mastery not just anybody can do. You can't buy this mastery off the shelf or in a self-help DVD or book. This kind of Mastery needs you to actually do something about it. We teach you exactly how to do it in this book. Address the past, let it go and connect to love whilst doing so, until you find the past is the past and the present is nothing but desire, inspiration, peace, joy and wonder.

But reading this book alone won't be enough. Talking about how wonderful the insight in this book is and sharing it with your friends as if you're so tuned into it won't do it either. Pretending to yourself and everybody else that you are one hundred percent giving it all you've got in every single moment, every moment, to achieve it certainly won't do it. Playing the blame game won't do it either, nor will playing the victim.

Feeling a positive energy rise in you that takes you to a better feeling place will do it if you consistently allow yourself to be taken to this better feeling place. If you continuously drive yourself to improve no matter what no matter how hard, and no matter what your Higher Self places before you. That WILL do it.

Because in your Higher Self you have someone that knows. Knows you, knows this Universe and knows how to get you out of that hole you've been in for most, if not all of your life. In your Higher Self is someone that will be distant and cold and confusing just to get you through whatever it is that you need to find freedom.

Yes that's right. Your Higher Self will not make this easy for you. Your Higher Self will not pretty this up for you with kind words of inspiration for you to continuously ignore. Your Higher Self probably won't talk to you at all if this is what you have experienced all your life because your Higher Self wants you to wake up to what you have suffered and endured and accepted all of your life. Your Higher Self will play the bad cop continuously no matter how much you ask them not to if that is what you asked them to do in your Soul Contract.

For your Higher Self loves you more than you could ever imagine and will do anything, anything to get you over that line.

So how do you become the Master of Your Experience?

Put down this book and just try. Try to go out today without feeling the need to hate yourself. Try to listen to everything your inner guidance has been giving you for years but that you have just been ignoring. Try to remember that you have your Higher Self next to you at all times. This invisible top of the range sports car that if you connect to and sit within, will give you a complete an utter unfair advantage. And for those that say to you that they don't like that you've got an unfair advantage because of this, point them inwards and tell them to start listening and they too will be connected in, they too will be Consciously Whole.

And what does it mean to be Consciously Whole? It means being connected to who you truly are, allowing and giving love at all times because of the fact that you are always feeling the energy of your Higher Self. At first, receiving your Higher Self will be like using an international electricity plug converter. In order to receive you'll need something to help Translation and to support the fact that you are not Emotionally and energetically capable of fully receiving the pure divine energy of your Higher Self directly. But once you have acted, once you have done something other than read this book and gone back to pretending, then a Change will come.

For once you get yourself to a place where fear and doubt no longer rule you, that's when you don't need that plug converter. That's when you can plug straight in and feel the awesomeness of your Higher Self and the awesomeness of who you truly are. Just you wait.

Just you wait. Just you. Wait...are you waiting for something to happen? Are you all alone again thinking that's not going to be me? Thinking I haven't got the courage or the support to do this. I've got too many ailments or issues to overcome to be able to get to a point that I can plug straight in. If you truly feel this then put this book down now and never pick it up again, until you're able to take a different perspective. Until then, save yourself the pain of feeling the victim any longer and go back to being mastered and not the Master.

For those of you that want to keep reading, just know that you are not alone, that you are supported and very much loved. Know that in your Higher Self you have the most wonderful chance to stop playing this game you've been stuck in and instead have a chance to make up your own game with your own rules. This is the power of the love that comes from your Higher Self and he or she will keep letting you use that plug converter for as long as you need it. And for as long as you keep wanting to use it, your Higher Self will be there.

But remember, your Higher Self isn't only here to send you wonderful messages and share joyous moments. Your Higher Self wants so much more for you than that and for as long as you keep asking for it and allowing it, your Higher Self will lead you in the direction that you need to go no matter how hard at times it seems for you.

Mastery of your own experiences starts with Mastering yourself and the Self. It comes with Mastering connection to your Higher Self and to your other Guides that may come along. It comes with Mastering your past, your present and your future by being Balanced Emotionally and Physically.

Ask your Higher Self today to show you how to plug you into him or her directly. Ask them to show you how to become

'Consciously' Whole with them and to truly get that unfair advantage over those that haven't gone through the pain and the struggle for freedom that you will have done to become Consciously Whole. Ask for life to made easy once you become Consciously Whole. Ask for them to love you like they've never loved you before once you do get through to the other side, and challenge them to then love you in a different way, a way not as trying perhaps but instead, in a way that makes you feel free and always loved.

Not just the tough love but a good dousing of 'in your face, obvious, can't get enough of you' love. Ask for people to see your light but for you to see your own light shine just as strongly inwards as it does outwards. Ask that you feel their love more than any other and ask that they help you make your life feel different, great, challenging, and for them only to ever keep driving you forwards and those that follow you forwards.

Ask for all of this and they will try to give it to you but know that they will also ask something of you.

Anything we hear you say! I'll be consistent, persistent, I'll never give up even when times are tough. Is this what you ask?

No. They won't ask this of you.

All they will ask is for you to listen. Not to listen for a voice or a thought in your head or look out for a sign. Just listen to yourself. Listen to yourself as you grow and as your words Change and your actions follow suit. Listen to that man or woman that you are that slowly starts to become someone else, someone who is proud and who is confident and who is expectant and who is determined and loving and only ever looking forward and never ever listening to the past or those that try to drag them back to it.

Mastery of your Experience starts from this point. Listen to yourself and listen to others and then act in accordance with your desires. Act in accordance with what you have agreed with that virtual and divinely spiritual sports car that you are currently driving or being driven in. Your Higher Self.

These are not just words that we give, these are intentions. Intentions that will set you free Emotionally and make YOU the Master. Not the angry Master or the controlling Master, for the only thing that you need to be in control of is yourself.

Become Consciously Whole and you will achieve this. Become Consciously Whole and you let go the chains and be let loose from them. Become Consciously Whole and those fears and doubts that you and others fling at you like a leather strap whipping at your back, will no longer be felt. Become Consciously Whole and the scars of past Emotional whippings are not even visible or remembered.

The Releasing Process will enable you to become Consciously Whole, and lead to you to becoming the Master of Your Experience.

EMOTIONS DON'T CARE ABOUT EXPERIENCES

Ever feel that itch or that pull to do something different? Ever been for a horse ride on a beach or snow boarding in a remote mountain location? Ever gone kitesurfing in Tarifa?

Ever felt scared to try? There are many that have been too scared and therefore many that have not experienced anything like the life that they wish they could have.

But forget about experiencing the best that life can offer what about those of you that are experiencing the worst of it? Some might say well, that's not me I'm actually ok. Yes things are tough at times but at least I'm not in a warzone or have just lost a child or a partner.

We say tell that to the person who has just jumped off a high balcony to their death because they couldn't pay their bills. Tell that person that what they were experiencing wasn't as bad as war.

You see, we all suffer, and whatever the experience, we all are impacted by it in our own unique way and because of that no one experience is worse than another. Literally nothing is worse than anything else when put into the context of an Emotional impact.

What was the last thing that happened to that person before they decided to jump off that balcony? Well let's just say that this person received an electricity bill warning that the supply was going to be disconnected thereby leaving the whole family without the ability to cook, bathe or even see in the night around the house. It's just a bill that wasn't paid and yet let's add another experience into the mix for this person. What if that person was also abused as a child but in such a manner that it went hardly noticed, in fact it was brushed under the carpet so as to not cause the family any embarrassment. That single experience which may not have been seen as much at the time may well have been the

OLIVIA & RAF OCAÑA

reason why that electricity bill was just too much for them to deal with.

The sense of unworthiness that would come from being abused, just lightly brushed on the knee by a strange man in the park could have started the seed of so much agony for that person. Fear of strangers, of men. Fearful of the dark perhaps as a result of constantly replaying the experience as he lay in bed alone, listening out for every creak around the house wondering if that person was going to come into their room in the night. This sounds over the top but this is how the seed grows in our mind especially when we are young.

Add to this an up and down career further driving down their unworthiness, perhaps relationship and marital problems causing a wedge to be created between that person and their partner. Continued paranoia that something might happen to them or their family, building up over the years because of their fears of the dark and fear of being killed by strange men and fear of losing their job and their marriage and the fear of judgement because of all of this.

And this is not even factoring in their constant anxiousness, worry and nervousness at every conversation, every situation and every person that they meet. Then there's the children. Their needs to be played with, to have fun, to have an awesome parent who dotes on them and gives them everything that they want and that can never say no to them for fear of a meltdown; the father not the children.

A story here that sadly is one we come across all of the time and this is without mentioning all of the other things that life throws at you on a daily, weekly, monthly, yearly basis.

Running out of milk, never enough money to go out, the mortgage, the house and domestic jobs, the death of a family member, relocation of your office to another country, the depressing and sad news that you connect yourself to every night on TV just to up your fix of Low Vibration and to remind you that things aren't as bad for you because you're not fleeing a war torn country.

Really? Are you serious? Are you really saying that your life isn't as bad as theirs?

Emotions don't care about experiences.

Never ever forget this. Never allow yourself to feel that your life isn't that bad and that you're ok and that things will be fine and it that it will all be ok once the summer comes and...

...YOU are suffering. You ARE struggling.

Sadly you are also struggling to do anything about it because you haven't realised just how tough your life has been and still is.

Mastery of your Emotional experiences comes with putting into place many different things as described in this book. Connection to love as many times as you can is vital. Yes connect to the pain in order to release it but keep a Balance. Be aware of your actions and reactions and catch those thoughts and those feelings in order to avoid continual self-sabotage but most of all, recognise that you have suffered and are suffering.

Don't suppress it any longer.

Allow your Emotions to rise and with it allow yourself to rise and be angry with it. Don't confuse our message when we say connect to love, by trying to act as this perfect Human Being all of the time. Let the anger surface. Remember, anger is love. Love for you. Not the spilling over with hatred anger, but instead just sufficient anger to say that's enough. Doing this truly is love for you.

When your children are outside playing and making too much noise because you're trying to work, recognise the anger in you. Connect this anger to your guilt because you feel you should be out there with them. But don't let the guilt drag you down. Tell yourself it's ok because you're busy, you've had a tough day, week, year, life!

Emotions don't care about experiences. And your time to play outside with them will come later.

Being the Master of Your Experience is about showing love for you in this way. It's about allowing yourself not to go shopping just because you're low on food. It starts with asking the kids to go and play upstairs on their own for a while as you sit and watch TV and ignore the messy kitchen or the preparation for that meeting that you have tomorrow.

Being the Master of Your Experience is about recognition of how much you keep putting up with but also how far you keep pushing yourself. How many times have you looked at a balcony and just for split second thought about jumping? How many times have you considered stepping out across that car, just in a flash of a thought and not even when in a seriously distressing situation outwardly. We suspect more times than you acknowledge.

Emotions don't care about experiences.

Your Emotions are tied to a myriad of actions and reactions and outcomes and they have no interest whether it's bombs that are going off somewhere nearby or whether the birds are singing quietly outside. Just ask that person that jumped off the balcony about how the sound of songbird early in the morning before it got light would link them to those early and scary thoughts of death by that stranger that brushed against them in the park when they were young. Just ask that person how unsweet the sound of songbird is because of the Emotions of doom and evil that were filling their body like a pouring tap, as they contemplated the rest of their awful day at work amongst all of this debt and relationship heartache that they held.

Don't let your Emotions drive your experiences, let your experiences drive your Emotions.

Yes you have suffered and yes you are suffering but it's not the way it was meant to be. You're not just one of those unlucky people that nothing good happens to. You're just one of those people that nothing good is allowed to happen to because of...well because you keep allowing this to be the way it is.

There are many ways to show that you are the Master of Your Experience but do try to recognise that there actually IS a problem that needs to be mastered. Give yourself some love and be prepared to accept that you too are in a warzone. An Emotional warzone that at times can be far more deadly than any bullet. A bullet can at least be dodged if given half a chance but there's no escaping your Emotions, they are going nowhere apart from where you are. You are carrying them with you everywhere you go and your backpack isn't full of cans of dehydrated food to go with your spare firearms and bullets. No, your backpack is full of confusion, worry, judgement, fear of loss, fear of being hurt, fear of death and so much more. And you don't need to go back to the barracks to fill up on supplies when your backpack is empty. Oh no, you have a constant supply coming from the Dripping Tap of Emotions that you self-generate and that you can't turn off and that fills you up day in day out, slowly making you heavier with sorrow, with hurt, with despair and without love or without an outlook that's worth living for.

Be the Master of Your Experience before your Emotions beat you to it and become the Master of you.

Olivia and Raf, Abraham and Jesus

RECOGNISING LOW VIBRATION IN YOU

How much you actually feel when you generate Low Vibration within you will depend on a number of factors. The primary consideration will be the amount of Low Vibration you already hold. The more you hold the less you will feel. If you are working with your Higher Self as part of The Releasing Process to release Low Vibration, they will commonly ramp up the specific Low Vibrational Emotions that they would ask you to consider letting go and in doing so, you can learn to understand what the energy of each Emotion feels like.

There are obvious Emotional reactions that most people feel, these would include fear doubt and anger, but there are so many more that you literally create minute by minute each and every day that can go unnoticed for years and perhaps a lifetime.

Look out for signs of dizziness as this is usually a tell tale sign that a Low Vibration has been triggered within you and is circling its way around your head and your body looking for a place to permanently land. This sounds somewhat sinister and in all truth it is. For the impact of this Low Vibration on your brain, your bodily functions, your energetic paths, nerves, nervous system, brain, bones, heart, liver, stomach, colon....we could name every single part of the human Physical and non-Physical body here but the point to understand is that Low Vibration in your body is not healthy for you if it is allowed to settle and grow in size.

Worth starting to take note of when you feel it we would suggest.

The Subconscious Mind and the Egoic Bodies, which we shall discuss in later chapters, are either independently or together working as the instigators of Low Vibration in you, with both having the ability to direct the command to your Emotional Bodies to produce it. You will recognise when a shot of fear or doubt has been instructed from the Subconscious Mind because you will feel it like a short but sharp energetic jab in the area below the bottom of your rib cage and above your hips.

The Emotions directed by the Egoic Bodies will be felt anywhere between the rib cage and just below the bottom of your collar bones. Note that only fear or doubt can be generated by the Egoic Bodies and therefore all other Emotion trigger requests are instructed by the Subconscious Mind. Also note that different Emotions will be felt in different parts of the Emotional Bodies. If it's anger for example you will feel the energy rise within you from your belly button area up towards the top part of your chest in an upward moving motion almost as if someone has used a 4 inch paint brush to stroke it up your chest. Anger can also be felt either side of this stripe in the lower abdominal areas.

All of these points are important distinctions to understand because those of you wishing to tackle whatever Emotion it is that has generated itself within you in order to let it go, will need to start becoming more aware of when it 'lands'. Catching the feeling of the Emotion can be difficult at first so catching the thoughts is another way to do it. Becoming more aware of what you are thinking may give you a clue as to what's going on in your Emotional Bodies.

But you might be surprised as to which Emotions you're actually generating.

Take for example the simple example of putting out plates of food on the table for the family which you have diligently cooked for them. You know that the kids detest vegetables, in this case broccoli, but you want them to have something healthy. In that moment you may suggest to yourself because of your thoughts, that you have generated the Emotion of judgement because of the complaints you know you will get from them. A fair assumption, but it's potentially just as likely that you may have also generated paranoia, hatred, fear of judgement, panic, anxiety, worry, nervousness, doom, evil (yes this is an Emotion), sickening, depravity, debauchery, fear of death and perhaps many others.

Maybe think about giving the kids pizza next time you go down the healthy dinner route? We make light of this but it is in fact a very serious point and an issue that affects every single person on the planet.

The 'Dripping Tap of Emotions'.

The Dripping Tap of Emotions literally fills your body with whatever Emotions your Subconscious Mind links to each and every experience. The Dripping Tap therefore can also fill you with High as well as Low Vibration. For the purposes of this chapter we focus on Low Vibration but know that the sooner that you can feed your Subconscious Mind with High Vibrational thoughts, feelings and Truths the better.

So with reference to the plate of broccoli how is it that we can generate these terrible Emotions from such a simple action. The answer lies in what has happened previously in your life experiences.

It's down to your Subconscious Mind and the way it works depending on its state at the time of creating the memories. Memories of activities and experiences are very loosely coupled together by the Subconscious Mind and due to this coupling of memories, often the Emotional reaction that we generate in the Emotional Bodies is not just that which we feel in the moment but also a whole series of other Emotions that form part of other past experiences that have been linked together. It's a potential that these other Emotions will not even be felt because the Dripping Tap of Emotions is just that, a small drop of Emotions that gets released, and so your real Emotional reaction to an experience is often not what you think.

So in our example with the broccoli, if this experience made you feel judged sufficiently, it's likely that it would remind your Subconscious Mind of other past experiences in your life where you have also felt judged by a family member. Your Subconscious Mind would therefore also group this current broccoli experience, and its related new memories, to the past memories of feeling judged in other experiences. So let's assume you lost a parent as a child. Often in this situation you can feel judged by others for being 'the unlucky one' and therefore an uncle or an aunt who would have wanted to give you their love and support at the time because of your loss could have connected you to this sense of 'unluckiness', and in doing so may have made you feel unworthiness and shame because you were the unlucky one to have this loss. And in feeling these Emotions you would have also felt judgement.

It's sounds far fetched but this is exactly how the Subconscious Mind works, especially when in a fearful state. So in general, if your overall Subconscious Mind memories were mainly fearful and your state of feeling at the time of the broccoli experience was generally fearful, then that experience would definitely be placed in the same group of memories as the loss of a parent.

And so the relevance of this is that whenever we experience something, we generate in ourselves the Emotions in the moment (which we feel), but also all the Emotions that were generated by any other past experiences that this current experience is linked in our Subconscious Mind, and remember these may not be felt – The Dripping Tap of Emotions.

So the broccoli experience being linked to the loss of a parent because of feelings of judgement from a family member would also generate in us the feelings we would have felt from that loss of a parent over and above the Emotion of fear of judgement from our children regarding the broccoli. These other Emotions could be fear, anger, hatred, unworthiness, doom, evil, fear of loss, lack of love, paranoia, confusion, worry, shock, despair, doubt, there are literally so many more Emotions that we could mention. And remember how many times you have tried to give the kids broccoli. In other words this isn't a one off, you are literally generating the Dripping Tap over and over again.

This is how the Dripping Tap of Emotions works and it can literally be deadly for us depending on what other experiences we have had in our life and how they have been grouped by our Subconscious Mind. Consider that we have only referenced one past experience here but think how many other past experiences could potentially also be linked here by the Subconscious Mind with reference to feeling judged by a family member, and therefore potentially many other Emotions would also be generated for the 'broccoli experience'.

And of course this is just on the subject of feeling judged by the family. We have many different experiences day after day, month on month, year on year and this will generate literally millions of different memories all of which link to Emotions. If many of these experiences are Low Vibrational then your Dripping Tap won't be helping your Vibration in a positive way. If you've just woken up from a nap feeling groggy and frustrated, or just come back from a walk with the dog out in the fresh air but are feeling sadness or really negative, ask yourself what is it that you have just seen or dreamt of that has triggered your Dripping Taps of Emotion.

We don't wish to not allow you to relax when you nap or sleep but these moments are some of the worst times, as your Subconscious Mind runs freely and undisturbed triggering your drip of Low Vibrations by stealth. The mere act of closing your eyes can trigger doom and fear of death as your Subconscious Mind is reminded of your fears as a child as you would lay there with your eyes closed thinking about your lost parent being cremated. Your thoughts then continue as you sleep, coming through as dreams...drip, drip, drip. And then when you wake up from this nightmare that you don't even know you've had, your first waking Emotions, again without you knowing, is fear of loss, doom and shock as you link back to childhood memories of waking up alone without your parent. You may have consciously forgotten this event but Subconsciously you will always remember it whilst that memory holds fear for you...The Dripping Tap of Emotions.

The Releasing Process that we teach around letting go of the past is the starting point to tackling the Dripping Tap of Emotions. Over time as you generate new Truths about the past, you will start to feel love and not fear for those experiences and you will start to control your Subconscious Mind through your new perspective of your Journey.

Know that no amount of conscious 'talking yourself up' will

Change the behaviour of your Subconscious Mind and so whilst we always recommend a positive mindset, it's the 'Feelsets' that will fix this problem for you and give you true Emotional freedom from yourself.

Olivia and Raf, Abraham and Jesus

17

HOW ARE YOU FEELING RIGHT NOW?

Some days you just don't have the energy to do anything other than clean your teeth and get back into bed.

Sounds like a great day.

Well why not? Relaxing in bed, maybe have the window open listening to the birds and wondering what you're going to eat from the fridge, hopefully there's something in there already made or leftover so you can nip back upstairs and get into bed again then maybe grab the magazine and reread it and later flick on the TV and settle in for the early evening shows.

Wow what a waste of a day.

Really? Why's that? You've spent all day relaxing working on your Vibration and generally feeling good. That sounds like Vibrational Mastery to us.

The day could have gone differently of course. Lacking in energy or enthusiasm for anything at all and therefore rather than enjoying the moments undisturbed in your bed, instead you lay there thinking through what you should be doing, working through your lists and maybe even doing an appreciation list to manifest yourself the perfect day relaxing in bed.

Or maybe you're laying there in your cloud of guilt and worry because you're not doing anything and you forget that it's sunny outside and you get straight onto your phone to see who has messaged you. Then you have a quick look at the news to see who was suffering the most that day and then in between your four cups of coffee you will have had just enough time to think about everything that you're doing wrong in life but how tomorrow you're going to do things differently once you get your energy back.

Sounds like a painful existence living that way, and whilst we appreciate it's not always possible to spend all day in bed, if you do manage to get the chance just make sure you take the most from it. It's a simple message but how many times have you allowed yourself to enjoy the times that you have had nothing to do?

Life has a habit of throwing us the odd curveball or two and for some they all come at once and don't stop coming. We will discuss in later chapters about the many wonderful Universal Laws and how to harness them in order to manifest all that you desire for the future. We also make reference throughout this book on how to feel amazing by letting go of the past and lifting your Vibration to something all together much more positive. But it's also what you do, or don't do about the 'now' that we also ask you to focus on.

In the moment, instead of blaming your problems on someone or something, or bemoaning your lack of luck in life, just sit quietly for a minute and stare. Stare at the ceiling, at the walls, out of the window, anywhere that makes you just switch off for a while. Switch off from the caffeine, the phone and the noise all around you.

Instead tune into your body and feel it gently slow down and allow yourself to relax and fall into a state of nothingness and stillness both Physically and mentally. Maybe a yawn will come over you at this point.

What happens then is something really quite wonderful.......................................Nothing.

Olivia and Raf, Abraham and Jesus

18

LEAP WITHIN

Leaping is that term used by so many for that moment borne out of inspired action when you are propelled forward, perhaps not as fully prepared as you had wished, but nevertheless ready to put fate into the hands of the Universe and go for it!

What an utterly awesome, fantastically positive and courageous place to be. Or is it?

For those of you that feel Emotionally unsafe, unstable, unsure. For those of you that haven't had success before whilst all others around you appear to be doing just great. For those of you stricken with fear because nothing in your life has ever gone well and never will.

We say leap within.

Leap within to that place inside of you that is nothing but pure positive energy, your Inner Being and your Higher Self await you there. For here are all the riches that this world has to offer. Trust, love, hope, truth and strength.

This is not a leap for the faint hearted and yet when safely landed it will bring you more joy, more wonder and more clarity than anything else in the world.

And do not feel that just because the word leap has previously filled you with fear that this is not for you. For this leap, whilst a difficult one, will never fail you, will never leave you all alone, will never judge you and will only ever see you as the perfect individual that you are.

Leap within to that place of vulnerability and feel the rewards. Leap to here with honesty and integrity and wash away all of your fears, your guilt, your shame, your hurt.

Leap within and unturn those stones that cause you pain and then move quickly on, quickly on to love. For in love you find your salvation.

Leap within and give yourself to you. Let all that you truly are flow from you and give all of this with love.

Leap within and let your suffering drive your desires and lead you to your destiny.

Never step away from your goal, never be steered from this path, either by you or by others and know that your Journey is eternal, full of growth for you and your Higher Self. Together you WILL see it through.

Leap within and allow your loved ones near and always be true to them. Never fear failing them. Your truth, your love is all that they need from you.

Know that your anger, your distress, takes you further from YOUR truth. Love is your guide back home.

Leap within.

Fear not this Journey for freedom is your gift. Fear not your life nor others nor yourself, especially yourself. Hold on to the love for yourself and never ever let go. The Soul in you that has suffered so is ready to stop hiding now, ready to peep over that wall and ready to jump over it.

Your time is NOW.

Olivia and Raf, Abraham and Jesus

19

"FREEFALL" - CONSCIOUS FEELING

We use the term 'Freefall' with many of our clients. Freefall comes from a place of ease, it is "Conscious Feeling", in other words being fully aware of how you are 'feeling right now'. When you are able to Master this you free yourself from those habitual or self-sabotaging thoughts that don't make you 'feel' good.

In order to Freefall the first thing you must do is get out of your head. If your mind is continuously leading the conversation with you then you are not correctly undertaking Freefall. With Freefall you allow your Inner Being and Higher Self to work together to literally lead you to what you are going to do now, not next, not later…now. You have ultimate control in Freefall with your Higher Self merely making suggestions via your Inner Being, and trying to connect you to what will make 'feel' good or better.

Freefall is about letting go of all control of what you 'think' you need to be doing. Some of you will say that this is impossible for those that lead busy lives, with jobs and kids and all the duties that comes with this. And yes, we acknowledge that it's not easy but it is possible and the more you let go of the control to plan, and know and set tasks in motion, the more you will in fact really 'feel' in control. Because when you Freefall you are leaving everything that you do down to what 'feels' best for you at the time and therefore in this knowledge comes a 'feeling' of safety, of love for yourself, and a 'feeling' that everything that you are doing is in your best interests.

Still there will be those that will argue with us that when you have a meeting to go to or the kids meals to think about, that you need to put thought into those things beforehand; what are the agenda items, do I have what I need for the clients, are there eggs in the refrigerator. But we say why think about these things now? Why not later when you 'feel' like doing it. Or why didn't you do it earlier when you 'felt' like doing it but decided to do something else that you 'thought' was more important.

In other words we are not denying that life goes on and that life comes with ownership and responsibility, but we are saying that letting go of the need to control it all IS the way to live. So instead of instigating control, act on that impulse, on that 'feeling' at the time, every time and in doing so you will always be doing what your Inner Being and Higher Self know is right for you 'at that time'.

So start first thing in the morning, which by the way is often the hardest time, as we lay in bed or sit by the breakfast table thinking about what we think we need to do. Instead get yourself into a mode of 'feeling' and connect to a sensation of gently falling safely and endlessly, forward or backward, either is fine, we use both. In this moment you are letting go for a moment and allowing yourself to 'feel' something. The key is to have a sense of energy momentum around you and by connecting to that 'feeling' of momentum you are taking the focus away from your head and those perpetual thoughts.

This momentum can take many forms in terms of pace. There's a momentum in just lying down, there's a momentum in staring out of your window and of course there's a momentum in following a 'feeling' of excitement as you rush to meet your loved one or to the laptop to write that next chapter, or to scamper out of the door to take the dog for a walk. All of these things should have one thing in common and that is that they 'feel' like the thing you really want to do 'at the time'.

Many of our clients struggle with achieving this in particular those with high levels of stress and anxiety as these Emotions will disconnect them from 'feeling' and instead keeps them in their heads. So we suggest that if you are one of these people then just focus on allowing.

Allowing with regards to Freefall means stopping any resistance to absolutely everything. Allow yourself not to decide what the kids will want for breakfast before you yourself get up. Allow yourself to get worked up at the thought of that meeting or presentation. It's ok to get stressed, to get angry to get deflated or to get fed up, whatever you 'feel' is ok. Which is worse, convincing yourself that by getting stressed you put yourself into a state of misAlignment and therefore to control that you must bury or suppress those feelings, or allowing that stress to be surfaced and displayed but then afterwards allowing yourself to know that it will be fine and that you'll find a solution or that it will just work it's way out of you over time.

Allow yourself to have that bottle of wine in the week because you feel stressed and if you're on your third bottle of wine in consecutive days then allow yourself to recognise that somewhere else along the line you're not allowing something else which is therefore causing you to want to keep on drinking. It's in this continual state of allowing that you generate this feeling within you of utter Alignment with what you want in each and every moment and that 'feeling' of falling from moment to moment in an easy and flowing manner. This is Freefall.

And as you make this more and more part of your life's routine you will find it so freeing and so liberating. Every moment becomes one to savour, just the simple action of staring out at the window at a small patch of green grass, instead of that rectangular screen in front of you can bring immediate connection to 'feeling' and therefore a new focus for you. And if the new focus is saying to get back on that screen then that's fine because that's what you will 'feel' like doing. But if that focus is saying lie down or take break from the office for a few minutes then do it. Leave the schedule for a moment and trust that it will be better for you in the long run and that you will actually get more done, whilst perhaps also enjoying yourself just a little more.

If you're unsure how to connect to with Freefall just try stopping what you're doing for a moment and allowing your mind to relax and run free. Let the thoughts simmer down until eventually you take yourself to a point of relaxation. Ok that's it, you're now in a 'Freefall State' where you can connect so much more strongly with your 'feelings' and what your Higher Self is leading you to.

Closing your eyes is helpful if you're struggling to slow the mind. Hold this state for as long as possible and see it as a mini rest for you. Now just wait, but wait without apprehension and instead wait until you 'feel' like doing something that 'feels' good to do in the moment. It may not be an action that has you spinning cartwheels of joy but it just needs to be something that's enough to motivate you into a more positive momentum.

A small of caution with this. Be wary of excitement when looking to Freefall. Something you really desperately want to do is not Freefall, it's 'thinking'. Because in that excitement you lead the conversation and therefore you are in danger of confusing what you 'think' would be a cool thing to do with what you 'feel' would be a cool thing to do. Allow yourself to connect inwardly through the Emotion of excitement and double check if it still 'feels' good to do. It's not to say that this exciting activity will not be a great thing to do but be aware of your true Emotions in that moment. Will the excitement just be masking a stress or a worry that you have about not doing that exciting activity; for example doing something with the children because you've been ignoring them all week because of work. Is Freefall actually just asking you to take a break and rest yourself for that day because you've been pushing yourself so hard.

Perhaps with this rest Freefall will lead you to do that exciting activity tomorrow when you are more energised and both you and the children can get the most from it? By the way, if you do follow Freefall and take the rest, make sure you do it without guilt or the generation of other Low Vibrations otherwise it defeats the object of listening to yourself and your Self.

There's so much fun you can have with Freefall but also from it can come so much insight and for this reason Freefall has been made a chapter in this book. For Freefall is not just a way of spending your day but it can also be a crucial tool for connecting to the Self for the purposes of self-discovery. Consider for a moment what you are doing when you leave yourself at the mercy of what 'feels' right for you. In this moment you are truly connected to you, to your Inner Being and through to your Higher Self, and in this connection comes so many other possibilities.

Freefall is literally the most advanced way of being that you can possibly live by and it could well be your saviour. When you master the ability to connect to your Physical Body, Emotional Bodies, your Inner Being and your Higher Self all at once it is possible to understand how connected, or disconnected you are in that moment.

There are many Physical sensations you can 'feel' when you have that sense of disconnection in you, when something doesn't quite 'feel' right. Perhaps there's a hollowness, a distance inside of you when you think of something or someone that you care for. In these cases try to find a way to draw nearer to your Inner Being, the Self, to sense which

Emotions you are feeling because your Higher Self, through your Inner Being will be offering you a Truth or an opportunity for new Truth. Offering you this opportunity perhaps to analyse or to understand and receive clarity and therefore to Change that old Truth and create something more positive from it.

As you become more attuned to this process it becomes automatic and you will recognise your Inner Being's offering for an opportunity for you to receive clarity on something that perhaps you hold within and need to release, or just the opportunity for another manifestation born from that understanding, from that new Truth.

Freefall when used in this way to connect to your Inner Being and Higher Self for clarity and Emotional releasing can really bring you a true connection to the Self, to Emotional freedom and to the manifestation of a better life.

Think about this for a moment. Freefall links you to positive manifestation.

Why? Because at the heart of Freefall is your Higher Self.

Your Higher Self who knows you so well, and who is fully Aligned to your Soul Contract and importantly has divine insight into what you are currently Aligned to from a manifestation perspective. Your Higher Self knows how Aligned you are 'right now' to all of your wishes and dreams and knows exactly where the resistance is to you manifesting them. And so by allowing yourself to Freefall, in other words to 'feel' what your Higher Self is suggesting, you are also allowing yourself to get closer and closer to all that you desire.

So remember to stay out of your head, don't think from the mind, think from the Soul, and FEEL your way to everything that you want to achieve in life.

Olivia and Raf, Abraham and Jesus

20

LET GO CONTROL LET GO NEED

Let go that need in you that yearns for the love of another. That person that hasn't loved you all of your life or ever at all in this relationship. Let go the anger at him or her. Do this and you let go of something. That something in you that pulls you in and drags you down and along and along and along.

That something is your need driven by a lack of love and anger. That something for men, women, children, drugs, gambling, sport, work, love, whatever. What's your need? What's your pain? What does your lack of love relate to? What does your anger cling to? Find these answers and you start to tackle that most frightening of Emotions.

LUST.

Just the word alone can fill some with fear, especially those that are so imprisoned by it. Lust, lust, lust. Dark debaucherous lust. Lust, lust, lust. Evil depraved lust.

But don't be fooled by these sinister words. Don't think that these words belong to nasty men or women that lurk in the shadows waiting for their prey to make itself available to them. Lust affects the majority of men, women, and children on this planet. For some lust never goes any further than the thoughts and Emotions that secretly and quietly eat away at them. For others it goes much further and of course can be harmful to others as well as themselves in such terrible ways.

But lust can be beaten.

Lust is the result of suffering. Never judge the lust of another. Such a harsh pill to swallow when you or somebody you love has been the victim of a lustful person. Lust is such a dangerous concoction and when the lack of love and anger levels are high, not even that high, the consequences for that poor person can be horrific. Lust in us grows gently but picks up a rapid pace if the hurtful encounters continue for a person. But know it only takes a single stream of tough consequences for your life to be blighted by it. Lustful experiences for those exposed to them will differ greatly but nevertheless the Emotion of lust will sap all that hold it within them if they allow it.

But lust can be beaten.

Next time you take a look at that man or woman across the street, or find yourself looking away awkwardly when you see a young child semi naked or wonder why you just can't get enough of that casual and social drug habit or why you spend hour upon hour in the gym or at work, look closely at your experiences and ask yourself where is your anger coming from. Ask yourself who in your life has hurt you so much either in a one time experience or over and over again. Lust feeds on these moments that dwell in your Subconscious Mind's memories and your Physical Body. Slowly over time it's energy starts digging it's long dirty fingernails into your body as you top up with more lack of love and anger.

But lust can be beaten.

Let go the need for that love that you yearn for and that you have never had. Connect instead to the love that you do have all around you. Find a way to see beyond the blame game, not easy to do but so simple if you allow it. There is so much love around you, both here on Earth and in Non Physical. Allow it in.

Follow the guidance in this book and then allow it. For if you don't, if you simply continue to look to control that lust, to hide and bury it then you will literally be sitting in a pool of guilt, shame, paranoia, panic, shock, nervousness, confusion....the list goes on and on. You know it does, you feel it, you fear it, you hate it.

But lust can be beaten.

Control.

Control.

Control.

Stop it!

This is you speaking not us. This is your conflict, that which bases itself in your Subconscious Mind. Such a beautiful thing is the mind and yet why does it make many feel like they're in hell.

Let go control of that lust NOW.

Let go control and you let go the need and you let go the conflict. Don't fight that anger any more but instead let it rise in you. Seek what it relates to and let it go. Find peace with yourself, love for yourself and then and only then find peace with those that have hurt you so. What drives their lack of love, their anger, their lust? Understanding this will help you to let go, not to forgive, you know we say never forgive, just find understanding, compassion, love and then forget.

For if you refuse to forget then you will hold onto that control. So instead find a way to not replay those sickening experiences over and over in your head. Why didn't they love me? Why am I not important enough? How could they have done that? If only they knew how much I'm suffering they would love me more I know it.

No they wouldn't.

They wouldn't because they couldn't love you any more. They may not show it but they couldn't love you any more. They too live in their own world of lack of love and anger and disconnection from the Self. And because of this they just can't bring themselves to show it to you. Too much hurt, too many arguments, too much judgement between you.

So instead love yourself the way you want them to love you.

Find a way to understand all that has been in your respective Journeys and then with love simply let it go.

But we hear you say, tell that to the person that was abused Physically, Emotionally, mentally, sexually or all of them. Say that to the person that can't stop that lustful urge for that fix of love in whatever guise it takes because of the relationship battles they have had to endure and that have fed this cesspit of lack of love and anger. This lustful pull within them that at times they don't even know is working its magic on them.

But lust CAN be beaten.

Let go the yearning and the need and instead connect within. Start here. Build back up your self-worth, let go the self-judgement and the paranoia and most of all STOP BLAMING. You came onto this Earth knowing there would be challenges and you did so knowing some of them would not be pleasant but you did so because the rewards were outstanding.

The blame is not yours to take on. The blame is not theirs either. God takes this blame remember, so allow him to take this blame and do not blame him for taking the blame! Start here and you will find this a much easier task.

Connect to love for you. Trust you. Let go the need to control who is responsible, the need to control how you react to them and most of all let go the need to control the lust in you, the anger in you and the hatred in you. Be brave with this and know that over time if you knock down those skittles of lack of love and anger and what they relate to, you will be free from this.

But in the meantime don't clench up when lust takes hold, simply allow love through in that moment, we mean self-love and not the fix of love driven by anger. Don't fight anger with more anger. Strength fuelled by anger only goes so far but strength fuelled with love is a winner. Your strength is in the allowing of your anger to rise, just a little and enough to affect you for a short moment and once connected to it, fight this with your Truths. Your Truths that are gathered as you go about releasing yourself from the past will tackle this anger if strong enough. And know when this happens your world will Change. Self-love and love for your Journey will now bring you a new strength over your lust and your fears of this lust.

Those dirty fingernails can grow pretty long over the years and decades. Don't expect an overnight miracle. You may become tired of trying to beat this, tired of trusting that this will go, tired of waiting for a Change. See this period through and keep dealing with your anger and watch when you trip into hate for this only strengthens the lust, especially the hate that you allow yourself to feel from others that probably doesn't even exist.

Be strong with this, be brave with this for the peace and Balance that you crave is literally just around the corner.

Olivia and Raf, Abraham and Jesus

2 1

WHAT IS LOVE

Love is vulnerable and scary at times. Love is help and support from those that care. Love is that anger that has protected you all your life from being hurt. Love is trust and knowing, knowing that it if it doesn't quite work out today everything will be fine in the end. Love is knowing that everything that happens to you is for a reason and at the right time. Love is moving forward. Love is letting go resentment anger fear guilt shame hurt sadness paranoia disbelief shock worry nervousness distress anxiety. Love is letting go those sickening depraved self-sabotaging thoughts. Love is avoiding conflict. Love is allowing and not resisting goodness. Love is hope. Love is strength. Love is faith. Love is hard. Love is easy. Love is natural. Love is listening. Love is giving and receiving. Love is cool. Love is generous. Love is freedom. Love is free. Love is costly. Love is acceptance. Love is family and friends. Love is enemies. Love is great and greatness. Love is the small and sick and weak. Love is the strong and powerful. Love is wonder. Love is bright and light and enlightening. Love is calm. Love is caring. Love is connection, to the Self and others. Love is laughing, love is crying, love is living, love is dying. Love is poetry. Love is your poetry your poem your sonnet your song. Love is you love is me love is us. Love is connection to every single piece of you because love is in every single piece of you and every single piece of you is love. Every single piece of this Universe and the Multiverse is love, love is God, remember. Every single thought, every movement, every Law that governs all that we do is love. Letting go and moving on is love. Waving goodbye to fear is love.

All of these things together into one single Truth is love. This Truth is love for me, this Truth is love for you, this Truth is love for God. This Truth is my freedom. Love is this freedom. Love is your connection to this freedom, living this freedom, allowing this freedom, feeling this freedom, becoming this freedom, becoming love. Become love, integrate to love, see love in everything, every person every animal every plant, every single fabric of your existence.

But never forget you. Never forget to love you. You you you you you YOU.

This is love.

You are love.

Olivia and Raf, Abraham and Jesus

22

CONNECT TO LOVE

So much in this book could be perceived as just being about connecting to pain and the past suffering, all in the name of letting go and moving on. Let's not forget the importance of this and understand that just solely focussing on the positive all of the time will not shift your Vibration to where it needs to go. Having said this just focussing on the negative all of the time isn't what's required either.

Desire is such a strong part of what is needed in us if we are to maintain Balance through periods where we are looking to make a Change and to shift Low Vibration. Love for the Self and for others is also critical.

The simplest of things can make a difference. That distressed email that you reply to, the crazy driver that you respond to, the grumpy shopkeeper or assistant. All or some of these things can occur for most on a daily basis and so imagine the difference you could make to your Vibration if you simply decided to not allow any of these to affect you.

Imagine if you created a Truth which you called via your Higher Self that was created with the intention of being used for the purpose of generating in you High Vibration in a moment. Let's say that Truth contained the Emotions of joy, calm, peace, hope, love, self-love, safety, assurance, certainty, expectation, confidence, desire, passion, trust, strength, faith, excitement, wonder and enlightenment. Now that's a real funpack of Emotions and in The Feelset Tools at the end of this book we detail exactly how to do this.

Call this Truth at any time and you will immediately generate these High Vibrations in your Physical body. For those of you thinking that this is generating falseness within you, a feeling that isn't real, note that it will not stop you from feeling the Low Vibrations that you may generate for yourself in the same moment of the experience. It will also not stop you from generating your own High Vibrational Emotions in the moment either.

It will however make you feel a little better should you not react as you would have wanted to for that experience. It will also remind you, just by calling that Truth, that you want to feel good and not be distressed by that email or that road hog or whatever it is that has caused you to feel stressed.

Connecting to love in each and every moment of your life is going to be a tough ask but trying to do so should be your intention. Generating a Truth which fills your body with High Vibration will help you to set high standards for yourself, not to mention that it will also massively help shift out lots of Transitional Low Vibration and stop it settling into your Stored Vibration. What's not to like?

Of course the generation of High Vibration from actual experiences is also great because of the memories that you will generate in your Subconscious Mind. For those of you in the Resistant and/or Psychotic Subconscious Mind State (to be discussed in The Bodies section) this is critical in helping you to train your Subconscious Mind as to how you want it to act in given situations. The more High Vibrational experiences that you can have as memories, the more Balanced the mind feels and therefore the less Low Vibration it generates through your Egoic Bodies. Likewise the Egoic Bodies themselves, which act more habitually, will be less inclined to generate fear and doubt in your Emotional Bodies if your habits are High Vibrational.

Which is a better example to set to your Subconscious Mind: You screaming at the driver that has just cut you up, or the acknowledgement that the driver has been foolish and a bit reckless, but that you have done that yourself when you have been in a hurry? We say acknowledge the latter and then call your funpack Truth to soothe you.

Low Vibration is generated by everyone all of the time no matter how High Vibrational you are. But the chance to fill yourself with High Vibration as often as you can should not be missed. So for those of you that lead busy lives and can't get out too much make use of the Vortexes of Emotion (also to be discussed in a later chapter) and generate Truths that you can trigger just sitting on the couch watching TV. Do this all day every day, there's just so much available capacity in terms of how much your body will be able to absorb with regards to High Vibration. You can do this on an individual Emotion basis or create a bundle of them to call as you wish. Be considerate of creating Emotions that you wouldn't necessarily wish to exert for a given situation. Your Higher Self can guide you but just allow yourself to be free with this.

Routinely connect to love first thing in the morning or at the end of your day, or when you can at any other time. You do enough connecting to pain during the day so try to some find some time for love. Treat yourself to your funpack when relaxing, journaling, showering, when in a meeting and getting ready to present to the board or just when the kids are running around screaming and having fun. There's no limit on how much love you can have so stop restricting yourself.

Be mindful of which Vibration that you are choosing to place into your body for each and every action. After a while it will become second nature. Well in fact it probably already is but perhaps it's the Low Vibration and not the High, so ask yourself, which is your Vibration of choice in this moment and if need be, Change it.

Let go the pain and suffering for just for a while and if you can do this consistently you will find that you will slowly start to unstick yourself from those things that hold you back and that you constantly carry with you. You will start to recognise behaviours in you that you don't like and that you wish to Change, and in time you will start to connect to love, to be more in love and to create behaviours and reactions to situations that evolve you and evolve the way your

Subconscious Mind reacts, and therefore the way that you react in every moment.

Turn off the Subconscious Mind Dripping Tap of Emotions. Turn on the hosepipe of High Vibrations and love instead!

We love you.

Olivia and Raf, Abraham and Jesus

23

LOVE OR HATE WHICH WILL YOU CHOOSE?

It sounds like a selfish position to take but if you always choose 'you', then by inference we say you always choose love. It's a choice which drives the least conflict in you which is always the best one to take and by taking this approach love is what you connect to.

Take for example a situation where a friend or a loved one has said or done something to cause you Emotional disharmony or distress. You may argue that it would be far better for your overall Vibration to shut them out of your life and put the whole thing behind you. And yet ask yourself for how long will you be able to deal with the spiralling thoughts and feelings as you play back the situation over and over, 'mindreading' how they may be judging you, or the scenario when you will eventually have to deal with seeing them somewhere.

For in the constant playing and listening and feeling of this movie to yourself, little by little your Vibration will spiral. And burying away your Emotions and refusing to deal with the situation can usually only be held out for so long before the Subconscious Mind warms up and starts that loving process of protection manifested as fear, resentment, sadness or perhaps guilt.

Resolving the conflict in this situation does not necessarily mean picking up the phone or messaging to try and make things right. Often taking a position which understands why the other person did what they did or has taken offence to something that was said, is all that is needed to start to ease the cycle of conflict within you, and in this moment you have chosen love. Love for you and love for the other.

And so does this mean that if you choose not to pick up the phone or you ignore messages and gifts or attempts by the other to reconcile, that you are choosing hate? Well you are certainly choosing to connect to pain and in doing so disconnecting, not just from the other person but most importantly from yourself. In addition you could start a whole new round of Emotional war games with those around you that you love as they seek to support you and take your side on a matter which they may not really understand or worse still, may not actually agree with you on.

This cycle of conflict can all of a sudden become a huge matter for all and this is particularly common in family disputes where loyalties are requested and those on the opposite side are criticised, at times creating a whole new set of arguments based on their own conflicts and as such triggering a new cycle of Emotional suffering. And so it goes on literally for months, years and in some cases sadly forever. Isn't this how wars are created?

We appreciate the extremity of this comparison but we do it only to highlight the depth and breadth of the pain that can occur from Emotional differences. And the conflict within is where it all begins, and therefore where it must end. So look to choose love ALWAYS. Look to take the action which leads 'you' to the most ease and consider that it may not be the action that feels the best in the moment but that may serve you and your Vibration better best in the long run.

And choosing love over hate is not just about the big stuff. Ask yourself what is the best way for you to respond to that unpleasant Customer Services Assistant or your partner who's had a long day that snaps at you when you ask them how it went. And next time you look at yourself in the mirror and you hear that voice in your head criticising your clothes or your size, just stop, but don't bury the thought. Stop, let go, and then allow love in.

This is difficult for some but it's a case of starting to try to retrain the Subconscious Mind that this way of working isn't for you. Feel or think something different in that moment, stay out of the slipstream of fear and instead jump into the lovestream, full of hope and positivity.

And don't be afraid to seek help and to admit that you just can't deal with something or don't know how to resolve something. In that moment you are choosing love again for yourself. Allow yourself to show vulnerability, cry, get frustrated and even give up for a minute. Give yourself a break, take a dip into the lovestream and come back to the problem refreshed and with a little more hope and enthusiasm. Simple advice and yet often ignored in the quest to just keep moving forward.

We love you. Do you?

Olivia and Raf, Abraham and Jesus

24

YOU MANIFEST EVERYTHING

We have heard this said a few times and yet whilst this is true it's not quite as you would think.

The Soul Contract is a manifestation source which contains 'some' predetermined outcomes and therefore there are experiences in your life that have occurred or that will occur that you can do nothing about. These events or outcomes were asked for by you before you came to Earth in a discussion with God and your Higher Self.

This means that no matter how hard you work at something on Earth sometimes it will fail, and in contrast some things you don't even work towards will just succeed.

So for outcomes that have haven't gone as planned or where you have caused yourself or others suffering in life, take your foot off the guilt, the blame and the failure Emotion pedals because sometimes you were just meant to fall down that hole. Of course everything else that happens on your Journey outside of the pre-manifested Soul Contract milestones and experiences, are also of your doing and form the wonderful tapestry of your Journey that you so craved to create as a Soul in Non Physical waiting to take your place on Earth for this mission called 'Life'.

Take comfort from this and start now to cherish everything that happens to you, good and bad, as a gift from God and a gift that you can grow from because this is what all of our successes and failures are manifested for. And this is how you always wanted it to be in this life.

Don't think that this excludes you from taking responsibility for these outcomes especially if they create pain for you and others. Ultimately you took every decision here on Earth to do, think or feel what you have done, thought or felt. But be kind on yourself and connect to the understanding that your life here on Earth is part of a much greater eternal experience. An experience that will ultimately lead to so much good, so much love and so much expansion for you and all.

Whilst your Higher Self will incarnate many Souls on this Earth there will only ever be one life as your Soul, as you. You will never return to this planet as a Physical Human, only as a Non Physical Human, and whilst there will be many more wonderful experiences for you eternally in Non Physical after this life, at this moment it is not planned for you to have a chance to have a good go at life on Earth again.

Remember this always. Know that you are now in control of most of what is manifested in your life, and that which occurs that was pre-manifested, by God on your request, try and accept with love. Your Higher Self will do all that they can to make this experience as magnificent as you wished it to be when you set out the details of your Soul Contract, and if you're able to connect to your Higher Self at all times the wonderful paths of light and love which lay before you, awaiting to be manifested, WILL be achieved.

Olivia and Raf, Abraham and Jesus

25

FEAR NEEDS TO STAND ASIDE NOW

Dear Diary,

The things that have happened in my life have at times been devastating and yet it's the little things that at times eat away at me the most. I could list out all the things and actions that I do or have done repeatedly based on fear but I just don't want to. I'm fed up with fear I've had my fill of fear and I know I have no reason to fear anything now.

I and we have been through it all it seems, literally name an Emotion and we've had it, name an experience and we've probably had something similar happen to some degree or another, and yet we are still here and we are still strong.

But we are fed up and we are aching to move forward and so fear needs to stand aside now. Fear has ruled me for so long but no more, I can't and won't allow it. I know my Guides will help me through this but I take this challenge on myself and right now I say to you fear "I DON'T FEAR YOU".

Instead I leap up and scream I love life, I miss life and I want life. Boy has fear ruled me, I feel it right now just how much it has held me back, Aligned me to pain and not to love. I must never forget this, never allow myself to be held back by this Emotion and I never will. I demand this of myself and of those Guides that have watched me suffer from it since childhood. I ask for their love and support to see me through my fears, always.

Olivia and Raf

26

GROWTH

Someone Else: Such a commonly used word is growth. And yet what does it really mean and how much do those that use it really connect to it. It's learning from your mistakes some may say. It's dealing with all that life throws at you and not looking back, say others. You may agree that it's about changing your life and becoming a better person, connecting to all that is good in you and those around you. Or is it just about being happy with your lot and living a life of ease no matter what?

God: Well in fact it's all of these things and also none of them. Because my growth is different to your growth is different to his growth is different to her growth is different to their growth. My past, my present, my future is different to yours is different to his is different to hers is different to theirs. So what growth means to me will be based on my own experiences and what I do as a result of those experiences, either now or later down the line, or both, in fact especially both. For growth comes when something Changes in us, for the better that is. A Change may be the result of a negative reaction and therefore perhaps a Change for the worse, and a Change for the worse is not growth but simply an addition to the opportunity for us to grow.

A period of suffering for you and perhaps those around you, which in turn may have created more suffering for you, may only result in growth after that suffering has had a chance to fester, to bury itself and to cause you as much Physical Emotional or mental pain as possible. For many of us the opportunity for growth may only come after a lifetime of suffering because your Soul Contract has dictated this, or perhaps you just hadn't taken the opportunity for growth when you were given the opportunity earlier. When we use the words 'hadn't taken the opportunity' perhaps instead we could say 'hadn't had the mental strength' or 'hadn't been Physically able' or perhaps just plain old 'we were so weighed down by the horror of our Journey that we simply feel lucky to be alive'.

Someone Else: Lucky to be alive. Wow now there's a strong statement especially when linked to the word growth. We come to this Earth to learn and love and experience new things, good and bad, so we can expand ourselves and the rest of the Universe and I'm lucky to be alive. Really!! How dare you do this to me?? How dare you make me suffer in this way when all I am is a person full of love and hope, and all that I ever wanted was to live a wonderful life. Instead you made me hurt myself, hurt others, go through experience after experience, problem after problem, disaster after disaster slowly and painfully disconnecting myself from all that I am, changing how I act how I feel how I perceive myself, how others perceive me and all of this in the name of growth!?

God: Yes. You asked me to.

Someone Else: But really? Did I really ask for this much pain this much hurt this much disillusionment this much sickening impact in my life? And did I really ask for it to go on for years and years and years? Why God why!?

God: Because I love you. Because you love you and because you are strong. Don't fear this don't hide behind this. Don't shirk it.

Someone Else: Don't shirk what?

God: Your Journey. The Journey you willingly and lovingly accepted and created before you even came onto this Earth. Don't see all that has happened to you as hurdles to hurt you. These hurdles love you and are desperate for you to jump over them.

Someone Else: I've tried so many times to jump over them but I always seem to clip my heals at the top and fall down. Over and over I try to jump these hurdles and when I eventually clamber over one, the next one appears and at times even bigger than the last. Hurdles this close together are for sprints and my life is a long distance Journey so why can't I just have a bit more time in between hurdles? A bit more time to rest, to recover, to prepare myself for the next hurdle?

God: Because I love you. Because you love you and because you are strong. Embrace this. Love this gift to yourself.

Someone Else: I just need to let go all of this now. I need to let go the past. I need a break. At times I feel like running just running so far away from all of this. At times I feel like I want to die, to just curl up in a ball and never come out of this hell I call my life, that you call my Journey.

God: Come on take my hand we're going for a walk.

Someone Else: Where?

God: To take a look at your Journey so far. Don't be afraid we're not going to relive anything we just want to take a look of what you've learned.

Someone Else: I'm weak God I don't know if I can see this all over again.

God: You can you are strong you are love you are hope, you are like me. Have faith in me, you.

Someone Else: Ok. Where shall we start?

God: Anywhere you like whatever feels right, that is always the place to start. From this place of feeling you connect to where the pain is, to where the opportunity for growth is. How about here perhaps, look at this point of pain and tell me what you feel.

Someone Else: I feel sadness I feel anger I feel shame I feel loss I feel betrayal I feel lack of love I feel guilt I feel unworthy I feel so many others things. This is why my life is a mess why my health is a mess, just look at what I've been through.

God: You have been through so much my dear friend and you have every right to feel all of these Emotions. You have every right to feel sorry for yourself and for the others also involved. You have a right to be frustrated and feel hard done by. You have the right to turn away from this as you have said.

But do you want to? Do you really want to run from something that you have worked so hard to create and that you have put your life and soul into, blood sweat and tears into? Do you really want to do this when now, right now you have the chance to reap the rewards of everything you have sown? Everything you have ever done, good and bad, has gone into this masterpiece that you have created. This masterpiece is full of so much of you, and now you decide to leave it here like a painting that you are dissatisfied with folded up and hidden in a box, rather than framed and hung on the wall, proud of what it contains and what it represents?

Someone Else: I so understand and feel what you are saying here but how and where do I begin? I've never framed a picture I've never used a drill. I have no idea how to hang this up even if I had the strength or the will to do so.

God: Look at that picture over there on the wall and tell me what you see.

Someone Else: I see a person in small boat with the sea in the distance looking calm and the sky above full of sunshine.

God: I see hope. I see love. I see you. I see a scene that won't always have been that way, a scene full of potential danger

153

and hazards and that at any time could Change. But right now I see a scene of peace and serenity and a scene without fear, in fact I see nothing but ease. This scene is within you, in fact it is you and this scene is calling out to you every single day in every single moment, begging you to connect to it. This scene is within your Inner Being, a place that has felt and suffered every moment with you, felt past mistakes felt past wrongdoings felt all of the pain that you have ever endured no matter how small. And yet this place has also felt all the joy all the love all the…

Someone Else: …Look I'm sorry to interrupt but these words are just not getting me out of here. Don't you think I've tried all of this mindset stuff? Words are great, feeling all this stuff is great but how how how do I break free of all of this without understanding why all this has happened, without being able to share this with someone to support me, without having the opportunity to make amends. You've seen my life you've seen what's happened to me you've seen how much I've been impacted, this is just an impossible task. Tell me how. Please!

Me: Excuse me I couldn't help overhearing your conversation and I wondered if I could help. I have suffered, too much in fact. I have been hurt, hurt myself and others too, too much in fact. I have felt lost, alone and without anyone to share the burdens of my Journey too, too much in fact. But I have done one thing differently to you. I have lifted myself off that couch, got out of that bed, searched myself, seen myself, Changed myself. I have been honest, too honest and this has hurt.

This has hurt me and this has hurt others but in the end this hurt made me stronger, because in this hurt was love, was purity, was all that I am and in this hurt came freedom. True freedom, not just relief or a few days of grace but REAL freedom. It wasn't easy, it wasn't quick and I was afraid, very afraid of what might become of me, of what might become of those that I love. But know this. I don't regret a single thing not one thing that has happened in my life right now. Every one of those things has made me better than who I was when I came to this life. Right now in this moment I feel so Aligned, so unchained from what held me back, so ready for whatever comes. I know these are just more words for you and I know that your pain may be a lot worse than mine has ever been, but maybe not. It doesn't matter who wins the pain contest. All that matters is that we both win, that we all win, that we all grow.

God: Wonderful words my friend.

Me: More than words God. These words have taken so much courage to endure and to overcome. I know that you have been there every step of the way with me just as you were when we agreed this Journey. I know what these words mean for me today and how much love I'm going to get from these words from now on.

These words show that I now know what growth means and I say this to you *Someone Else.*

Take your gift of suffering and unwrap it now. Take this gift and share it with all, but most of all share it with yourself. Your life can be the gift box you always wanted. Don't look at the gift box wrapping or the size or the weight. Instead open it, take a look good inside and you might just find a whole bunch of surprises in that gift box. Unravel each surprise with care for some may be tightly wrapped and may be difficult to undo. And in the unwrapping you just might find some sweet treats to see you on your way. Some sweet treats to put that smile back on your face, to warm your heart and perhaps to inspire you to create some more sweet treats of your own.

This, *Someone Else* is growth. A sweet treat that only you can unravel. A sweet treat that those that you share it with will appreciate so much. And a sweet treat that fills you with love, so much love, connection, ease, truth, compassion and most of all freedom. Freedom to be who you want, when you want, how you want, without fear. Free from the past, free from the now, from tomorrow and free to be running towards all of your greatest desires.

Run now *Someone Else* towards that scene you looked at over there on that wall. That scene that looks calm. I know what it took to sail there, and I also now know what it takes to keep it there, to stop the boat from drifting away into stormy waters and to know when the sun is going down and when it's time to shelter a little until the sun comes up again.

My boat will always be in this scene now, I will always be in this scene now. Thank you God for helping me frame this scene, thank you for helping me hang it up. I could not have done this without you. I will never be without you.

Thank you for helping me keep my boat afloat.

Olivia and Raf, Abraham and Jesus, God

27

GROWTH FATIGUE

As we write this chapter we have literally just come out of an intense three weeks of growth. A period where so much has been gained and yet so much has been taken from us. The Physical, mental and most of all Emotional burden that comes with obtaining vibrational freedom and true spiritual connection. Obtaining feelings of Alignment, wonder, happiness, utter love and understanding for yourself and of those around you can be just a wee bit draining.

In our experience, a specific period of growth is often longer than three weeks and can take several months, and in that time often we will strap ourselves tightly in and prepare ourselves for what we know may be a bumpy ride. A ride with peaks and troughs, and as has always been the case for us, a roller coaster of a Journey that has always been worth it.

So what do we mean by 'growth fatigue'? In our case it's that moment when you realise that apathy has started to creep in and that instead of picking up that book you were reading, or writing that next chapter, or planning the next event or day out, you just much prefer to just settle into the couch watching series 5 episode 14 of that TV series that you first started watching only a few days ago. It's also that point when you realise that this apathy has been around for quite some time, potentially weeks and that as a result, your Vibration is affected and that you are starting to become disconnected to parts of your Self.

And yet for the past few weeks or months, all that you have done is spend day after day listening to your body, to your Guides, to your loved one, trying to understand what today's learning will be and how you need to fix it in order for you to move on and 'grow'. And you've managed to do this successfully day after day, so successfully in fact that now you have forgotten what it felt like to go a day without some kind of hardship or challenge and so each lesson completion and understanding has become just a tick in the box as you set yourself in readiness for the next hurdle to jump over or hoop to spring through.

It's at this point that something needs to Change, to stop. The continual cycle of growth can become tedious, frustrating, disappointing and upsetting, all of which saps your desire to look beyond today. The dreams and the manifestations seem like an ever distant reality and with the apathy now comes anger. Anger that you are stuck here constantly having to prove or improve, continuously on that wheel like a mouse in a cage, a locked cage.

So what needs to Change?

The simple answer is to take control. Recognise that you've reached a point of growth that will serve you for the next part of your Journey and that you just need a timeout. But this simple answer is not that easy to implement. Because for all the learning you may have achieved, growth fatigue can in fact put you back where you started, in other words in a Low Vibrational state of being with an overactive Subconscious Mind and a whole host of spiralling thoughts and Emotions.

Know that at this point you already hold the key to solving this. You have already passed this test and it's a matter of going back through your growth experiences and drawing on the lessons learnt. Have faith in what you have achieved and don't allow yourself to fall back into uncertainty. The wonder of your growth Journey is that you have accumulated a whole bunch of keys that have opened many doors for you and trust now that the doors you will come across in the next phase of your Journey can all be opened by one of the keys you already hold in your hand.

So hide the TV remote control and let the wonderful life that you are creating for yourself take you and fill you with love and joy and excitement, and feel the desire creep back in. Feel the anger creep away as you slowly slip back into normality.

That place where not everything is a sign and in fact it's just an ordinary thought or perspective given by your Conscious Mind on nothing in particular. Trigger more and more of this normality with thoughts and experiences of High Vibrational impact. Nothing big just normal stuff and soon you will start to feel your Physical Body energetically lift and grow within.

Be prepared to deal with the habitual Conscious Mind and even Physical cellular reactions, in particular if the growth period has been for a longer stretch. Just keep remembering that you have all the keys, and very importantly that your Higher Self is with you. Have trust in yourself and in this new skin that you find yourself in and as your energy returns your desire to move forward builds and so the cycle of goodness and love flows through you and all that has recently gone before you now becomes a wonderful, perhaps epic experience that you can look back on with pride.

Pride that you saw it through, pride that you have Changed and pride that on the way you have grown closer to yourself and those that you love, and perhaps also made a whole bunch of new Physical Human and Non Physical human friends.

Olivia and Raf

28

CHOICE + ACTION = ALLOWING

I choose me! So there.

I don't care what you do to me or say about me or think about me I still choose me. I don't care what I do to myself or think about myself or say to myself, I still choose me. I don't care if I mess things up I still choose me. I don't care if I upset you because I choose me and it's not going to make me fear you or fear what you might do to me.

I'm on a mission to get past all of this stuff (and that's me being polite about it). For if the Truth be known I've had just about all I can take of all the other stuff. I'm bored with it now, honestly this is so tedious. Aren't you bored with it? Somebody just pluck me from the sky and transport me to somewhere, anywhere, just take me away from my past thoughts my past negativity and my past 'ever so loving' Subconscious Mind that 'ever so lovingly' protects me by making me constantly feel fear or doubt or confusion or just about anything else that it feels is going to keep me safe. BORING.

When are you going to start listening to my Conscious Mind? The part of me that has moved on and Changed and left all of this 'stuff' behind. Seriously I'm not kidding Subconscious Mind, get on board or I'm off. I'm off! Meaning I'm going to stop listening to you and no matter what you do or make me feel, even if you bring me Physical pain, I'm just going to ignore you. That's how much I just don't care for your Subconscious Mind protection any more.

And the same goes for you my Guides and Higher Self. I'm so sick of hearing the same things from you. Honestly I get it! Now leave me be to become something else and stop dragging me down for heavens sake!

If you make me lie down on that bed one more time to contemplate one more piece of guidance, one more piece of advice that covers the same old ground I'm gone. Seriously I'm gone and what I mean by that is that I'm going to start ignoring you. I'll listen to anything that you do or say that is useful to me and the rest is gone, passing me by, straight into that folder named 'just not interested any more'.

Ok?! Are we clear? Seriously are we clear? Don't do the silent thing on me where I have to spend hours, days, weeks wondering what the heck I'm supposed to have learnt this time.

Right that's it now. I want no fancy ending to this chapter or words that make me well up and cry. This is a plain and simple message that I'm done. I'm through with these trials and tribulations and I'm moving on whether you or my Subconscious Mind are coming with me or not.

I've made my CHOICE and I'm taking ACTION right now and I'll keep making those RIGHT CHOICES and taking those RIGHT ACTIONS to make sure that my choices ALLOW WHAT I WANT to happen. I've spent too long making my RIGHT CHOICES and then taking the WRONG ACTIONS and therefore ALLOWING THE WRONG THINGS.

Ok, are you onboard with the program? Are we cool? Great.

Olivia and Raf

29

WONDERLOST

In a café talking with a stranger: I've been writing this book all about feeling good and Change and all that kind of stuff but I've got to this section of it and I've no idea what to write. All I know is that I feel a bit lost and a little confused. Nothing is quite happening for me today, in fact things have been a bit stop start for me for weeks...no, months now. Yes I've been doing some really good stuff, in fact I've actually learnt loads and there's been days where absolutely nothing could stop me from climbing that mountain of ambition and becoming the truly great person that I know I was always meant to be.

But today, like many recently, I'm just not on my game. Don't get me wrong the desire is there but things are just not quite hanging together. I'm doubting myself, making a few mistakes, nothing major just work stuff but it's all just a little bit...well you know. Or do you? Maybe you don't, sorry to assume, I didn't mean to...gosh I'm sorry, honestly I don't even know what I'm...tut.

I've been trying to lift myself probably a lot more than I realise lately and I guess this has all just culminated in me not quite being on my game. Gosh sorry I'm repeating myself again here aren't I? The thing is I just don't see an end to it all, you know, all this growth and stuff. Don't get me wrong I love it, well...no yeah I do love it but right now I just can't be bothered with it all.

You wouldn't believe the number of times I've picked myself off my couch and tried to feel different but for whatever reason...well you know. I tried taking the kids out to the park the other morning to get a little more connected to them because all of this growth has left me feeling a bit isolated from everyone. I sit there staring up at the ceiling processing stuff, learning stuff, releasing stuff and to be honest I know I've come so far. But yet I just don't feel any different in fact, don't tell anyone but I actually feel worse.

And yes of course I appreciate the bigger picture here but right now I just don't...well, you know. I mean I've gone through so much stuff, cleared myself of the past Low Vibrations, well most of them, and I can't help feeling like I've put a lot of focus on it that I've forgotten how to just be normal. Do you know what I mean? And I think my general mood is starting to rub off on the other half so together we're like this couple who are like just hanging around waiting for something to just happen I guess.

I really don't know what to do, all I do know is that something has got to Change because I'm not putting up with this for much longer. I can feel myself getting frustrated and even angry at times, I'm not sure at who, life in general I guess.

I suppose I'd better go and make dinner soon. There's some chicken in the fridge so the kids can have that and maybe me and my better half can have some beans on toast.

Anyway it's been nice talking with you, sorry I didn't catch your name? Oh, you didn't give it to me, fair enough. Well sorry to have wasted your time with my boring story maybe we'll meet up here again sometime? Oh ok, you don't come here very often, no problem well good to meet you.

Bye.

Oh wait! You forgot your hat it's raining out there so it will come in handy. Oh it's not your hat? No problem, maybe I'll just hand it to the person behind the counter.

Bye again.

On the way home: I wonder what's gonna happen on that drama we've been watching. I really hope that couple finally gets together, I'm getting fed up with watching it. In fact, the sooner we get through those remaining episodes the better so I can finally get away from the TV and get on with achieving something. I can really feel something awesome is going to happen with my job now, so maybe that will happen soon anyway and then I can just stop watching the TV. Yeah that's it.

At home: "Hi is anybody home?" Oh good I'll sneak a couple of those biscuits before anyone gets back. I wonder what's on

TV just quickly. Hmm, nothing in particular. Ok, maybe I could have another go at that chapter...nah I'm just not energised enough now I'll have another go tomorrow.

Tomorrow morning in bed: Darling I've had the worse night sleep I don't think I'm gonna be able to help with those things you wanted me to do today. I was going to maybe have a go at that book we've started but I'm not sure the ol' juices are quite flowing do you what I mean? Oh yeah I agree, it's going really well I reckon not too much more to write now...well, maybe, I'm not really sure in fact.

In fact I'm not really sure about a lot of things right now if I'm honest. I just seem to have lost my mojo and it's really affecting me. In fact when I think about it what I'm writing right now in the book is just a load of nonsense. I've really not got much inspiration for it at all. Don't get me wrong I'm really trying but...well, you know.

(Wonderlost).

Later that day: What the heck am I doing? I have so got to snap out of this. Since when did I become this person hanging around the house waiting for everything to fall into place perfectly? Since when did I let myself become so dragged down by life? It's like fear just rules my world right now and I have to let it go. I'm not in that bad a place, it's certainly been a lot worse.

A voice: Let go

Same voice: LET GO

Same voice again: Listen to yourself. Just stop my love. Yes, just let go. Feel. Feel the emptiness, the hollowness of your present. That's it feel. Feel that love within.

Let go. Please. Let go of the past. Feel your present. You are special. Those tears are that special. Don't doubt it, just allow it. Embrace you. I love you. I am you and you are me.

Later that afternoon: Hi kids! How was your day? Oh wow that's sounds like just the most amazing audition so when will you hear if you got the part? Oh it will be just so amazing to see my little girl up there on stage you are just perfect for that role. And just know that even if you don't get the role you were after it sounds like you'll get offered something. Either way I'm just so proud of you, come here give me a big kiss. And what about you my darling son did you get any feedback on that science homework? Really that's just awesome I'm just so proud of you! You worked so hard on that piece and not only that, you're now an expert on white and red blood cells! You know what, why don't you both come and help me with dinner. It's only chicken but we can add some peppers and garlic and maybe some chillies to make it a little more spicy and you guys can do all the chopping. Sound good? Yay!

Later that evening: Hi son how's it going we haven't spoken for a couple of weeks what's happening with the job?...Just hang in there fella we're all so proud of you and can't wait to see you soon, take care, bye. Hey darling I saw that link you sent me about that mountain walk I'd SO love to do that with you and the kids. They'd love it and then we could swing into that restaurant that we've always talked about and have a lovely lunch there maybe? Yeah? Cool!

Same voice again: Allow that to be enough my love. Forget your job, forget greatness allow this to be enough. Let go the guilt let go the fear. You have done enough. You are enough for them all.

That's it. Well done my love. This will all take time to sink in. You have come so far just allow things to settle. I know you want so much more for yourself. That will come I promise. It really is that easy you know.

Next day in the café with that stranger: Oh hi again how's it going? Listen I'm so sorry for dumping on you a little the other day I wasn't in a great place but you know what, I spent some quality time with the family and realised that those are the things that make me shine the most. All this other stuff I'm doing will happen I know it but for now I'm just going to sit back and enjoy whatever comes. Listen what is your name by the way? Awesome name where are you from? Oh how interesting I've always wanted to go there. I'd love to grab lunch and find out more if you're free soon? That's just great...well can't wait for that lunch I'll see to you soon.

Same voice again: It really is that easy. I know you don't feel it inside but keep making that choice and it will...

...Hey what's up? Been here before haven't you. That feeling is coming back isn't it. Tired of this now right? Never ending right? You were good earlier right? But now...I know my love. You're thinking you need more time, perhaps a little more to learn a little more growth needed before that good feeling comes.

Have faith my love have faith, all will be well for you. You will see, hope WILL return for you if you continue to allow and believe. Continue living your life in this Changed way, you are doing all that you need to do now. Your honesty and courage will see you through to the end, to that place you want to feel. This Change that you are undertaking won't always feel like you are making progress, even as you near the end of it, but you'll see, all will be well for you sooner than you think.

Lunch in the café a good while later talking with that stranger: Well thanks so much for a wonderful lunch you've really had such an amazing life, you must come over with your partner and meet the family. That's great, speak soon then. Bye.

That stranger thinking to himself: Wow, that guy was so shiny literally shining from the inside out. There is so much to be miserable about but there is something about that person. A calmness, a softness in the eyes, like someone wise, truly wise and almost knowing. No small talk just a nice and easy conversation. Sounds like they've been through a lot in their life, so much suffering going way back to childhood and yet I noticed the way he talked about his wife and kids, there is so much love there. That is really really nice to see, so nice to see. They are working on something pretty special too it just seems there's a bit of writer's block at the moment. I think they just need to talk about their experiences because from what I heard there's a whole lot to say. Whatever happens, I know it's going to work out for them. Things these days can be so hard now, lives are so crazy and yet he took the time to come and talk to me in that café, invited me out to lunch and how quick the time went, what a great conversation. I can't wait to read their book when it comes out.

That voice again: See that wasn't so hard was it. You were nervous about meeting up but you ended up having a lovely time. He thought you were great by the way. It really is that easy you know.

Well, what are you waiting for? You've seen how easy it is to be....

...."Be what" you're asking right?

Be with your friends be with your family be around town be in a park be funny be heard be excited be loving be loved be simple be smart, be with me.

Oh, who am I you ask? I'm the one who's hat you found in that café. You see I left it there for you actually. I've got so many hats. I've got so many hats in fact that often you won't even know I'm the same person. Well actually I'm not just a person I'm so many other things. But there's one thing I always am.

Clear, I'm always clear. Clear?

Sorry I don't mean to confuse you.

Oh ok then I'll say it. I'm God, of course I am. I'm sure you'd guessed already because of the hat thing. No? So let me explain you see...

...Oh my love. You're feeling lost again I can see.

Let go, just let go. Take my hand. Here, put on my hat, and remember what I said, you are nearer than you think even if it doesn't feel like it. Just keep going and have hope that this will end soon.

Now let go my love. Walk, run, jump, be happy, be free.

I know you've got a chapter to finish. But this chapter won't give you what you want. There'll always be another chapter to write there'll always be more challenges. Just be, my love.

A couple of weeks later talking to the other half: Safe. I feel safe all of a sudden. In control, strong, the Master of my Experience. I feel like in this moment, I sit here having truly let go the past, truly created a Truth to forget all that has gone before, created a Truth to love myself. And do you know what darling? I'm actually starting to believe I'm finally moving on. Those fears that have blighted me since forever don't seem that important any more, in fact right now just holding my dog and patting him and feeling that the love is what's important. Creating a world around me where peace and joy and truth and love exists is all that matters to me. And you know what, I actually KNOW this because of my Truth, I know this because of everything that I've added to this Truth. I know that everything is going to be ok. More than ok in fact, it's going to be unbelievably awesome. For the first time in my life I love me. All of me, every single part of me, past present and future. What I've learnt, what I've healed, what I've manifested just fills me with such utter wonder.

Yes wonder that's really the word for it. Wonder at how blessed I am to have suffered all that I have. Wonder at how strong I've been to work through all of that suffering, to heal, to grow to love. Wonder at the guidance the support and the love shown back to me whilst I undertook this Journey of healing. Wonder at the connection I feel inside, the connection I have to every single part of who I am, who I truly am.

Gosh, I am so lucky. So lucky to have trusted myself to go through this, so lucky to have you by my side, so lucky to have God by my side.

That voice again: You my love, you have shown me something here today. You and many like you have shown me why it is that I love this planet, that I love with every part of my Being. You and many like you have given to me all that I ever wanted when I created this planet, this Universe, all other Universes.

You see you, amazing you, magnificent you, and the others like you have one thing in common.

Love. Love is in every single person on Earth but what you have in common with these others is that you all have risen to the challenge of love. You have given yourself to this challenge, without fail, ever. You have chosen love above all other. This love has taken you on a Journey, a difficult Journey, a wondrous Journey, an enlightening Journey. And you have shown to yourself that anything is possible if you have love.

For it is this love that has bonded you to everything, to all understanding, to those that you love, even those that do not show their love or allow your love, or feel unloved by you. This bonding extends beyond what even you yourself realise. The energy of this love within you travels to the far reaches of this Universe, and beyond. This is the power of your love, the power of their love, the power of all love.

That hat you found in the café the other week. I said I'm always clear so it's best I clarify something. I said it was my hat but it's not, in fact it's yours. But I wear it. I wear it because that hat represents all that I have allowed for you to experience on this planet, this wondrous planet, this challenging planet, this loving planet. And all that I have allowed you to experience is not your fault, good and bad. Yes, you must take responsibility for these things that you have done but know they were all part of this Journey that you must rejoice in. Know that this Journey was your wish, your request to me before you came to this Earth and I granted this wish with only one condition. And that condition was that you grow. You live you learn, you grow. You experience hurt and joy, you grow. You remember that it was not your fault and let go the fear, you grow. You feel, you give, you allow, you grow.

Did I mention it was not your fault? It was not your fault, none of this was your fault, their fault, anyone's fault here on Earth. The fault lies with me, the allowing of this Journey and all that you have experienced lies solely with me. Can I make this any clearer my dear friend? Only responsibility lies with you. The responsibility to learn to heal to grow, I cannot make this any clearer or simpler for you.

And so my love you have done this. And now this hat of yours that I wear Changes. For this hat represents for me all that you are and in the wearing of it I carry a piece of you with me. If you feel pain so do I, if you feel joy so do I. Know that I will always wear this hat of yours, know that I will always cherish it and all that it represents.

And what does it represent this hat? This hat represents so much, not just you but also me, and I am everything that there is. Therefore know that in the wearing of this hat of yours YOU represent everything that there is. Yes you are that important, and what you achieve on this Earth and in this life is that important.

But know that your achievements are not scored on money or cars or jobs that you have had. Your achievements are not scored on what a good person you have been or how you have always been kind and generous to others. As I have said your achievements are scored on growth. If you have hurt someone how have you grown? If you have been judged by another how have you grown? If you have felt unworthy how have you grown? If you have failed or not loved another or not been loved how have you grown?

And why is growth the benchmark for your achievements? Because growth is LOVE.

Choose love in every moment and you will grow. No matter what has happened to you or to another, choose love and you WILL grow.

Shortly after: I hear you now God. I feel the Truth of you and feel you within me. I thank you for your guidance and support on my Journey. I thank you for showing me how to let go the past how to let go my fears and most of all how to connect to me. To have total faith in me to know me, to not fear me, to love me.

You have placed upon this Earth a child and that child has now become a man. But that child still lives strong in this man for it represents the love that I have for myself. That child at last doesn't just peak his head over that wall of hope but instead climbs to the top of that wall and with all of his might, all of his love and all that he is, that child gives himself to himself, to others, to you. That child is love, that man is love, that man knows that we are all love. And that man now jumps down off that wall and runs freely on his Journey without fear and without chains and with nothing but love coursing through his veins.

(Wonderfound)

But that man is not just me. That man is everybody, every man woman and child. And this chapter is not just ours, this chapter is theirs too. This chapter can also be their life, their Journey, their growth.

God: Let go now, ALL of you, please. Let go my loves. Let go. Go live. Go love. Go GROW.

Just go be...

(Wonderstays)

Olivia and Raf, Abraham and Jesus, God

30

RECONCILING THE UNRECONCILABLE

There are many instances, many examples that so many feel are just not possible to move on from. That you have experiences that are just not ever possible to be acceptable in any way shape or form to you and therefore you feel things need to stay as they are.

Even in hearing the words that all that has come to pass is not wrong, for those who have significantly suffered this can feel like a Universal joke. For there are many situations, even as an observer of life, where you can look and say, "how can that be acceptable?" "How can that be for the 'Greater Good'?" The short response and consistent response is that it always is, was and will be. Even if you never fully get to see the evidence of it, it just is. For you may only see the stone enter the ponds watery surface, turn around and walk away and never see the number and extent of the ripples within the pond. Never see how far reaching they become, nor the impact of the stone as it Journeys its way to the bottom of the pond.

The famous contrast. It is essential for growth. Essential for Change. Essential for expansion. Essential for the Universe, essential for you here in your Physical experience and essential for your Higher Self and the Collective you are within. Again, you may say "I don't care about the Universe/Higher Self/Collective etc, why has *this* happened to ME!" And it is in this moment, that if you are able to bring yourself further along the path to a place of understanding that you will have stretched and grown beyond what you ever thought possible for yourself.

We wish to give you an example of the feeling. There are many, many specifics to choose from. So many terrible events, atrocities, decisions have been made over human history to pick from. So many moments that could have been different, so many paths that could have been taken. Pick up any history book or even look at a recent news story to see one. For those who have suffered loss, abuse, betrayal, deceit, violence at the hands of others. For anyone who has watched a child suffer terribly, for those who are the survivors of any kind or the ones that were left behind, this reconciling the unreconcilable is for each and every one of you who struggles. Who holds the suffering and all of the Low Vibration that it brings.

So we have gone general, for in order to understand the unreconcilable, the Emotions that drive this depth of feeling are what describes the point that you reach in order to move forward from. This is what an unreconcilable event or series of events feels like.

You feel utter despair, such total oblivion by what you have experienced that you just want out. Out can mean over the top of the balcony, burying yourself under the duvet indefinitely. Just walking out the front door with no belongings never anticipating to return or, booking a one way flight to the middle of nowhere so you can be as isolated and as far away from all that you know as quickly as you can.

That you feel that everyone near you can't do anything, not a thing, to help you. That you are trapped, inside this knowing, inside this feeling and it is breaking you, literally from the inside out. As much as you tell yourself you are stronger than this, you can handle this, the internal shattering continues to a point that you are truly in pieces.

When the foundation of your world does not feel solid, does not feel like a foundation at all but rather a weight, a weight of endlessness that could drown you, not support you. When no matter how much you are loved, you don't care, you literally don't care for that love cannot reach you. For you cannot fix the brokenness in this moment. The darkness is shutting you down.

The light is so diminished you wondered if it ever shone before and you sense in this moment that you will never shine again, for nothing will ever, ever be the same. The numbness is welcomed but you fear that you can't feel anything. The event that triggered this, replays over and over and over again to the point where you feel that you could lose your grip on reality. The words, the impact, the hammering, the movie of it. Round and round it goes. On one heck of a loop.

Unreconcilable.

You try to reach for reason, for some semblance of sense. For some angle that you haven't found before, some truth to be revealed, almost like you are looking for treasure just to be disappointed as you continue to surface nothing. Dead end after dead end.

This is the unreconcilable.

Yet somehow, somehow, some spark of light starts to glint within. All that you are, it is within you always. It is calling you. Always. It is your beacon. It isn't asking you to fight. It is asking you to allow. Allow your love and your connection to who you truly are. This Emotional event, this was meant to be. Even now, as this is being written, it is totally understood that these words can feel completely inaccurate, trite and further crushing. There can be arguments made as to how this could never be the case, but it always is.

For taking an unreconcilable situation and finding a way through it, which you can truly, takes you to a place of growth like no other. No other. You can read words but the true teaching is by the living, the experiencing. Growth matches your experience, and for anyone who can get out of this abyss of Emotion gains greatness, Mastery of your Experience and something that no words could ever teach.

So, if this was meant to be, imagine in this moment that no matter what Change was made however big or small, it was inevitable. In this inevitability, let go. Let go of rationalising it. Let go of forgiving it. Letting go generates faith and hope. Faith in the inevitability. Faith in the ultimate outcome that growth is in motion. Hope that there is an end to it, that reconciling this situation is possible, that you can find your way through it. Letting go releases the resistance, resistance that there is no hope, resistance to resolution.

Focus solely on gaining an aspect of understanding, understanding for you first. In this understanding of your very own Journey, your aspects within this event, your Emotions that have been created, your thoughts that have been shifted and Changed because of it. Once this understanding is underway, the light within grows brighter. The lifting of the despair is starting and the triggering of relief, however small is happening.

Then, and this takes faith too, focus on the Journey of others involved. For they too have been part of the inevitability of the situation and often, when we are dealing with unreconcilable situations, this will involve others. So, they too being on their Journey, they made choices, they are responsible, there is freewill after all, but remember the inevitability. A series of circumstances, Emotions, thoughts, conditions, situations that all moved and shaped into this reality. This is the Journey that they too have taken. With this understanding, connect to any small part you can of their experience, even if not fully understood, even a peak at an understanding is a start. The moment that this happens, YOU will feel relief. You will feel a further spark, a further ignition within of love for yourself. Of love for the Journey, even though it still hurts, it is part of you now.

Be brave, be fearless in your determination to understand and to feel connected to the Truth of the situation. The Truth of how you truly feel in the moment. The Truth of this reality is important, for often we look to predict the outcomes over situations to say "If *this* happens, I could never get over it" but the Truth is, you can. Your Truth, how you feel now, then the next now, this Truth is your guidance and your reality. How you feel will evolve as you continue to connect further, further to the Journeying, further to the inevitability, further to the understanding and further to the growth.

You can reconcile the unreconcilable. It is the key to your freedom.

Olivia and Raf, Abraham and Jesus

31

WHEN YOUR GREATEST FEARS ARE REALISED

That feeling in the pit of your stomach that there is something wrong, something really wrong. It's off, the situation, the words being said to you, the circumstances, the feeling. You squash it down. You rationalise it. You listen to the words and you let them be enough, or you placate yourself and tell yourself everything is going to be alright – the Universe always provides and everything is always working out for the best. That feeling starts to move away. You distract yourself, you 'move on', you disregard it. Time ticks by. That feeling. It's still there. It's fear.

What are you afraid of? The thing you fear, that it is true. That it is your reality. Sometimes it is.

You don't want to be the one to say, "I knew it!" for this fear being realised is going to feel like the ground has opened up underneath you. It is a very rare human that can have a fear fully realised and welcome it in with a casual surrender and a note to self that there is growth to be understood. Fear doesn't work like that. Fear grips you. Fear resonates long and low and fear sits and waits. So what if you "knew it" in the moment but you chose to 'unknow' it. You chose to remove it from your reality in that split second and you chose to soothe instead. You wanted for things to be different, so wanted for things to be different.

Sometimes they are not, sometimes your fears are realised.

When the truth of the fear is ignited, when you understand that this is your reality, feel what you feel, whatever that is. Don't rush and run to squash it, to stop it, to silence it. For in this moment, you have every single right to feel a huge range of Emotions, from disbelief, panic, anger, frustration, betrayal, hopelessness, despair, shock, horror even and many, many other Emotions are warranted depending on the situation. Yes, this is Low Vibration but yes, this is human.

When you uncover something that you felt was wrong, when somewhere deep inside you knows that there is something not right and you were right all along, that tight lid has just been ripped off and all that Low Vibrating fear is going crazy within you generating all of these Emotions. So feel them. In the moment, allow yourself to release the resistance of fear and let the truth penetrate and ALL the feelings be felt. Feel them and even name them, each and every one. It may take a little bit of time but in this allowing, you are being true, you are being Aligned to your Emotions, you are not stalling them, nor stopping them nor hiding them. You are simply feeling them.

These Low Vibrational Emotions can feel overwhelming but

you are fully capable, always without exception, to allow these feelings to surface and to understand them as it is happening. You have total and utter capacity to hold this Vibration as it occurs and more, do not fear fear itself. Do not ever fear the truth, for once you have revealed these fear based Emotions, this is where you baseline. You now know the truth. You are now no longer in conflict within. Your fear that you have been holding, squashing, managing is now out and you know exactly what it is and you know why you felt it.

The truth will set you free.

You may not feel it in that moment, but here is the first place to start. There is nothing like the truth. You can deal with any truth. There is always, always an Emotional solution to every single situation. So start here.

And yet having found the truth, having dealt with it and in doing so removed the Low Vibrational Emotion attached, fear of death fear or failure fear or abuse or fear of betrayal, perhaps there may still be something within that stops you allowing yourself the freedom from it. In this moment look to your Subconscious Mind, for it is your mind that is king in this moment and so powerful can be it's grip on you. For if the experience that has created the fear was strong, devastating and perhaps something held and suffered from for many years then its power over you will be great, even in the face of utter faith that your fears will never be realised again.

And this as always will blight every part of your current life and how you think feel and act in all of your every day situations. With fear of failure a simple trip to the post office could be littered with spiralling thoughts, not knowing what to ask for, will the parcel arrive on time, will they like what's in it when it does arrive. But what of something more serious? What if the loss of a loved one at an early age is still with you. This terrible event would have triggered a whole raft of Emotions and perhaps impacted you and others close to you for years if left unresolved. And yet even if resolved and the Emotion attached to that experience understood and released, for many the fear of death could still remain. The Subconscious Mind remembering just how painful that experience was for you will be creating the energy of fear at every moment, gripping to you and refusing to let go despite your faith.

So what to do here? How can you break this wall of fear down? How do you set yourself free from this powerful Emotion that sits underneath the surface of you influencing you, worrying you, controlling you in every way and in everything that you do?

Time.

Perseverance.

Hope.

Trust.

Courage. So much courage.

Faith in your guidance.

Love.

Connection to your suffering.

Strength.

Allowing.

Time.

And that day will come. Allow yourself to feel it, allow yourself to let go. Feel the new Truth of 'you' and your determination to find a way, and move on from your greatest fears.

Olivia and Raf, Abraham and Jesus

32

THE WORLD DOESN'T WORK IN MYSTERIOUS WAYS

If we said everything that has happened to you so far in your life was meant to be many of you would say, "well yes we've heard that expression", and many others of you would say "that's nonsense! I mean what the heck happened to free will?"

Whilst there is of course utter free will involved in everything that you do, there are elements of guidance that gets given along the way that perhaps you don't even register as guidance and just put down to intuition. There are also of course the pre-manifested Soul Contract milestones in your life which we have previously discussed and these you are led to by your Higher Self and God but always through the process of free will.

How can this be, you might ask? Pre-manifested situations but I still have free will?

The process whereby you are able to find your way to the pre-manifestations is complex to explain but we will seek to do so at a high level in this chapter and commit to providing further detail on this in later books. Every action you take you have a choice over and from this perspective you always therefore have free will. If a person is meant to meet a certain person in their life, perhaps an eternal Soul Group husband or wife, then the path to this meeting and their subsequent falling in love is 'aided' by the Higher Selves of those two individuals that are meant to meet and be together.

A decision to just up sticks and fly across the world to a country you've never been to will not be forced upon a person in order to ensure that meeting of their future and eternal partner. However if there has been a yearning to travel or a sense that this person needs a Change in their life then this is where the Higher Self influence comes through.

For example have you ever done something because you just felt you had to even though you weren't sure why? This is potentially the influence of your Higher Self guiding you in accordance with your Soul Contract. Remember also that your Soul Contract is yours and yours alone to approve before coming to Earth so this influence is only what you had asked for before you came to Earth. So that person flying across to the other side of the world leaving behind friends and family may feel trepidation and nervousness about it but if it is something that is meant to be your Higher Self will enable in you the determination, or love needed to get on that plane.

This should not be seen as control in any way. You would still have the choice to not get on the plane if you felt really strongly about it or were convinced not to go, but if the drive is there within you to do it then it will happen. And if it doesn't happen then another way will be found for the two people to meet if this is what was meant to be.

Often the pre-manifestation is set up in a way which is much less difficult for it to go wrong. For example your eternal Soul mate that you are destined to marry will be born in the same country, region or even town. Or, you could be born in an area that specialises in something that links you to a specific job type or role and from here opens up connections to people in your Soul Group that you are destined to meet, or to locations of work where your Soul Group members also reside awaiting for your meeting. Not everyone in your Soul Group needs to meet you in person though. A Soul Group member of yours could merely influence you by a book of theirs you have read or a film they have been in.

Within the pre-manifested milestones are of course your own manifested experiences and encounters. These have less influence from your Higher Self however if they form part of the Soul Contract, both the Higher Self and your other Non Physical Guides will play a part in guiding you as and when required in order to Align you to the Soul Contract.

So when you Align to the truth of your Soul Contract and the influence of your Higher Self and Non Physical Guides it's easy to take a much simpler perspective on your life in terms of everything that happens in it. There is no influence on it in any other way. Previous lives will not impact you and your decision making. Your Higher Self will have had many previous lives on Earth but yours will be unique and therefore there are no influences of karma from a past life.

What you do in this life influences this life alone and this should be your focus and not how it may affect you in another life. 'You' won't have another life, but of course your Higher Self will as has been discussed. The lessons and experiences and growth from the life you are currently living will be remembered and held energetically to some degree for your Higher Self's next incarnation, but we urge you not to focus on this and instead keep it simple.

This life is your life so enjoy it as much as you can and know that all that is happening is meant to be in accordance with your Soul Contract and the decisions that you have made along the way. In other words if you chose to go right instead of left that was meant to be. If you asked someone to dance rather than stand at the bar and fear the answer, that was meant to be, or if you took that job rather than stay in your not so exciting old one, that was also meant to be.

It was meant to be because you chose it and for no other reason. It was not meant to be because somewhere in your Soul Contract you were supposed to meet that person or take that job. The pull to that person or job, if it was something that you requested in your Soul Contract, would be strengthened by your Higher Self in terms of your feelings towards doing something about it, but they won't force you to do it and therefore whatever action is taken in this scenario is because you chose it and therefore you wanted it to be, and therefore for this reason it was meant to be. And if you chose not to ask for that dance or that job then it wasn't meant to be because you alone decided.

You will eventually have to find a way to this person or this job if it's stated in your Soul Contract and so your Higher Self will begin to influence how you feel about certain things until such time as the circumstances are right and synchronised for you. The way this works is extremely complex and sometimes actions that you take or people that you meet are manifested and organised to occur on a certain date and time right down to the very second. This may sound far fetched but it is absolutely true and hence the reason why we would prefer to detail exactly how this works more thoroughly in a separate future book publication.

For now just know that it's really quite simple how your life works. You get out of bed, you do stuff, you go back to bed, and in between that time period, all of it is yours to choose as to how, where and who to do it with. Don't fear what you do or don't do and how it may influence you or others in this life or beyond.

Make the most of every moment knowing it's you and only you that makes the decisions in your life and it isn't any more complex or mysterious than that.

Olivia and Raf, Abraham and Jesus

33

GOD CREATED US IN HIS IMAGE

Yes he really did. We speak not of the image that we see in the mirror but the one that we FEEL.

God's energy is our energy. The energy of our Inner Being mirrors that of God's.

When you trust, you trust as God does. When you love and hope, you feel it as God does. Feel strength within and this is how God feels strength. Connect to truth and you will connect to the same truth that God feels.

You understand how every Emotion in your body feels and therefore you also understand how the Consciousness of God feels these Emotions. And in general how does God feel?

Special. That's how God feels. Special because he has so much faith.

Be immersed in faith and you feel exactly as God does. For God has faith always. In you. And me. And them. And us.

God created us all to have faith. But faith requires trust, love, hope, strength and truth. Without all of these there is no faith. Faith is all of these and *only* all of these together.

So when you next look in the mirror have a look out for God. Look beyond your clothing and instead go a little deeper, much deeper if need be. Look into your eyes and see what you feel.

Go on take a look now it won't take long. How long can you hold your own eyes in that mirror. Not long, too painful or awkward? This is a strong sign that Change is needed, that perhaps fear, paranoia, anger, shame, sadness, hurt all blight you and that they all sit buried deep within you. This is a powerful exercise of discovery if you have the courage to do it.

If this is hard don't worry keep trying, keep working on the Self and you will eventually feel more at ease. And once you can hold that stare for a little longer, ask yourself again what is then reflected back to you, what that person is saying. Is there pride in what you have achieved or are you just focused on the number of grey hairs? Do you feel a strength in you that wasn't there the last time you stared closely at yourself? Is there an emptiness there or is the self-love starting to come through?

Sharing this space with the mirror can be a little unnerving we know.

Why do we ask you to undertake this exercise and what does this have to do with God's image?

Well, God undertakes this exercise every moment of every day. He's felt the same awkwardness, the same shame. At times this exercise hurts him so, but he never stops looking at that reflection. And this perhaps is the greatest likeness we have to God. The need to feel a connection to our Self.

For it is this connection to the Self which indicates how we really feel about who and how we are. And even when we feel shame this is no reason to become disconnected, but merely a time to reflect, heal and grow. This is how God treats this reflection exercise and this is how he always stays connected to his Self. Constantly changing, constantly reAligning, constantly Self reflecting.

He asks of us to attempt to do the same as often as possible, and this is why he allows us to feel the way that he can feel. Do not fear looking at your own reflection. Know that whatever comes back is an opportunity for you. Know that it is an opportunity to strengthen your connection to your Self. This is your path to peace and joy and wonder in those eyes that you stare at.

Let the light from your mirror reflect back into you and reveal to you all that you are right now. Allow this light. Feel this light. Love this light. There is no shame in feeling shame from this light. Do not fear feeling *any* Emotion from this light, only growth comes from this light. Feel good from this light. Feel enlightened from this light, for this is what you are; special, awesome, perfect in every way.

Yes, perfect in every way. God created us in this image, his image. Do you feel him in the mirror yet?

Olivia and Raf, God

34

FAITH IN US

To have faith in oneself is perhaps a commonly used term however less practiced is the term 'faith in us'. What do we mean by this statement?

Well this term reflects the faith one puts in others and in this instance we are speaking of Non Physical Beings. Non Physical Humans know everything there is to know about the wonders of the Universe and its magnificent entities and energies. But those on Earth rarely take the time to consider just what it is that lives amongst them in their own dimension and other dimensions as well.

We wish for all of you that have ever asked the question "Does God really exist" to ponder for a moment to ask another more relevant question we feel, which is, "Does God really care"? We say this not in a derogatory sense but in the true sense of God being a loving and kind entity.

The answer to this is of course YES! And furthermore, God is willing to prove it. Ask of God anything that you may wish to have and it shall be given. Go on, try it, try it now and see what happens. Ok so perhaps not everything can be given immediately but we can guarantee one thing, and that is that everything WILL be heard immediately.

The answers that you are looking for will also always be given but not always in the way that you might prefer them. For if there is no benefit or learning for you then perhaps then there is no growth. And it is in the giving of our answers that perhaps the faith in us diminishes. For what is not given soon after, or in a preferred manner can be taken as not being heard, responded to or acted upon. But know there could be nothing further from the truth. Know that it is our absolute joy to respond and to give you something that may help you on your Journey.

So where does this leave those of you that still need something more to have faith in us?

The answer is exactly where you were before but without having asked anything of us, and therefore one step behind those that do have the faith in us. And so for those of you that still question, please try asking of us and keep asking of us, for Faith in Us, Non Physical, comes over time, and over time comes the knowing. Trust what you feel, and feel your way into this faith, over time.

Abraham and Jesus, God

35

FAITH IN YOU

The Emotion of faith can be manually triggered through your Vortexes of Emotion held within your Inner Being and we shall describe in a later chapter how you can do this. But you could try feeling faith in something now. The question being, faith in what?

During our own Awakening Journey the word faith came up so often between us as well as in conversations with our Guides. In those most challenging of moments and darkest of times what was it that kept us going, believing, driving forward, even though there was no end in sight? It was faith.

But again we ask, faith in what? The answer to that is faith in you. Faith in yourself means that no matter what, you will see it through, without an understanding of why, how, what or where. Faith is that feeling that when faced with no answers to these questions, that you will still WANT to carry on, with no idea why and with no specific feelings within you driving you forward. But instead, there is a momentum, an energy within you, getting you out of that bed, making you unturn those stones and almost begging you to find a way.

And so it is by acting with trust, love, hope, strength and an Emotional energy on the truth that you are seeking to understand, that you are propelled forward with faith. In turn as these Emotions take hold within you, the faith that you hold in yourself begins to pull at you. And with this, the momentum begins and the cycle continues as those Emotions begin to light up and grow, and in turn so does the faith in YOU.

But we must remember that with faith in oneself also comes a responsibility to oneself. A responsibility not to have faith blindly, but instead with direction and purpose. A responsibility not just to leave it to the Universe, but instead to affect the outcome of your needs and desires. For without this intention, each door that you open will bring back the same answer. Open those doors in a different way and as a different person and you will get a different answer, and a different outcome to your needs and desires.

Olivia and Raf, Abraham and Jesus

36

I KNOW WHAT IT'S LIKE TO BE DEAD

Sublime. Full of the most powerful loving energy. Happy, so so happy. Easy and relaxed in all situations. Understanding, mostly of yourself. Feeling connected to all that you are, who you are and what you are. And most of all completely and utterly FREE!

How do we know this? Because we have achieved a High Vibrational percentage of above ninety five percent and in moments have been at one hundred percent. For ninety five percent or above is the percentage that all Non Physical entities run at.

The phrase 'run at' makes them sound machine like and in fact that's almost what we had to become to reach our own High Vibrational levels. Raf in particular came from a starting position of consistently at twenty eight percent, a very low place to be, but Olivia also reached low thirties at times during her Awakening and so for us there is so much pride on what we have been able to achieve Vibrationally.

And it really is an achievement. But this is not said to boast, because every single person reading this could attain what we have achieved and even getting fairly close to our figures it would bring you so much nearer to feeling what your Guides, your Higher Self, your ancestors and friends in Non Physical all feel like in every moment.

And let us tell you it's worth trying for these High Vibrational figures. Anything above seventy five percent consistently would be awesome and this would put you in the top five percent of people on the planet Vibrationally. For in these moments of the highest Vibration you have a sense of total and utter Alignment, excitement and anticipation for all that is good and loving in this world. Nothing seems to phase you and those hurdles that jump out at you constantly during your average day just glide into a lovestream, often just taking care of themselves. Because the amazing thing about working to achieve a High Vibration is that once you have learned to become so highly tuned to yourself, and so understanding and trusting of the Universal Laws that govern and effect your own energy, everything just clicks into place.

At this advanced level of Vibrational Mastery you have also understood most of what has held you back. You have analysed and let go all of those previous painful experiences and you have learnt how to truly connect yourself to love and choose love in every moment. And so at this stage most of what is felt as a Low Vibration can be linked by you to an understanding and a Truth, and therefore The Law of Truth automatically works with other Universal Laws to let it go, without further analysis and without further pain in the trawling through of the memory of an experience. This is The Releasing Process in full flow and action.

Think about that for just a moment. If you're prepared to work at your Vibration hard enough and for long enough to see a radical Change, your gift to yourself is that managing your Vibration becomes simple in comparison, automatic at times and therefore your life automatically becomes easier, happier, smoother, GREATER.

So here's a thought, a suggestion perhaps. What if we were to tell you that your Vibration right now was one hundred percent? How much would you go out of your way to protect it by ensuring that you reacted to everything in the least conflicting way for you? How little would you question yourself for fear of dropping into Low Vibrational thinking and feeling? How quickly would you move on from those negative thoughts that pop into your head about those painful past experiences? How much more positively would you act on the basis that this is how one hundred percent Vibrational beings behave, waving at the security guard with a smile rather than doing your usual head down don't look at me act? How much more in control of yourself would you feel as your Vibration drops for a moment and all you did to resolve things was to gently and lovingly coax yourself back to the understanding that whatever you just felt wasn't real and doesn't belong in your body and is just your Subconscious Mind trying to protect you?

Ok then here goes. "Abracadabra!"

There you go you are now running at one hundred percent High Vibration. Well what are you waiting for....SMILE. What do you mean you don't feel like it, you're a High Vibrational Being, go on get out there and show 'em!

No? Ok then, we admit we don't do magic tricks. But we do know magic when we FEEL it. Magic is love, magic is allowing, magic is flow, magic is joy and magic is amazing, amazing! Amazing when you try and amazing when you believe.

So why not believe?

Believe that you are right now one hundred percent High Vibrational. When you believe you are you will act like you are and you will protect every cell within you to ensure that you always remain that way. And most importantly you will start to FEEL that you are. Not always, perhaps not often at first but the more you believe, the more your body will start to believe because it will feel the Truth. The Truth of your intention to believe that you are one hundred percent High Vibrational. And with that, for even the lowest Vibrational people amongst us, you will start to feel better.

And the great thing is you don't need to be dead to feel like Non Physical, nor do you need to die trying. But you do need to try.

Perhaps more than that, you need to fight for it and keep fighting for it. For your Vibration is your life's work. It's not just for Christmas and New Year. It's for now, it's for later, tomorrow and beyond.

Don't wait until you die to feel like the dead.

Olivia and Raf, Abraham and Jesus

37

WHEN IS IT YOUR 'TIME'?

By 'time' we mean death. Your death will come eventually, no big news there but 'when' is the question that many of us spend so much time pondering over or worrying over or even planning for!

Planning for your death seems counterintuitive to us as it's not as if you're going to be there at this funeral party or event, well not Physically anyway, well not Physically in the sense that you'll know what's going on from your own body.

Non Physically of course you may be there at your funeral but this really depends on how long after your death the funeral happens, for there are matters to discuss with God and Jesus when you transition to Non Physical after your death. These discussions will catch up on how you got on in the life that you led and review those matters that were important growth experiences for you and your Non Physical Collective.

So when is it your time to die? Is it controllable and do you have a say in it? The simple answer to both is 'yes'.

We have spoken of Soul Contracts and pre-manifestations and therefore for many your death can be predetermined, by you. The event of your death is not only in your own Soul Contract but also linked to the Soul Contract of others in your Soul Group in order to help them grow. A girl that dies young because it was stated in her Soul Contract sadly impacts the lives of her parents and siblings and friends, and this is all part of jointly formed Soul Contracts. The death of this girl could not have been stopped by anyone on Earth in this instance as it was pre-determined in her Soul Contract. So whether it was a road accident, a fall or a terminal illness unfortunately that poor girl was going to die at some point early in her life.

This is an extremely painful but important point to understand because often people blame themselves for a death. What if I'd been a healthier parent, or if only I had been there at this time to help save her.

Your 'time' is also often very much up to the manifested circumstances generated by you. Again an obvious statement perhaps, but why is it that given it's so obvious that we don't take more care to avoid it at times, rather than just planning for it.

This chapter is not about listing out all of the things that you could do to live a longer healthier life. In fact we are not suggesting you Change anything about your life. This is not to say we are dismissing the importance of how you live your life in terms of the length of it, but merely wishing not to impose any judgement against you.

So what are we trying to say in this chapter, what's the message for you?

The message is that you need to start living it instead of worrying about when it's going to end and then planning accordingly. Ask yourself how happy you are in each and every moment that you spend each day doing the things that you do with the people you do them with, and in the places you spend time in, with them or yourself. Are you truly getting the most out of each and every single moment or do you have an underlying undercurrent of sadness or anger or guilt or hurt or....the point being are you happy, relaxed and enjoying that moment if it's a moment that should be being enjoyed.

We're not suggesting you fake it. But recognise the Vibrations that continuously run in you and make sure that as many of them are High Vibrational and if not, then try and do something about it. Recognise when you're at a birthday party but for some reason you are not quite getting into it and ask yourself why, so you can Change it. Feel your underwhelm when you've just got that payrise and work out why you're not popping the champagne.

Death is a terrible thing when it comes at the wrong time but until that time comes try to stop thinking about it. That's yours, theirs, anybody's. Start planning for now and tomorrow and the day after and so on, but slow yourself down when you get to the planning stage that involves burials or cremations.

That time will come. You will get your time. But it's not your time yet.

Olivia and Raf, Abraham and Jesus

38

RETURNING HOME

When you eventually transition back to Non Physical it will be a joyous time for those of us who are not on Earth. The sadness for those that you have left behind, we of course understand and often we too will feel their pain and their Low Vibration, in particular the Higher Selves of those Physical Humans left behind as well as the Guides of those Physical Humans.

But your transition back to Non Physical is coming back to old friends. Friends that have been watching you, at times not so far away from the Physical Human that was you on Earth.

As has been previously eluded to, your first meeting is with God and Jesus, not Jesus Christ, but his ascended Soul that forms the head of what we term the Christ Collective Consciousness. Because of the size of this Collective it's not unusual for the returning Soul to actually be part of this

Collective, but of course there are literally thousands of other Collectives in Non Physical that the returning Soul could also be part of (we will discuss Collectives in more detail in a later chapter).

And it's with these Collectives in mind that this meeting with God and Jesus takes place. For before you are allowed to return to your eager and excited friends and ancestors in Non Physical the opportunity is taken to understand just how things went for you during your life on Earth and to collate the understandings and learning that you had so that it may be passed on to all the other Souls that form part of the particular Collective that your transitioned Soul, you, belong to.

And it's this meeting that should be in your awareness for everything that you do whilst here on Earth living this life of yours. Not just because it will be a meeting of great joy and insight but also because it's the meeting that looks to understand just how much you've grown whilst you were on Earth.

The discussion with God and Jesus won't be a judgemental one. No, this meeting is all about reviewing all that you asked for in your Soul Contract and assessing what you managed to achieve from it, which paths you chose and what you did and didn't do on those paths.

If your life was one of personal suffering, how did you heal from it? If you chose to hate instead of love and inflicted on others great suffering, what took you down that path and what could you have done differently. And this information isn't just collated for a nice report but instead it is given back to the head of your Collective and the heads of other Collectives within that Collective in order for this to be 'known' and used by the Souls of future incarnations of Physical Humans.

This knowing is what forms part of the information that is passed onto every single Soul that is a Higher Self in each of those related Collectives. The Souls within those Collectives whilst they have a chance to understand what was learnt by you will not absorb this 'knowing' like your Higher Self will. For it is the Higher Self that will incarnate a new Soul to Earth and therefore will need to ensure that this 'knowing' is energetically passed on to new Souls.

So what is this 'knowing'?

It's an energetic capture of key aspects of what you learnt from influential experiences in your life. This energetic knowing is shared across the Collective but as stated is most strongly absorbed your own Higher Self as well as the Higher Selves of those in your Collective that are the nearest to your own Higher Self. Think of a hierarchy within the Collective and the nearer that you are on the tree to each other the more you share energetically.

So those moments when you act a certain way but you don't know why, or when you acted not consciously but more intuitively, know that this is heavily influenced by the energy within your Inner Being and that of your Higher Self. And it's this intuitive reaction to something may have come from a learning from a previous life, that knowing, that would have been passed across from either a past life of a Soul of your own Higher Self or from a Soul of a nearby Higher Self to your own in the Collective hierarchy.

If you have ever been strongly Aligned to the lyrics of a songwriter or the book of an author or poet, or the jokes of a comedian and just felt something about that person and their points of view that so relates to the way you feel, then ask yourself could the Soul of that person be in your Collective, and perhaps even close to your Higher Self in the Collective hierarchy. The energy within our Inner Being influences our personality so ask your own Higher Self to clarify if you feel something like this. It can be an exciting discovery and fascinating to see how that Physical Human acts, thinks and feels so similarly to you. And of course this other Soul that you just feel so Aligned to can also be someone that you know, someone at work, a neighbour or an old school friend.

Coming home to Non Physical also doesn't have to feel like you've been away for the time you've spent on Earth. For those of you that are able to connect in a more conscious way to your Higher Self, your Guides and your Ancestral Guides whilst on Earth, the conversation when you transition to Non Physical just picks up from where you last left it when you were at home on Earth. This is the wonder of remembering who you are whilst you are on this planet, and the wonder of remembering why it is you are here right now.

The worlds of Physical Humans and Non Physical Humans have been too far apart for far too long now. For thousands of years spirituality has at times been treated as such a taboo subject for many, and for those that have showed the spiritual connection many have been feared or just thought of as strange. A person discussing or displaying their spirituality may find that their good friends suddenly keep their children well away from them or worse still just have them burnt them at the stake.

And yet which is more strange, that person that takes the opportunity to connect to their Higher Self and give themselves access to all that the Multiverse has to offer in order to be the best that they possibly can be? Or that person that is perhaps so disconnected from themselves, fearful and doubting of everything, and suffering as a result of it and refusing to reach out to someone that could truly help them just because that they cannot see, touch or smell something that has not been defined in a dictionary or online as being one hundred percent real.

Perhaps it's time to stop making spirituality taboo and a conversation killer. Perhaps it's time to turn the tables on those that seek to point fingers or pass judgement on something that they do not allow themselves to believe in. Perhaps also it's time for all Physical Humans to recognise that they have Non Physical Human friends right here right now and allow them in to help make their lives better, their relationships better, their work better, innovation better, projects better, everything about their life better, and this world better. Surely it's strange not to seek out your spirituality and your Higher Self in order to have this all made possible for you? We suggest the time has come for it to be taboo that you are not taking advantage of this wonderful possibility.

Connection to Non Physical humans and our Higher Self and

therefore to the magical, insightful and powerful information that this Universe offers is the only way to a 5th Dimension Earth.

We can't wait for you to be with us again here in Non Physical but would rather that you connected to us now and not when you transition. Returning home to Non Physical needs you only to remember, death is not required.

We love you.

Olivia and Raf, Abraham and Jesus

WHAT IS A SOUL?

Consider a Soul to be that part of you that is your Inner Being. Your Inner Being is made up of some elements of the energy of your Higher Self, with the remainder being topped up by a brand new energy created by God.

So imagine a huge pot of soup and in this pot are various different ingredients topped up over time by each life that your Higher Self has incarnated. Imagine now a ladle taking a single scoop of that soup and placing it into a smaller cup. This cup is for the energy of your Inner Being, your Soul. Just to the right of this huge pot of soup is a small saucepan cooking up a brand new flavour of soup. Imagine now, that saucepan of soup topping up the smaller cup of your Inner Being, until it reaches the top. In essence the huge pot of soup is your Higher Self's energy, the new soup made in the saucepan that was poured into the smaller glass is your Soul's unique energy, and the mixed concoction in the glass is what makes up the complete energy of your Soul; in other words you energetically.

A Soul is such a precious gift of creation for the Higher Self and the Soul's incarnation onto Earth then places the challenge upon the Higher Self to find a way to connect to the Physical incarnation of that Soul (the Physical you). That challenge is to communicate with that person, that Physical Human, you, in order to help them remember who they are and what it is they came to Earth to do. Years can be spent doing this, diligently sending signs and messages for that Physical Human to pick up on and respond to.

The signs which can come in the form of feelings, nudges, songs in the mind or downloaded thoughts are often put down to something else. Ask yourself next time that you speak with authority about a subject that you have very little knowledge on, or when you give an opinion so accurately on somebody that you hardly know, where this insight came from, for it just may have been from that greater part of you, that which is your Higher Self.

And know that the sooner that you can pick up on these signals and start to engage with, and allow connection from, your Higher Self the sooner you will become who your Soul truly is.

For all that you are, is all that your Higher Self is, and all that he or she is, will be all that you are. You are literally that connected and every single thought feeling or Emotion that you have ever had will have been felt and known by your Higher Self. Remember this the next time that you feel sad, lonely or isolated and without love or a friend. For your

Higher Self has always been with you and always will be. In your corner, singing your praises and urging you to become the best Soul that you can be.

Those of you that feel down and out, or perhaps are living a life full of bad luck and suffering and generally just feel that this is just your lot, think again. Your Higher self will have lived many lives as many Souls, some with suffering and some with joy, some quite ordinary and some perhaps notorious. Remember that no matter what each previous life experienced before your Soul, all of that learning from their previous Soul incarnations has found its way into to your energy, into your Inner Being. And therefore know that unless you are new Soul created from a newly created Higher Self, it's most likely that one of your Higher Self's previous lives will have gone through something similar to what you are experiencing in this life. Connect to this and allow yourself to find a way to all that you desire knowing that the energy within you links to previous Souls that perhaps also found a way.

Remember that you only get one chance on this Earth as you, one Soul as you. Your Higher Self will incarnate many Souls out of his or her pot of soup but they will each be individual and new on Earth as that Soul.

Only one chance then. Only one go at this. Only one you. Glorious wonderful beautiful you.

What is a Soul? You. You are a Soul. You are a Soul that has been carefully and lovingly cooked up by God and your Higher Self in order for you to live a wonderful life. A life which will stumble across tough times but that will always be given the opportunity to find a better path. Find that path, fight for it. Your Higher Self will push your Soul all that they can but only you can unturn those stones and only you can reach for something glorious. Only you can allow yourself to pull yourself out of that hole and only you can ensure that you never let yourself get back into that hole.

Only you can decide to be great in this life but don't feel you are doing this alone.

What is a Soul? You. You are a soul. But know that with your Higher Self if you can connect to him or her that you become Consciously Whole. Everything that you were meant to be and so much more should you wish it awaits you. But know that it starts with you. You. Precious you, perfect you.

Your Soul is yours to do with what you wish. Let it fail and die if you want, or maybe instead you might like to let it flourish, blossom, exceed, explode and take by storm all that is available to it. Live for your Soul, fight for your Soul, own your Soul, love your Soul, never doubt your Soul and never ever ever ever compromise your Soul.

Your Soul is yours and yours alone to cherish. Your Higher Self makes you Whole but you hold the keys and you lead the way to become Consciously Whole. Never shirk this responsibility. This is your Soul not theirs.

What is a Soul? A magnificent thing of beauty lovingly created and nurtured until it was ready to come to this amazing planet. Now go lovingly nurture it for the remainder of the time it has on this planet. Dovetail your amazingness with that *of* this planet. Fight for your right to be amazing, unhinged from fear and full of love. Use every ounce of your Soul's divine energy to drag you out of those holes and onto calmer more peaceful and wondrous places.

Then, when you feel that divine energy rising in you, calling you to fight to love to wonder to discover to innovate, get your skates on and just go.

Go. Go...Go!!!! Now THAT'S a soul.

Olivia and Raf, Abraham and Jesus

40

A NEW SOUL IS BORN

When we think of life, new life, we think of that moment of birth, when that beautiful baby is brought into the world. The newness, the beauty, the wonder of this little Physical Human, with the world at their feet and the all the possibility and wonder of what they will experience and who they will become is evident to all.

In most instances, that beautiful baby is a powerful Soul whose Higher Self has experienced through its other Souls a Physical life many, many times over. Sometimes the Soul is brand new and therefore is a brand new Higher Self, and each time when this occurs, that brand new Higher Self Soul is in fact not born at all in the lifetime of the parents who created them. A new Soul is created into a Physical Human at the point of conception, sometimes carried for weeks, sometimes longer before a miscarriage is experienced and also in some cases of course, a termination is completed.

In both instances, miscarriage or termination, the experience of loss for that baby is indeed still part of your Soul Contract, as hard as that is to reconcile for many. There are two other situations which are equally distressing and impacting, which is an Ectopic pregnancy and Stillbirth. These two represent significant Physical impacts for the Mother, the Father and family who are also Emotionally affected as these are Emotionally distressing experiences.

One final situation that we wish to also address is creation of life when there wasn't consent. Again, this is incredibly difficult for any woman to reconcile, not only the act itself but the follow on Emotional and Physical impact of this if it has led to pregnancy and often, the traumatic decision for termination.

If any of these situations have happened to you, please know that there is so much love for you, so much compassion and understanding from Non Physical. We hope that as you continue to read that this resonates deeply within you to know that all that you suffered through the loss of your baby has indeed not ended in that loss, but instead the creation of new life, and that it did take place, it did matter and it was for a reason.

Why are New Souls Needed?

There is unique energy within the Soul of you here on Earth. As you are now familiar with the Higher Self understanding, you will recognise that you are still a new aspect of that Higher Self's energy. Your Higher Self will not ever be the same again because of you and this is special, celebrated and ultimately incredible for our Universe. This then leads to the new life combination of you and another, a specific blend, never seen before life force that is generated by the energy that is you and them, right here, right now in this Physical experience. Does your Physicality matter? Your DNA? No. This is not a consideration, nor a minutia of impact or importance when related to the Soul Creation.

Does God play a part? Yes, absolutely. This starts with your Soul Contract, which is where this Soul Creation is determined and the equal partners in this, the male and female energies needed are agreed and decided and this is known and understood, alongside the understanding that this new Soul will not live a Physical experience this time. God is also a part of the Physical creation, as with all things, God is the creator and creation and therefore participates in the ultimate creation of this New Soul with you.

Each New Soul has a purpose for being created and this purpose is understood at the time of the Soul Contract and each New Soul that is created immediately expands the possibility of the Universe. As that New Soul grows in Non Physical understanding this too generates growth, huge growth and expansion. New is needed, always. Newness and uniqueness equates to endless possibility.

Where do New Unborn Souls go?

There is an unknown Archangel, Archangel Nicholas who is the carer for all New Souls that are created. Archangel Nicholas resides in the Ultimate Dimension with God and is an Almighty Omnipresent Energy. His energy transcends all Dimensions from the Ultimate. This means that all New Souls are welcomed and nurtured by Nicholas and each New

Soul is 'taught' and shared with in order for the greatest possible understanding of All That Is. This isn't just done by Nicholas, as your Higher Selves are also able to share with the New Soul as are Collective Consciousness Beings including Jesus and Abraham as well as many others.

When the parents of that New Soul transition from Physical to Non Physical their Soul will reunite with the New Soul that was created for the first time in this way. This is a very special and looked forward to event and one that we hope brings you great comfort, hope and love for there is nothing but love here in this reuniting of energy. Even if the New Soul has fear attached from you in this moment here in Physical, for perhaps given the conception situation this was something very difficult for you to suffer, please be fully reassured that on your re-emergence to Non Physical, you do not feel this way, that as you are released from this suffering (and as we have offered within this book, you are also able to do this whilst in Physical!) all there is, is love.

The next phase of growth for a New Soul, working as a Higher Self Soul, is the Physical experience of its first Soul and this is created just like all others. A Soul Contract is agreed with God, the Soul Group also agrees and participates in the Physical Experience with that New Soul. This is eagerly anticipated by the New Soul.

Even though you did not get to hold that precious baby, to nurture and take care of that little one, you still have a connection, you still have the ability to love the Soul of that child and they will also be with you, so often should you allow them to be. Once you have become familiar with your connection to your Higher Self, if this situation applies to you, you are able to call and communicate with that New Soul any time you wish without any Physical impact on you. Your Higher Self will facilitate this for you when the time is right, but all you need to do is ask.

Olivia and Raf, Abraham and Jesus

41

CREATION OF A SOUL CONTRACT

As has been stated, everything in your Soul Contract was agreed by you, your Soul that is, before you incarnated in this life. Your Soul Contract is an agreement between you, God and your Higher Self in the first instance and nothing that is stated in that Soul Contract has been forced upon you.

This is a key point of understanding and therefore for those of you that have found your Journey so far a challenge or a struggle at times know that this is exactly what you asked for. If it has been a wonderful experience so far then this also is exactly what you asked for and what was allowed and agreed to by God.

Your Soul Contract is agreed with ancestors up to the level of grandparents, that is, those Souls that will be your grandparents in the forthcoming life. The Souls of people that will be friends or other relatives in this life that are in your Soul Group, whose Higher Selves your own Higher Self will have had eternal relationships with, are part of this cross Alignment of Soul Contracts. This is another key understanding.

So all that are involved in an overlapping Soul Contract have to agree to the contents of it. The first point to note here is that none of these can incarnate until agreement has been reached and therefore this gives you an indication that Souls are not just generated when conception occurs between the Physical parents of that Soul, but instead it can indeed be many years from the creation of a Soul in Non Physical until they day that they are Physically conceived on Earth.

And so the connection to your Journey and the understanding that nothing within it is your fault or the fault of others can now be perhaps better understood when you become aware of this process of Aligned Soul Contracts.

And so when you were ready to enter the Physical world of Earth you will have been fully aware and prepared for what was about to come and this includes the paths that would be presented to you and the choices that you could make. Not all choices of course for the majority of your choices are manifested whilst you are on Earth. It is the key milestones in your life that we speak of and those points where decisions or a series of decisions and events could lead you down a specific path would be known to you.

We, Raf and Olivia, feel deeply honoured that we are able to receive information directly from God with regards to the Soul Contracts of others and often provide this information for the people that we work with. The paths of a Soul Contract are presented to us as either dark or light, representing either a path of fear or love. Often the paths can be shown intertwined as dark and light, other times the path is a grey mix and at others there are two paths shown that a person is currently walking. These are just a few examples of how the Soul Contract paths are shown to us, and beyond this we also see the future paths for that individual, shown to us rather like a tree with different dark and light branches.

Along these dark and light paths are a number of different milestones that get described to us and these represent the pre-manifested and pre-agreed points on a person's Journey that WILL occur. Again this is another important point to remind ourselves of, for often we blame ourselves or others for things that occur in our lives when in reality there is nothing that could have been done about it. The specifics of a pre-agreed milestone event on your Journey is most often not one hundred percent defined and therefore it is left to the free will manifestations to crystallise that milestone into what actually occurs.

For example a Soul Contract milestone could state something such as 'disconnection from a parent' which is a reference to an Emotional disconnection of some kind between you and a parent. Now this could manifest itself in a number of ways such as continuous disagreements as a result of more general Journey level experiences resulting in a lack of love between you both, or it could be something more serious where a parent or child abuses the other in some way thereby creating a lack of trust, lack of love, hate and potentially so much more between them. The early death of a person can also be specified in a Soul Contract and perhaps it may also be specified that it could occur due to an accident or a terminal disease. The actual terminal disease is rarely specified so again this is manifested on Earth and could be any number of diseases that sadly cause that person's death.

But there is also so much wonder in your Soul Contract and again much of this is pre-manifested before you come to Earth. It is the reason why Souls agree to undertake elements of suffering, particularly in the earlier parts of their life on Earth because the growth from those harder experiences often lay the seeds for entry to the paths of light and all of the wonderful milestones that are along those paths. We speak a lot of recognising growth as part of your suffering along your Journey and if you can find a way to heal, to move on and let go, the wonders that await you can often be beyond your wildest dreams.

Because of course growth is also driven by experiencing wonder and love and so it's another reason to get past the challenges of life as quickly as you can because growth from wonder is so much greater and expansive for you than expansion from suffering alone. This growth is beneficial not just to you in your life but also to your Higher Self and at times your Guides if they also have Soul Contracts which are tied to yours. The expansion of your Soul on Earth before you transition back to Non Physical is possible as is the expansion of your Higher Self although usually the expansion which leads to ascension through higher dimensions comes after you have transitioned back to Non Physical at the end of your life on Earth.

The Alignment of your Spiritual Guides to your Soul

Contract is an interesting one. They are tasked with supporting you and whatever you have agreed within your Soul Contract and it's a role they willingly take on and feel extremely proud to be part of. Often their own ascension or expansion is tied to how well you do on this Earth in terms of your growth and whilst it is you that is always their primary concern in terms of what can be achieved on your Journey, they also feel the joy when you heal and experience wonder because it also takes them to a greater place of understanding and experience and ability.

Know that there is so much love around you on this Journey of yours. Know that there are so many in Non Physical in your corner supporting you when times are tough and rejoicing with you when life is good.

Never feel alone. Never forget that you are here to learn and expand not only yourself but your Guides and the Universe as a whole. This is how important you are.

Olivia and Raf, Abraham and Jesus

42

CAN YOU REALLY CHANGE?

Yes of course you can but the question is do you 'really' want to?

Not, "yes that would amazing but I just don't know how". Or, "well let me just get beyond this phase in my life and then I can properly focus on myself".

Real Change comes at a cost, not a financial one but an Emotional one. Real Change requires courage, hope, support and most of all love. Love for yourself, love from you, love from others and love from you for others.

Align yourself to this understanding and you WILL succeed. Be prepared to go to those tough Emotional places, ask yourself those questions that you just don't want to hear the answer to, act with honesty and integrity throughout and trust that in doing so you raise yourself to a new place, a place where nothing but love can eventually be found.

Yes it will be difficult, yes it comes with risks. For in undertaking this real Change you risk everything that you perceive that you are and everything that you perceive is important, as well as everything that you wish not to lose. But ask yourself what it is that you are actually losing by continuing to live a life within yourself, a life as a shell within a shell, a person that at times you yourself do not recognise let alone understand.

Well, understand this. That nagging feeling that you have right now as you read this. That feeling is telling you that until you truly allow real Change you will always be living an untruth. And this untruth will cling to you, harass you, annoy and frustrate you in every moment. Sometimes gently but felt as a constant tension never quite allowing you to feel at ease, like a monkey on your back. At other times this untruth will be in your face like a snorting rhino egging you on, goading you to step out of that shell and face the consequences if you dare.

That monkey and that rhino make real Change pretty challenging we fully appreciate. But at least they bring to your attention the untruth which you carry. It's the silent, constantly eating away at you untruth which is the one to wary of. For this untruth allows you to carry it without facing or acknowledging it, like a spider tucked away in the corner within you. This silent untruth allows you to continue feeding it, expanding it and if left unchallenged it will eat you whole.

Instead, try something different, try anything in fact. Turn away from fear and take a dip in the pool of love, self-love.

Real Change starts here and always here. Many of you will have tried so many different things to heal and to grow and to Change your lives. Many of you will have tried so hard at this and yet somehow many of you will have been unable to effect real Change.

So what is REAL Change?

REAL Change is felt. A REAL Change brings fear at the thought of getting it. A REAL Change could lose you everything that matters. But what if what matters isn't real either? What if what matters is something cobbled together, built on thin ice and held up by endless rolls of string or tape? What if what matters only matters because you have nothing else, because you have no other choice or because it's better than having nothing at all?

But REAL Change will never leave you with nothing at all for with REAL Change you have yourself, you have access and connection to the Self and with it nothing but love to indulge in.

Start with love and that spider retreats backwards a little. Start with love and light blinds that spider just enough to keep it still long enough for you to see it, know where it is and most importantly know what it is. And what it is when you shine that light across its web is afraid. Afraid to be hurt, afraid to show itself, for any kind of exposure will see it killed, squashed, eaten. Start with love and that spider will soon find another home, a less fearless home.

Love, always love. This is your greatest weapon against that spider, as well as that monkey and that rhino.

For that monkey and that rhino work together. Both are afraid but together they conjure up in you feelings of anger, frustration or aggression when you challenge them and when you try to address them. For within you lives another to address them. Another which IS love, is ONLY love and only ever wanted to be love. This other is you. Special you, funny you, free you, forgotten you.

So start with you. Not him not her not them, just you. REAL Change starts with you. You deciding that enough is enough. You building a life on solid ground, not on thin ice. You wanting, wanting with every part of your being to salvage you and all that truly is you. And from here you connect to what really matters, what really is worth keeping and what really doesn't matter.

And what really doesn't matter is what you lose from this point for it's likely that it wasn't real. Save what's real, protect what's real, allow what's real, do everything within your power no matter how afraid you are, no matter how much it hurts, to create real. Real love. Real happiness. Real everything. REAL Change.

And when you have effected REAL Change you will know. Oh yes you will know. To the very core of you it will be felt. REAL Change brings freedom, is freedom. REAL Change is possible. Possible because it is only in your hands. No other can influence or effect your own REAL Change. Yes they can support you and of course help you to achieve it but in the end it comes down to you, just you.

Turn your back on that monkey and that rhino, open your doors and windows and let the light shine in on that spider and then just keep walking. Keep walking with the breeze blowing through your doors and windows, cleansing you, invigorating you with each and every step. Know that the wind will blow strongly many times over but do not be tempted to close those doors. Know that at times the light will seem too bright, too revealing but do not allow those curtains to be drawn on those windows.

Instead reach for love, for you, special you, funny you, free you, but not forgotten you.

For REAL Change never forgets you, but rather rejoices you, worships you, allows you to be just you, the REAL you.

Can YOU really Change?

Olivia and Raf, Abraham and Jesus

THE GRASS IS GREENER ON THIS SIDE

Ever looked over into the near or far distance at a beautiful looking spot with trees and grass and flowers wishing away the seconds as you connect to how much better life looks in that place and then thought to yourself, wow I'd love to be there right now in this moment, relaxed peaceful and away from it all?

Ever visited that place? Most likely not, but for those of you that have, you probably found that when you got there the grass was actually a bit damp and full of insects the bees around the flowers were making you anxious and that dead frog by the small pond nearby was freaking you out. Not untypical occurrences when out and about in nature and of course part of what makes it special.

So why could you not relax there? Why wasn't it as wonderful as it had seemed from your bedroom window? And why was it that your own house up there on the hill seemed so much more attractive to you when you were looking at it from a different perspective down by the pond?

Sadness, loneliness, lack of love, lack of self-love and other Emotions no doubt will all have had an influence on this. These four Emotions alone have the ability to trap you within a world, an Emotional prison of your own doing, that makes every scene in the distance just a pretty picture on the wall. A picture that you dream of going to but in reality you will never get to. Not that you won't be able to get to that location Physically but Emotionally it will never happen unless you make a Change.

For what that scene in the distance, that pretty picture represents is something that you can never have because it doesn't exist. Whatever it is that the scene reminds you of it has gone, passed by months or maybe years ago and what's even sadder is that what you think that scene represents to you from the past was probably never that in the first place.

Nostalgia.

Now there's nothing wrong with looking back on past days with love and fondness and joy but when the memories of the past draw you towards them like a magnet almost begging you to come back to them, there's something wrong. There's something wrong because wanting to go back to old times means you're missing something that you 'think' they gave you and could give you again.

Well think again.

Think about the ants and the bees and the frogs and remember the reality of what those memories really gave you. Pluck away those moments of fun or joy or love that you felt from those memories and remind yourself of what lay underneath at the time. Remind yourself of what views you were looking out at from of your window at that time, those scenes from the past wishing that you could be in instead. Remind yourself of the sadness, loneliness, lack of love and lack of self-love that you also felt back then.

We've managed to make you feel pretty awful about your past now haven't we? Well actually it's you that's done that. Yes you've had good times and of course you will have felt so much joy and love in your life at times but ask yourself why you don't feel this way now. Ask yourself why you keep looking out of that window or reading through that magazine or at that TV advert just wishing that person could be you.

Maybe a Change of job or a Change of location will help, what the heck let's move country and be in the sun! But no matter how warm that sun is, the brightness in the sky will not be matched by the energy within you. That sunny scene will be even more painful to look at when you stare at it locked within your Emotional prison. The Change of country may even take you to a place by the sea where you can feel free at last. But just wait, when you get out into that sea up to your shoulders with nobody around, that freedom will feel isolated, scary and very, very sad.

Nostalgia. Beware of it.

Beware of what it entices you with. The rich pickings of a better life just like days gone by that in fact link you to something not so nice.

Your sadness.

Your sadness could have formed as early as the day you were born when you couldn't feed properly or perhaps you were that mother that couldn't feed her child, both will be affected by sadness because of this. The lack of love or self-love felt in these moments can be the start of a wonderful relationship with hurt and sorrow and pain and suffering.

Sadness in your life builds easily as you have problems with friends at school or you have to move town and make new friends when Dad loses his job. Then as you get older and you struggle with your Physical Changes and can't get a boyfriend or girlfriend your sense of unworthiness grows, as does your loneliness, your lack of love and self-love, and of course your glorious sadness. Throw in a couple of failed relationships perhaps a divorce, some estranged children and some money problems and we have the perfect recipe for nostalgia.

So what's the answer to all of this and how can I stop the sadness?

This book describes perfectly the high level approaches to letting go the past as part of The Releasing Process, and that is literally all you need to do. Let go those memories that in all honesty probably were never quite as you remember them. Let go the need for love from those others that will never give it to you. Start to focus on generating love for yourself and from those that do show it to you, and most of all let go of that anger.

Yes anger.

We deliberately haven't mentioned anger until this point because it's the anger that you hold that keeps you tied and strongly gripping to these past events and memories. The anger that you still feel now for being hurt and let down and unloved. The anger that you hold that takes you into your daily cell of sadness and feeling sorry for yourself and blaming everyone and everything else for it. That anger that puffs you up and holds you in place and stops you from collapsing when you connect to your sadness.

Find a way to let go of this anger about your hurt and your sadness, and you find a way to make that scene from your window a reality, a reality within you. Let go of that anger and that distant scene doesn't look that good from where you're standing anyway. The grass in your garden will have less weeds, less sticks and less creepy crawlies!

Your garden will be full of love if you do this, and it's love that will lead you away from your Emotional prison. It's love that will place your garden on the map. Your garden will be full of fun and vitality and joviality as children or dogs or even adults run around in circles chasing butterflies and running from bees with laughter. For of course your garden will have bees and insects and creepy crawlies but what fun you will have discovering them and what fun you will have running away from them because there will be no anger in your heart. Without that anger you won't need to run inside the house waiting for them to fly away on their own whilst you stare into the distance wishing that you were in that much calmer looking place by the pond. Instead with love in your garden you will embrace the variety of your garden, the lovely smelling flowers with the not so lovely prickly bushes and with love, not anger, you will prune back the prickly bush, tend to it with joy and a smile on your face and know that with a little care and attention everything in your garden can be rosy, literally.

Love is what will make 'your' grass greener. Love is what will take away your sadness and your anger. Take down those mental pictures now and let go of your nostalgia. Instead ask yourself why you feel drawn to it and from this place look to replace whatever you are seeing in that picture with something real, and better! There will have been real things in that scene from the past and real love too but that doesn't exist now it's gone.

Let go the sadness of that scene, we know it's hard, as it means so much to you but ask yourself just how much good there really was in that scene and instead ask yourself how you can reconnect to whatever brings you sadness from that scene. Ask yourself, what's lacking for you today and then find what's missing and make it your reality now. Whether it be a lost child, friend, parent or lover that connects you to sadness over that scene, bring what they used to represent back into your reality now in a different way. Perhaps connect to them in a Non Physical way through your Higher Self, or find a new lover or just cherish the one you have even more.

Whatever your choice, just always remember to do it with love for you. It's you that needs to Change for that scene to Change. Connect to the love for you, the love for the son or daughter that you are, for the father or mother that you are, for the friend that you are. Connect to love for the courage in you, for the determination in you, for the passion in you.

Time now to let go of the sadness and the pain for something that isn't even real any more. Instead it's time now to find something real.

Real love, real people and the real you.

Olivia and Raf, Abraham and Jesus

44

UNDERSTANDING ADDICTIONS

Addiction is a word that brings to mind someone who is out of control with a desperate need, or that is engulfed by a sordid world of debauchery and depravity.

But addiction is a lot closer to home than you realise. We are not talking about one too many drinks on a Monday night or that uncomfortable social drug habit that you might seem to be forming. Addiction comes in many forms and is driven by Emotional needs and not Physical needs.

For most addictions are formed long before the symptom appears in whatever form it takes, whether it be sex, drugs, gambling, love, whatever. Your addictions are just around the corner if you are someone who is lacking in love or who is angry, fearful, hurt, lonely or all of these and many more.

Addiction is born out of isolation. That feeling when you sense that nobody cares or understands or is just too busy to care or just too hurt to be able to care. Have you been without love or been unable to hold down a long term relationship with a committed partner? Ask yourself why. And then ask yourself why you can't stop obsessing about that person that you couldn't keep hold of and what it is that makes you feel that this person is the best person that you ever had, and how you know that you could never get anyone better and that you truly believe that they love you and that all of the lies and the hurt they put on you are because they are broken and that it is you and only you that can fix them if you could only get them to answer the phone and stop avoiding you after months of chasing them. Then ask yourself why you hate them so for ignoring you. Remind yourself of the thoughts you have of what you're going to do to them or yourself if they don't answer that damn phone.

Or next time you're in a bar looking across at that person wondering if they like you, ask yourself why you yearn for this so much. What pain are you holding that makes you feel so drawn to them?

Or when you choose to lose yourself in that drug haze or that gambling rush or in that dark and sad place with that prostitute. Ask yourself what the heck you are doing there and why.

And when you get the answers to all or some of these questions, if you get the answers, then take a step back from yourself and realise that whatever it is that has driven you into this dark hole of fear and anger and lack of love for yourself is slowly draining the life blood from you and making you into an addict.

An addict for love.

Yes love.

Pure and simple innocent love.

This sweet angelic Emotion that connects to everything that we are and that fills our hearts with joy and hope and freedom, is the reason for your doom. This wonderful energy so entwined into all that is God and that shines light on all that embrace it, is the reason for your personal hell.

Damn you love.

I hate you love.

You owe me so much love, love.

When are you going to give me your love, love.

Well if you can't give me your love, love then I'm going to get it somewhere else. Yes I mean it, I'll show you and then when I'm in bits Emotionally and when I've ruined everything that I have and hold dear, and destroyed any chance of me coming back from it, then, then you'll be sorry.

And then I know you'll love me finally. When I'm nothing but a shell of who I truly am or used to be. I know that then you'll come back to me and show me your love, love.

Why are you judging me love, why do you laugh at me and look down on me. What have I ever done to you love? All I ever asked for love, is your love. Why can't you see my suffering love, my eternal suffering at your hands love? Can't you see that this is why I take these drugs these men these women these children these long hours these hopeless and sad activities that keep me away from my sadness, love. Can't you see that it's because of you that I lust for all of these things that give me that fix of love that you can't give me, love?

Let go the anger my love.

What did you say love?

Let go the anger. Let go the hate. Let go the need for me because I'm never going to be here for you in the way that you crave it. The sickening way that you crave it, crave me.

Look within you my love for I am in there. Feel me inside your heart that's where you'll find me. Don't look to another's heart for they cannot guarantee me to you. Only you can give me fully to you, my love. There are so many others around you that have my love and can give some of me to you, and from them you should seek and accept it but not before you have allowed me in. My love for you is the strongest, the purest and the best, for you.

Don't drown or suppress me in a haze of drink or drugs or sex or other habits. Fight these. Fight these needs because they do not serve you beyond the quick fix. And I am not a quick fix, I am a permanent fix. I am a permanent fix to fight your fear and your lust and your anger and your doubt and your confusion and your paranoia and your unworthiness and your worry.

But I am not available to you in the state you are currently in.

I am never available to those that deny themselves me and instead seek me in other forms because they can't have me in another way from another they seek it from. I am not here for you just because you desperately need me either. Your desperation for me doesn't make me any more sympathetic to your plight. What attracts me, real love that is, to you is your recognition that I already exist within you and that nobody, nobody else needs to supply me to you no matter how much you think they owe me to you.

Get this into your head now and quickly before you lose the real me forever and in doing so the real you. Put down that weed that needle that drink that women that man and go home to your family and don't swing past the gym for the fifth time this week. Stop. Stop. Just stop.

Stop running away from what you fear you are or what you fear you are not, or what you fear you have not got. When you need your fix don't come looking for the substitute for me in whatever it is that you do to get that high of me.

I'm probably talking to you by the way. Yes YOU.

You, that person that is dedicated to their job and their career, or is running marathons or is buying the latest clothes or constantly spending to remodel your home. Yes you. You are the addict. You may not be mainlining heroin right now but you are merely a more refined version of that person.

Recognise your need for love, your yearning for love, that quick fix of false love and go and find the real stuff. The raw unrefined uncut stuff that will give you the biggest and best high of all.

Recognise your addiction. Recognise why you have it. Free yourself from the need for it and come find me.

I'm here for you, right inside of you. Some of you will need to dig a little deeper to find me but know I'm there.

Next time you look across that bar or through that magazine or pick up the phone to text your dealer, I'll be calling you. I'll be pleading with you to take a look at yourself and hear my call.

Hello, is it me you're looking for?

Olivia and Raf, Abraham and Jesus

45

ACTIVATE YOUR JOURNEY

Ok I'm ready…

Let go the fear, let go your protection, let go your need to be safe to cross every 'i' and dot every 't'. Oh hang on that's the wrong way around did anyone see me make that typing error, is anybody hurt by what I just did? I hope nobody judges me for messing up just there, I'm sure I can cover it up and make myself look good anyway.

You know maybe I should just start that sentence again. I'm not sure it's that funny anyway and this is a serious book with serious intention and a lot of people counting on us and so…gosh is that the time already? Where has the day gone? I tell you what, I'll start this chapter tomorrow when my mind is fresher and my energy is perfect and the temperature outside is not a smidgen under sixty eight degrees Fahrenheit, well you know how my arthritis plays up in the cold.

Ok I'm ready...

Let go the fear, let go protection, let go your need to be safe...

...hang on, I've no idea what I'm going to really write about in this chapter. Maybe a good night's sleep will help get the creative juices flowing and I'm so much better in the morning. I know I've got that client at 10am but as long as my energy is fine after that I'm sure I can give this a better go and to be fair right now I'm keeping everybody waiting on that TV series that we're watching, there's only seventy six episodes left to download so we're getting to the crunch parts now.

Ok I'm ready...

I'm honestly getting so tired now. I've been sat here for ages trying to think of what to write so I have really given this a good go. Today is just not the day I guess, and there are only twenty three episodes left to go of that TV series now, so I may as well finish those and be clear headed and fully focussed on this chapter before I attempt to write it.

Ok I'm ready...

I'm starting to get really annoyed now I've spent so much time in front of this laptop trying to write something and all I can think about is that stupid TV series. I need some fresh air.

Hang on, I've just written four paragraphs of this chapter, that's a start isn't it? It feels like a start and it sure looks like a start. Ok well if I just keep going with this, just keep writing before I know it the chapter will be over won't it?

And then I'll be on the next chapter and then who knows what will happen after that. But to be honest who cares I'm just loving the fact that I've got something to write about in this chapter, so the next chapter can wait.

In fact everything else can wait, the TV series, the dog, the car, the hairdressers, everything! Tomorrow, the day after that, the week after that, Christmas, my birthday it can all just wait a minute because I happen to be in my flow here and you know what right now I am loving it. Loving the tingles as my words inspire me. Loving the fact that right now nothing else matters. Loving the fact that I am feeling like a writing beast, like a machine, wow I'm good!

Actually I'm better than good I'm great, in fact I've never been better. I've never felt better and...hang on remind me of what I just said there again? No seriously how on Earth did that happen I mean did anybody notice me or what I just said? Did I just make a fool of myself? This just isn't me I'm not sure what came over me. I wonder how many episodes of that TV series are left I'm really going to miss those guys when it's over.

No, no, no! No way is this happening again I've come too far in this chapter. This chapter that I have literally given tears for, suffered for. There's just no way I'm going back, nor am I going to stop here. The next chapter for me is just around the corner and as it happens this chapter was easier than I thought. All I had to do was stop thinking about it, stop trying to make it perfect, stop fearing it. STOP JUST DOING NOTHING.

LIVE.

LOVE.

BE FREE.

BE PROUD.

BE YOU.

ACTIVATE YOU.

ACTIVATE YOUR Journey.

Olivia and Raf, Abraham and Jesus

III

LEADING EDGE INSIGHT

46

YOUR BODIES

We have multiple bodies? But surely there is only one? This is phraseology, a way to introduce to you a new concept and make you aware of the different Physical holdings or placements within your Physical being which may have at times felt illusive or intangible. This reference, this illustration is truly leading-edge thought and an introduction to a most specific rationale that will help drive Change and connection within you. Your Bodies are your Physical Body, your Subconscious mind, your Conscious Mind, your Egoic Bodies or just simply your Ego and your Emotional Body and combined together they make up Yourself.

With all this talk of the Inner Being, how does that play in? Your Inner Being is also referenced in this diagram but it is separate, something that cannot be impacted by Your Bodies. This is the eternal part of you, the you that is connected to

All That You Are, your Soul, your connection to the Universe through your Higher Self, your Source Energy. It is pure, positive energy. It is your Intuition, your navigation system and your internal compass. It cannot ever be impacted by anything that you do, say, think or feel. Your Bodies however, are impacted by what you feel, what you think, what you believe, what you allow or disallow, the conditions that you place yourself under, your practiced and habitual patterns.

The current information that is being shared with us is very focused on the Physical and this is on purpose. For now is the time for you to become fully aware and in tune with your Physicality, ALL of the parts of you for this greater understanding ultimately will help you with Emotional understanding and also with Physical Alignment.

The insight shared on Your Bodies will not be found in a biology or anatomy book, nor will it be found specifically using the tools and techniques for current Physical scanning and imaging. This is not to say however that this will not be able to be found using greater energetic and frequency measurements in the future should our incredible science and medical friends wish to explore this in a new way and for anyone reading this in such a field, this is also an open invitation to explore this further.

For us to share this with you in this way, it is incredible to receive this kind of amazing insight but we also know that as anything like this often comes with further questions. We know that so many people need evidence. So many people want to see an ultrasound, an x-ray or MRI scanning as an example of this evidence with a label to say – look, here it is, it really does exist. As with much that is written in this book, there is no other reason why this is being published other than it has been given. For anyone that has come to understand these Bodies, it is somewhat life-changing. You FEEL that this is true when you engage with this fully. For each of you that normally needs evidence in order to believe, just give this new insight a go. Feel it if you can and feel into these energy placements within your body.

The terms that are being used, these are not new. What is new is the awareness and understanding of the Physical placement and positioning within the body, the interrelationship and the access options that you now have with this Physical understanding.

The illustrations that are shown were received as channelled drawings. These are very specific but also quite simple in their appearance, as with so much that we are given these have not been altered in any way but they have been replicated in order to be printable. These came thick and fast these drawings and with them the most incredible insight as to the relationships between the Bodies and a whole new way to understand how your energy works within you.

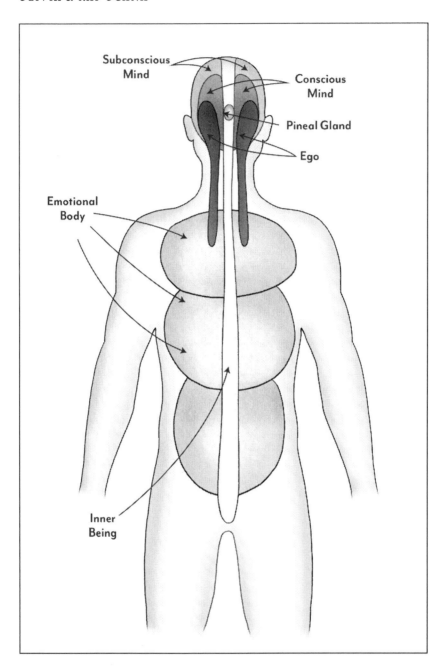

The Subconscious Mind

This is formed of two parts, both right and left aspects within the mind and is the 'container' for the Conscious Mind and the Egoic Bodies and therefore can influence both of these bodies.

The Conscious Mind

This forms a larger energy holding on both left and right aspects of the mind and where the logical thought processes are managed and maintained. The Conscious Mind is the container for the Egoic Bodies and can be heavily influenced by both the Subconscious Mind and the Egoic Bodies.

The Egoic Bodies

This is a flexible energy holding and therefore can increase and decrease in size within the container of the Conscious Mind. The Egoic Bodies have direct connection and therefore full access to the Emotional Body and can influence and be influenced by the Emotional Body as well as be activated by the Subconscious Mind.

Emotional Body

Running from your collar bone to your pelvis, your Emotional Body is the generator of Emotion. Emotion cannot be 'felt' anywhere else but within the Emotional Body, however it can be translated into thoughts in order to understand the Emotion, both Conscious, Subconscious

Emotion is also stored as Vibration within your cells throughout your Physical body and this is not only contained within your Emotional Body.

Your Physical Body

We detail your Physical Body in a separate chapter and in doing so, we wish you to understand the utter importance of your Physical being. This is not just a shell, a vessel for you to take care of and discard when you are done with your Physical life. This Physical Body of yours holds the very key to unlocking true and total Alignment and the tuning into your Physical Body provides the ability to hold Alignment, to notice and quickly, when you are in or out of it. For you are full of cooperative components, all working together, so beautifully. These are your cells. Your incredible, regenerative cells but is also the space that holds the impact of your Physical life on Earth. For Your Bodies (Subconscious, Conscious, Egoic and Emotional) residing within your Physical Body are wholly impacting it, all of the time, both in the positive and the negative. So, on goes your capable, regenerative Physical Body, Balancing and rebalancing as the impacts come and go as a result of your Bodies.

Your Physical Body stores your Emotional Vibration. When you experience Emotion, this fills your cells and not only the cells that reside within your Emotional Body but the cells that fill your Physical Body. When you repeat that Emotion, in a loop, the Vibration sticks, it holds, it takes up space. Everyone on the planet has experienced positive and negative Emotion for this is the joy of being human. How many of you can truly understand what impacts these 'feelings' have on you? So many references are made to Vibration, to the ability to heal oneself, and the fundamentals of this is, and always will be, what you FEEL impacts you, truly. What you think, matters and it matters in particular if it makes you feel something. You can not only influence your cells, you are able to control your thoughts, reduce your Subconscious Mind and Egoic Bodies well-meaning protection and understand your Emotions and thus, absolutely, you are able to heal.

Residing within you, not only are your body systems, your anatomical perfections and imperfections but your Physical Body hosts four of the most incredible energy holdings that have never been explained to you in this way, but as you come to read, understand and connect to, you will feel like you have always known them. You will start to understand just how they interrelate and how they work.

Your Physical Body is beyond precious. It is your history book. It is your record of moments, the holder of secrets and the truth. It is yours and yours alone to fully connect to and understand and in doing so, by taking this ownership, by truly understanding the power of what it is capable of, well, this can lead to things you never dreamed possible. Is it possible that the human body has a much longer shelf life than is currently on record? The answer is clearly and absolutely, yes. The human body and its regenerative capability has not reached its full potential. This understanding is in its infancy by those you share the Earth with but there is the ability to extend life beyond the current age limit and it starts with the understanding of your own influence, it starts with an awareness of All That You Are. It starts with true connection, with maintaining that connection always. It starts with moving to Alignment and putting your Alignment at the forefront of every moment.

Olivia and Raf, Abraham and Jesus

47

YOUR SUBCONSCIOUS MIND

The leader of the mind pack, the Subconscious Mind is a phenomenal energy holding within you, one that holds the energy of things you often don't consciously acknowledge and will remind you and hold you in a particular Vibration until these things are addressed. Your Subconscious is a route to uncovering essential understanding of your Vibration and once you are able to further understand the Subconscious Mind and tap into the understanding of how it works and use The Releasing Process, it is the way to enable letting go permanently Low Vibration Emotion. Truly allowing you to move on from the past and allowing your 'now' based experiences to be truly you, the Changed you.

Your Subconscious Mind holds the Conscious Mind and the Egoic Bodies and therefore can influence both. Your Subconscious Mind, along with your Physical Body is your Vortex, a term commonly used by Abraham through Esther and Jerry Hicks (more is outlined on this in the chapter Manifesting Bigger).

Your Subconscious Mind will not allow you to let go of something that you do not fully understand. It is in the understanding of an Emotional experience that you are able to release the Low Vibration Emotion that resides within, in particular when you connect to new understanding or perspective and when you are able to create new Truths associated with that understanding. Your Subconscious Mind will play the part in understanding fully if there is Low Vibration within you, it knows entirely the Emotions that you have experienced even if you have rationalised them with your Conscious Mind. Your Subconscious Mind will not allow you just to be rational about it, your Subconscious Mind will always want you to know the reality of those Emotions relating to that experience, the reality of that Low Vibration within.

The Subconscious Mind commonly alerts the Egoic Bodies in order to trigger the request for Low Vibration and in doing so will start to inflate them as part of a self-protection mechanism. The Ego can also do this on its own when over-inflated and habitually so, triggering requests for fear and doubt Emotions. In general though, if you have Low Vibration that needs to be addressed, it is the Subconscious Mind that is behind this and not the Egoic Bodies. The Subconscious Mind, through the Egoic Bodies is responsible for generating the requests for all Low Vibration that is felt in the Emotional Bodies.

WHAT IF I REMOVE ALL MY LOW VIBRATION ? CAN THE SUBCONSCIOUS MIND STILL CREATE LOW VIBRATION ?

Your Subconscious will not ever manufacture Low Vibration within, however when in a particular Subconscious Mind State, it will influence you based on your past experiences (more on the Subconscious Mind State chapters shortly). The Subconscious Mind is there to act as a record holder of the truth of your experience. It understands every Emotion experienced at the point in time and it knows where that Emotion is stored energetically within your cells. Not only does it hold the 'map' of your Emotional experiences, but it also holds the memory.

This is why the Subconscious is so critical to become tuned to, for it will not allow you to kid yourself. It won't be aggressive about it, but it will find a way to let you know that something needs to be understood or to be cautious of based on your previous patterns of behaviour. For example, if you are not able to connect to love, love for others and love for yourself. You will know that this is the case if you think of a situation or another person and feel Low Vibration such as fear, judgement, guilt or blame as examples. This will give you an indication that you are still holding onto the past and your body is looking for freedom from it.

Your Subconscious Mind is looking for your connection to self-love and a connection to your understanding of your Journey and that of others. Without this connection, it continues to seek its stores, the memory stores and the Emotional stores of Low Vibration. This is for clarity on your

Emotional experiences and understanding, whether that understanding has Changed and also whether you have let it go. If you have not fully let go of your past experiences, the Subconscious Mind can loop into seeking mode, so it will continue to sort and source the Emotional experiences that you are triggered by and continue to alert you to it.

This is why, so very often, it feels like you can't move forward or move on or, why it feels like you are having a consistent and persistent Emotional experience. It is also why you feel like you are being dragged back, even when you have 'dealt' with the stuff that has plagued you. This can build and build over time, where your body creates a number of methods in order to handle this Vibration within you. This can include illness (mental and Physical), it can include true disconnection from the Self, it can increase self-destructive behaviours because of it and also it can cause Egoic Blocks which stems the continuous flow of High Vibration from your Inner Being through your Vortexes of Emotion.

Without the letting go, without the understanding, each time you re-create or re-trigger the experience of a particular Emotion or set of Emotions (for example, you generate guilt, fear, loss, worry) this then links to previous core experience Emotions. We describe this further in the chapter Understanding Low Vibration and the Cellular Impact, but where this is exceptionally important for you to connect to is how the Subconscious Mind connects you to these 'like' experiences, how you get triggered and why you get triggered. How you can go from feeling relatively ok, to watching something on the television that generates a whole host of Emotions. Let's explore this very example even further.

Picture a lovely Saturday night, you are settled down after a great meal with your partner and you are having a glass of wine, nothing bad has happened in your day, there's nothing wrong at all in fact, you are feeling pretty good. You decide to watch that series that you have been enjoying. The moments tick by, there are a couple of scenes and everything is great and then BAM!, out of nowhere there is a reference, a glance, a look, an argument then brews, feels familiar, feels like it's yours, the pressure is building, the fear is rising and you are watching the screen but it is like your life. Horror, fear, guilt, shock, disbelief, betrayal, anger, loss, worry, sickening, all activated, all flowing through you, all connecting you to YOUR moment, remembering the words of YOUR story, the memory of what you know about YOUR life. Except it isn't your 'now' experience. You were just watching the TV.

Often, in this example, you start to spiral. Your Transitional Vibration is impacted and you have gone from feeling good to feeling really bad and you keep feeling bad and you can't shake it. Your Ego is triggered into Self Protection mode and your Subconscious Mind says 'don't worry, I know what to do' and so triggers the Spiralling thoughts. Taking this potential real life example further, your partner may ask you "Are you ok?" and then you start to verbalise it and generate more and more Emotion, attracting more and more of it to you as do they in response to your Emotion and the triggering of their own Emotion. So, you both go from having a relaxing and generally 'fine' time to feeling really quite terrible wondering where the heck this all came from.

Sometimes it is more subtle. Sometimes you just have this creeping feeling of dread that seems to sneak up on you, or a consistent feeling of guilt in seemingly every daily situation. Perhaps you suffer from anxiety, so you have days when it is manageable and days when it really isn't, but it falls under the all-encompassing umbrella of Fear and Anxiety and you notice that consistency of Emotion and continuing to connect with just good feelings and ease is becoming more and more difficult. This is the Subconscious Mind. It's telling you it's time. Time to Let Go. Time to Move On. Time to Change.

There is no talking yourself up or talking yourself out of these situations. A positive Conscious mindset will only get you so far in this situation. Regardless of what you might say to yourself about those scenarios from that TV show, if you are in the wrong Subconscious Mind State then it will just reference the potentially hundreds of thousands of memories it is storing for similar experiences to those happening on TV where you have had something similar happen. It will know that you still hold some level of fear for those memories and will also know that you still hold Low Vibration within you that are attached to those fearful memories.

This is why the Subconscious Mind needs total understanding, full awareness of why you haven't been able to shift out of it just by 'thinking a better thought' and why you can't hold that good feeling for long enough for it to make a difference. The interrelationship of all of The Bodies is vital, the letting go and understanding of your Emotional experiences essential, and the Mastery of your Experience is what we all should want to enjoy and enable within our

Physical lives because, it equals freedom. After you have fully read and understood The Bodies chapters, do start to look at The Releasing Process in The Feelset Tools section of the book to take action, to start connection in order to create Change within.

LOVE AND FEAR MEMORY PROFILING

This is key to understanding EVERYTHING about your Subconscious Mind. When you live through your life experiences, the Emotion that you generate in that Experience is profiled within your Subconscious Mind as either Love or Fear. This is WHY! This is why, for so many, Fear is such a predominant Vibration and why Fear profiled Memories are haunting and recycling, why more 'like' fear-based experiences are being attracted to you literally by The Law of Attraction and also why this is stopping you from holding a consistent Vibration and stopping the Balance within, keeping that Alignment so elusive, keeping your Manifestations away from being realised into your current experience.

Perspective is so critical here, because one person's perspective of an experience and another's can be wildly different. It is all to do with your Vibration at the time, in the moment, for you feel what you feel when you feel it – never as someone else tells you to or when someone else tells you to, you are truly the only absolute FEELER in the moment. You may be taught to suppress your Emotions, but you still FEEL what you feel, even if you think you have 'outsmarted' your Emotional Body. You can reflect on an experience and the Emotion can Change (more on that in a moment) but no matter what, that experience is profiled and stored in your Subconscious Mind based on that perspective.

Now, what was your Perspective? Was it Love in the moment, even if you initially felt Low Vibration Emotions such as hurt, anger, disbelief, did your perspective understand that it was a growth experience, or one that was 'given' and therefore had Love attached to it and therefore AS you experienced the range of Emotions THIS was the outcome, the outcome ultimately was Love? Or was there no understanding of Love in the moment and therefore the default setting is Fear? Was your perspective "I can't believe this has happened to me"; "How did I not see this coming?"; "Why is my life so difficult"; "I never get what I need"; "Oh MY GOD, how am I going to deal with this?"; "What is this going to mean for me, for my future?" Fear, Fear, Fear, Fear and more Fear.

Your Subconscious Mind State, which we shall talk more of shortly, can heavily influence these thoughts and even make you feel something that is just not your current reality or perspective but is reminiscent of past experiences. This is the power of the Subconscious Mind, and why we repeat, talking a good game won't be enough in isolation to stop the generation of Low Vibration in some circumstances.

Emotional Mastery or being the Master of Your Experience. This doesn't mean you will never experience contrast again, that Fear will never raise its head at you but what it does mean is that you will recognise it IN THE MOMENT and you can look to *feel* Love. In one particular Subconscious Mind

State, the Expectant Mind State, this will allow you to *Change* the profile of this Emotion before it is stored as Fear and instead, it will only be stored as Love. In other Subconscious Mind States, it won't.

The Releasing Process teaches you how to overcome this for *any* Subconscious Mind State. BELIEVE that this is possible. Believe that this is all part of your greatest understanding in this Physical experience and that *you* have the power and possibility to use this understanding to utterly free you and ultimately Change your life to one of wonder.

Keep reading and also reference The Feelset Tools section which will provide further guidance on The Releasing Experience.

CHANGING THE EMOTIONAL PROFILE OF YOUR MEMORY

As your Subconscious Mind is your record holder, your library of memory and Emotional history, what happens when you truly understand an experience and let it go? How do you stop from going back to that same Emotion again and again if you trigger the memory? Or can the Emotion attached to a memory Change or be 'forgotten'? For when we say forget, this means forget the connection to pain. You can still access and observe the memory, but it doesn't trigger the original Emotion any longer. That part is almost like watching a movie with the sound turned off. Also, you have to really search for the memory, rather than it replay on a loop in bright colour like it used repeat on you. You also have no Fear associated with the review of the Experience like you used to.

In the Understanding of the Experience, in the letting go of the Low Vibration, in the creation of a new Truth for that Experience, the Subconscious Mind will now re-profile that stored Memory and archive the Fear aspect and re-label it. This means changing the profile of that experience to Love and in particular as it now knows that the held Low Vibration has been moved out from your cells, it no longer associates the Emotions related to the Fear based experienced as stored Emotions, but sees now that you have High Vibration in its place.

You do not need to do anything differently through The Releasing Process in order to do this, this is all part of the 'How' this happens, but it is fantastic understanding for you so it can answer the many questions that you have about how this works.

IN THE MOMENT CHOOSE LOVE

This is the Ultimate Mastering of your Experience. No matter how High Vibrational you are, you will still experience contrast, for this is the joy of being Physical, the joy of continuous Expansion and Journeying through your Physical life, creating more and more Desires on your path. You can, however, once at you are predominantly High Vibration, swiftly move away from contrast and the generation of 'in the moment' experience based Low Vibration , to a fast understanding of that 'now' experience and the growth associated with it. You will ultimately then feel love for that experience and the growth associated.

This is in the moment, feeling Love. Love for Yourself first, love for the Self, love for others involved. What this then does is Change the Transitional Vibration if it is relatively in the moment, from one of Low Vibration such as fear, shock, shame, sadness, loss, lack of love to Love. If you catch this and truly feel it in the moment, then your Transitional Vibration Changes also and the Low Vibration in your Transitional Vibration moves away. The Experience you have just had is stored within your Subconscious Mind as a Love labelled experience.

This can happen when you have already let go of a lot of Stored Low Vibration to become predominantly High Stored Vibration and, when you have a number of strong Truths that you can connect to. This is so you can feel love for your Journey, you understand the concept of growth and how it has truly served you, and you have stopped blaming yourself and others. Even if someone is having a terrible day and treating you badly in the moment, you may not actually feel any of the Low Vibration Emotions that you used to but instead, feel compassion or even understanding for them. But only after you have felt compassion for yourself in the moment to say, 'hey, I haven't done anything wrong here and this isn't about me, it's about them and how they are doing'. This stops the negative Vibrational impact in its tracks. To do this verbatim just because you really want to live like this, you won't be able to necessarily until you have got that broader understanding of your Journey, Growth and Blamelessness.

For those who are starting their Journey of Vibrational Mastery, this may feel like it is totally unachievable but it absolutely is, no matter who you are, no matter what you have experienced, this could indeed become your reality. Feel the Truth of this, connect to this and you are already starting to experience it. Go take a look at The Feelset Tools section of the book and get started with The Releasing Process.

LOCKED AND HIDDEN MEMORIES

Lost childhoods. We understand that for many who have experienced extreme Emotional contrast as children that their childhood memories are almost inaccessible. They can't recall detailed memories, even happy ones, from early on in their childhood, it is like their childhood starts at a certain age (later than most) and they don't remember a lot before this. The concept that we are about to introduce about Locked and Hidden Memories isn't of course, only relating to children and childhood memories. This can be an experience at any time in your life of intense and consistent Low Vibration Emotion and huge suffering which leaves this period of your life's experience unobtainable in detail.

We will however look at this specifically with childhood in mind as this is so very common and for those who are predominantly Low Vibrational, often the core experiences and Emotion stem from childhood. For childhood experiences where so much has been lived in fear and therefore all like experiences, are 'Marked' as Fear within the Subconscious Mind. The more experiences generated like this, if they are more of the same type of experience and similarly generated Emotion, the more that goes into the bracket of 'to be forgotten' rather than 'to be reminded' and therefore is 'Hidden' from the Conscious Minds recall.

You are Consciously aware of the overall experience and the timeline in some cases, but it is the details, that you cannot get to and you also often don't wish too. Part of the reason the Subconscious Mind is marking it as 'to be forgotten' is that it knows that the remembering of it will cause extreme suffering.

The understanding of this mechanic of the Subconscious Mind will allow the Emotional releasing process to be further activated and explored. In particular this can be exceptionally helpful when using your Higher Self in order to access those Locked or Hidden Experiences and bring these forth to you in a way that you may find difficult to do on your own without this guided support. There is more detail on The Releasing Process within The Feelset Tools Chapter within this book.

Olivia and Raf, Abraham and Jesus

SUBCONSCIOUS MIND STATES

There are three Subconscious Mind States; the Expectant, Resistant and the Psychotic. The Expectant Subconscious is absolutely where you want to be living but often, when you have lived through a variety of contrast, those who have predominantly Fear based Subconscious Mind labelling, a volume of Egoic blocks to the Vortexes of Emotion and who are also predominantly Low Vibrational will often not be in the Expectant Subconscious Mind State and will often be inhabiting the Resistant and sometimes flip to the Psychotic Subconscious Mind State.

This moving back and forth between Subconscious Mind States is very common, so if this is you, know that this is where the majority of people are and not to fear this or feel disappointed if you find yourself moving between them. The reason that this is being highlighted to you in this way is for utter clarity and understanding that this is why you often are not able to react and respond to things in the moment the way some others do, or more importantly, the way you wish to. This is also why sometimes you can and sometimes you can't. It can be as simple as where you are in your Subconscious Mind state of being in the moment that will allow or disallow you 'handling' things or Mastering things. But even if you are in the Expectant Mind State at the time of a new experience, if the memory of a similar previous experience is held and labelled as Fear because it was created whilst you were in the Resistant or Psychotic Mind State, then that past experience will heavily influence the Low Vibrations that you generate for the current new experience. This will occur even if you hold a positive outlook on this new experience. We speak more of how this works in later chapters but we have termed this effect the 'Dripping Tap of Emotions'.

The reason you can flip between the states will primarily be about the core things you need to address:

1. Fear vs Love labelling of the Subconscious Mind

2. Egoic Blocks to your Vortexes of Emotion

3. Conflicting against Truths or not creating Powerful Truths (ie. Law based Truths)

4. Lack of Desire (again, created with The Law of Desire)

5. Predominantly Low Vibration either Stored, Transitional or a combination of both

6. You are swinging Emotionally and not able to maintain Balance

You do not have to be a Master of Your Experience in order to visit the Expectant Subconscious but do know that with Vibrational Mastery this will be the predominant state of being for you. How do you get there? You need to address 1-6! Find out how in The Feelset Tools section of the book.

THE EXPECTANT SUBCONSCIOUS

The Expectant Subconscious is the absolute best state of mind possible, one you will have experienced many times in your Physical experience and one to be actively aware of moving towards as often as possible. This wonderful state of being is when your Subconscious Mind will wait in the moment, expecting you to act/think/feel love when a contrast situation occurs *and* when a High Vibrational situation occurs. We state that explicitly because in the Resistant or Psychotic state, even a High Vibrational situation may generate fear. This is an important distinction of this particular mind state.

When you are in Expectant mode, you focus on 'in the moment' Vibrational management. You are not generating past fears nor activating them either, this 'waiting' that your Subconscious Mind does is allowing you to act in the moment, expecting you to act in the moment with love first, love for you, love for others.

So why is this the utopia? This allows you to BE who you are right now and in the moment. It isn't activating habitual patterns and behaviours and ways of being. It isn't activating the ego and generating new fears. It isn't wary of the current now situation and actively mirroring the past. It is clearly you, you now, not you then, not you as you were, but YOU now.

THE RESISTANT SUBCONSCIOUS

Sometimes, you just keep tripping into Fear. You are going about your day seemingly ordinarily and then you are set off, you don't even really understand why but that dripping tap of Fear starts. This is the Resistant Subconscious Mind State.

This is a very, very common Mind State to be in and for some, for most of the time in your daily life. This is particularly when you have more Fear Labelled Subconscious experiences than Love Labelled and/or when you have multiple Egoic Blocks to your Vortexes of Emotion. In this Mind State it is also hard to shift yourself Physically and you aren't able to look at small things and feel pleasure or joy. You have that undercurrent of Low Vibration Emotion such as prolonged anxiety and fear or a state of being, such as apathetic, frustrated, irritable, disappointed as examples.

You can recognise if you are in this state if you are consistently, for a number of hours in a single day, feeling fear, reacting to things in a 'big' way and a way not warranted for the actual experience. Think back to a moment when maybe the phone rang and you saw who was calling on the ID, or the email drops into your inbox, or a Physical letter arrives in the post or you check your bank account and your Emotions go spiralling...fear, anxiety, anger, worry, nervousness, hatred, doom, lack of love, lack of hope, fear of death (yes, really for some people!)...we could go on. Think how big a reaction this is, based on what action has just occurred.

If you are in the Expectant Mind State, you would feel in the same experience (if you allow it), determination, support, hope, love, safe, strength, faith and expectation. You may say, this couldn't be the reality because you don't know what is inside the letter or the email or you have a lack of funds in the bank account, but the 'what it is' is irrelevant. Regardless of the circumstance, even one that is totally contrast based, perhaps something difficult that needs to be dealt with, the Expectant Mind waits for confirmation from you that you are able to Emotionally handle this situation with love.

By you actively choosing in the moment and feeling in the moment you can say to yourself "it's ok, I know that this call/email/letter/bank Balance is just a point in time, that this can be resolved, that in fact I am actively working on resolving it, that I choose and feel love for myself in this moment, that I am fully supported, that the solution is here or it is on its way, that I am not resisting this and I know that the outcome is going to be for my greatest good in fact, that I welcome dealing with this *now* because I like to deal with things in the moment and not put them off, that I am strong and resilient".

We do not expect you to have these feelings verbatim nor rehearse this and then try to apply it, for the most important thing is that you feel the truth of what you are saying in the moment. What we would like to impress here however is that it will be something similar if you are in the Expectant Mind State and perhaps this will help you to feel just when you have been in that Mind State because you will relate to this in some way and acknowledge either the Resistant or Expectant Mind State within your own experiences.

Back now to the Resistant Mind.

So, the Resistant Subconscious Mind is actively in a Fear State, meaning that you are expecting Fear and when you are going about your daily Emotional experiences, it will 'trigger' the existing fear based Emotions and family of Low Vibration Emotions linked to similar experiences to remind you of a Fear Labelled experience. These loosely coupled Emotions are placed into a virtual container in your Subconscious Mind, otherwise known as Vortex Groups.

This triggering of grouped memories is almost like that library filing system is stuck searching only through the Fear labels and the 'like' experiences to serve you. This is why such a loosely coupled 'like' experience can trigger such a host of Low Vibration Emotions and so quickly; this is the Dripping Tap of Emotions in full flow. One conscious experience triggers a series of other experiences and generates for you their related Emotions (more on this in a later chapter).

Likewise if you are feeding it with habitual or spiralling Conscious Mind thought patterns in the moment this just exacerbates the situation. It is also why, once you move into this Mind State, that you stay there for some time, and depending on how long you stay there...the harder it becomes to shift to the Expectant Mind State. This self-perpetuating cycle is one to be truly aware of, and one to connect to. This also helps you to see exactly what is happening and why, so feel relief right now in this moment, that you aren't ever to blame here (for God asks to take the blame remember) and this is just reflective of your past experiences which you are absolutely able to shift and move forward from.

How to move out of the Resistant Mind State? First, seek Balance in the moment, then with your Higher Self, pick one of the other 1-5 Feelset processes (found at the end of the book) listed at the start of this chapter to begin with and if you are stuck, start working on the Egoic Resistance Feelset which is part of The Releasing Process. If you have things coming up in the moment, courageously see it as something that needs to be addressed and understood. This won't mean that there is only one experience to manage, but at least you know you have made a start on this process to ultimately create lasting Change within.

The shift doesn't happen overnight, in particular for those who have been living in the Resistant Mind State for most of the time, and also for those that flip between Resistant and Psychotic. Remember, this mind state that you find yourself in is about your Vibration and your Emotional experiences to date. What happens from this point on is where you can Change your perspective and allow that permanent Change for you.

THE PSYCHOTIC SUBCONSCIOUS

Surely not...the Psychotic Mind is only for those seriously mentally ill isn't it? We wish you to connect to this new understanding of the terminology in this way. The Psychotic Subconscious Mind State is where you are in an *extreme* Fear based mind state. As with the Resistant Mind State you are able to generate Fear without even knowing it and totally subconsciously, which means it can be even when you are resting, dreaming or asleep even. It can be when you are smiling outwardly and inwardly utterly, utterly gripped with fear, panic, hurt, sadness, loneliness...the Low Vibration list can go on.

This Subconscious Mind State often flips between Resistant and then into Psychotic for periods and therefore you don't feel the reprieve, the Emotional Balance, that equilibrium that is so wanted. It is entirely possible to move through all three Subconscious Mind States in one day, and this is also key for you to understand just how much you can rock your own Vibration and now link this to your Transitional Vibration understanding, and how in a day you can have these extremes.

For those of you not living in the mind state permanently, you can recognise that you are in the Psychotic Subconscious Mind State when you feel trapped, like there is literally no way out of your Emotions, where they are so utterly overwhelming that you start to have 'dark' thoughts. You want to remove yourself from literally anyone and everyone and you feel no love even when there is so much love around you.

This Mind State is also where and how those who drive themselves to the thought of suicide or almost deliriously start to think how it is the only way out. You feel that it may be the only option to relieve yourself of the horrendous locked down, Fear-based, extreme way of being that you find yourself in, or, you want to run away and hide from your life. Even if it isn't something you actually attempt, you almost feel those types of thoughts start to come up.

This is serious. This is important to recognise within you. This ultimate extremity of the Subconscious Mind State is not where you want to be, but even for periods, short periods, many of you will recognise this Mind State. It is when this Mind State truly takes hold and stops moving even back to Resistant over a concentrated period of time that people lead themselves to attempt delirium in whatever form that takes. Something to just make it stop. This black pit of doom, it literally feels like it, and something that no matter what you try, it doesn't work, it doesn't stop the pain. The thing is, *you* are putting the lid over that black pit. You have control. You have the ability to Change. You have the courage to do this too. It takes one moment at a time when you are in this state, one step, one Change, then another.

You need to try and connect IN. This means, feel you. Feel you darling one. Feel you in this moment. For there is light, pure light, unwavering light, unwavering love flowing through you in this very moment. Love that is accessible, you just have forgotten. Love that is everlasting. Love that connects you. You are never, ever alone. You have access to All That You Are and All That Is at All Times! Believe. Believe in you. Trust you in this moment. Trust that you have this love. Trust that you have this support. Trust that you will get over this moment, and the next and the next. Trust that Change can happen for you. For it can, it truly can. Through this experience, you are growing. It won't feel like it, we understand, it is painful, and hard and extreme, but YOU are growing, stretching and evolving like never before. Do not waste this powerful opportunity that you have in your hands right in this moment. Allow it to be what it is. Allow it to be the platform to step forward from. Now...what is it? What are the Emotions? What is the experience? It's part of your Journey. Find out. Get to it. Understand what it relates to. Release it. Love you for it. Let God take the responsibility for it and the blame. Give it over. Hand it over. Relieve yourself from it. It is just your responsibility to grow from it.

All stirring stuff. But for some of you this will feel and sound like an impossible task. Some of you will have tried all of this and spent years doing it. Some of you will still wake up with extreme fear and go to bed in the same feeling. Some of you will have been in this Psychotic Mind State for most of your life, permanently, and will literally feel fear in everything that you do. Even the High Vibrational activities will be carried out with extreme fear undertones.

Know that this is your Subconscious Mind triggering and linking every single thought to a negative experience from the past. Know that this is not your reality but sadly the reality of your past, no doubt accumulated over time with probably a handful of extreme experiences that would have manifested the way you feel, act and react for everything that you experience today. Death, abuse, loss, constant judgement, broken relationships and a series of failed

296

ventures are just but a few examples of what can trigger you into a Psychotic Mind State permanently. And in this Mind State comes anger, self doubt, unworthiness, fears, so many fears, paranoia, shock, despair and depravity as your Subconscious Mind plays over and over to you your past in every possible moment and in the most sickening of ways.

This Mind State is not the domain for psychopaths, but it is the mind state for the mentally disturbed, and that could be you. Going about your day trying to be positive, always trying to see the bright side of things, smiling when you can. But within, and not too deeply, lies a darkness that you just cannot shift and that has taken you to a point of complete disconnection from love and hope. Do you know this feeling?

Know that you're not alone and that The Releasing Process IS your saviour. Together with the love of your Higher Self and the creation of new strong Truths, over time, you will find a way through this.

And when you start to feel some semblance of Balance and start to feel that you are moving back into Resistant Mind State, then you need get to keep working at it and do not delay. Don't take a momentary reprieve of moving back to Resistant from Psychotic as a reason to rest and relax as you truly don't want to be in this Mind State either. You need to reduce the Psychotic Subconscious Mind State at all costs, so you need to act.

How? You start to address those Fear based labelled experiences prevalent through your Journey. You connect to your Higher Self to serve you all that you need to understand and you start to shift your Vibration. You let go. You release the past. You release the blame, the responsibility too, no matter what you have done, no matter what has been done to you. You remove those Egoic Blocks to your Vortexes of Emotion and you start to allow love, you start to create and generate love for yourself. And slowly, you shift, you release, you Change.

Be courageous. You are love and you are loved.

Olivia and Raf, Abraham and Jesus

49

YOUR CONSCIOUS MIND

Your logic centre, the processor, the space that thinks now, now, now. Your Conscious Mind is what we have consistently been taught to allow to be the master. How many phrases about "Mindset", "Logic Prevailing", "Thinking First" can you think of? Our Conscious Mind is essential, critical to our humanness and truly a wondrous part of our incredible Physicality. It is the Balance of the Conscious Mind and the ability to truly understand the habitual impacts, the connection of the Conscious Mind with the other Bodies and how to calm and refocus from a consistent 'thinking' life experience to a more 'feeling' life experience that we want to share with you.

The Conscious Mind at times can be at the centre of spiralling thoughts, the centre of habitual thoughts and easily influenced by the other Bodies in order to generate these thoughts even when the habits are understood.

HOW DOES THE CONSCIOUS MIND INTERRELATE WITH THE OTHER BODIES?

The Conscious Mind will think through a situation. You may be Emotionally impacted by a situation, and logically, using your Conscious Mind, you are able to intellectualise it and mentally confirm if it has impacted you or not. No matter what intellectualisation you are able to achieve, you cannot stop the truth of the experience to be understood by your Subconscious Mind, which is utterly profound and wonderful if you think about it for a moment.

You cannot rationalise the Emotional Body, you feel what you feel when you feel it. It just is. Through your living experience, these Emotions are not thought through, they are felt. The Conscious Mind if allowed to be predominant alongside the Subconscious Mind, will keep you very much 'up in your head'. But no matter what your Conscious Mind 'tells' you to think about an experience, your Emotional Body will still feel whatever Emotions your Subconscious Mind truly understands about that experience.

The Egoic Body and the Conscious Mind, led by the Subconscious Mind, have become the strongest energy holding for many, rather than the Emotional Body being the strongest. This has happened over time, and if you are able to observe a child, watch the nature of children and see that they are indeed led primarily by their Emotional Body rather than by their Conscious Mind. Children FEEL often. They can experience several Emotions sometimes in just a minute and multiply that by a child's entire day, it is very feeling centric. Children naturally express their Emotions in the moment – unless they are stopped, unless they are told otherwise (usually by adults!). So, this is often the source of the switch, the Change between being Emotionally led and switching to Consciously thought-through in the moment. Children are taught to do this. It is highly likely that you were taught to do this.

Where does this start? It starts by Consciously 'controlling' your Emotions and your Emotional responses. Consciously rationalising your experience and thinking your way out of the Emotion. Squashing down the natural rise and swell of Emotion, controlling your response, controlling your reaction, controlling the depth and duration of the feeling. When this happens, the Conscious Mind is leading and in doing so, it triggers the Subconscious Mind. The Subconscious Mind responds by adding it to the list of Emotional experiences that it needs to protect you from, it is literally 'doing its job' and the more control that gets applied to your Emotional experiences, the more inflated the Egoic Bodies become, the more self-protection gets activated. The consequence of this control is disconnection. Disconnection from your Emotional Body and the ability to feel your Emotions in the moment, understand them and let them go in the moment, which in turn stores that Emotional Vibration for 'later' understanding. This impacts you Vibrationally the Subconscious Mind understanding the experiences therefore labelling these with Love or Fear.

STOPPING THE SPIRALLING THOUGHTS

One of the most common Conscious Mind experiences for those who have become more disconnected from their Emotional Body is consistent periods of Spiralling Thoughts. These thoughts start off as one thing, often self-critical, accusatory, self-pitying, blaming or judgemental types of thoughts and then they gain increasing momentum and start to add more and more volume, velocity and almost kinetic energy as they start to swirl and spiral down, down, down through a negative cycle of more of the same kinds of thoughts. The depth of your disconnection and the duration of habit of allowing the Spiralling Thoughts to be your current way of living, will depend on how often this occurs on a daily basis. For some, this can happen almost every moment, even in a good situation. Imagine just how mentally exhausting this is! For others, it is through specific periods of your life or in a particular situation that always triggers it.

Notice. Notice that this is what is happening. Notice. Be fully aware that this is what you are allowing.

This is total and utter self-sabotage. But, in this self-sabotage, in this spiral, you have a big clue that is being generated as to what is happening and why. The busyness of these Spiralling Thoughts and then the connection to the feelings that then become reactivated, your Emotional Body will end up holding the underlying Emotions such as lack of love, fear, disbelief, hurt, anger, rejection and many, many more that the Spiralling Thoughts are activating.

When you notice, stop the thought in its tracks, and then

allow yourself to become disconnected from it. Find Balance and distraction from it. Literally. You may feel that you aren't able too, that you can't but you always, always can. It may take some practice, you may try it once and then the Spiral keeps going, but stop it again, and again and again.

Now, how do you FEEL? What are the feelings that these Spiralling Thoughts are connecting you to? By stopping the activity within your Conscious Mind and the Spiralling Thoughts that are activating, you have an opportunity just to feel in the moment. You may feel many Emotions all at once and these may feel overwhelming to you because within this your connection to your Emotional Body may be bringing up a number of Emotions here. But this is ok, you can do this, you can manage this experience.

Name the Emotions. Every single one. Name them out loud, write them down, articulate them. You are acting as an observer here, you don't need to get to the bottom of it all right here and now but these Emotions, these are big, big clues for you of where to start. By capturing them in an 'awareness' little book or stack of paper, you are committing this new insight about you down, so that you can, whenever you feel Aligned to it, feel your way to it to better understand these Emotions, these experiences and ultimately let them go. There is more about this in The Feelset Tools section of this book called Creating an Awareness List.

UNDERSTANDING HABITUAL THOUGHTS

Physical beings are creatures of habit and this, when combined with the power of belief within can truly generate practiced, habitual thoughts that are incredibly self-sabotaging. Habitual thoughts are those that are triggered in any given moment but are almost pre-programmed. They have been thought so often you see, that your Conscious Mind just 'does' the thinking for you without too much active participation on your behalf. It has been often thought that it is your Subconscious Mind that is generating these habitual thoughts but instead, it is indeed your Conscious Mind that is doing so. These thoughts are deliberate conscious thoughts, practiced, and for some, constant. These thoughts are influenced overall by your Vibration, by your beliefs, by your past.

Let's take a practical example. If you were to stand in front of the mirror, observing your Physical self, what thoughts take place? Do you have self-admiring thoughts? Do you compliment yourself? Or, do you berate yourself? Do you generate a stream of negative Conscious thought about your body, your face, your hair, your clothes, your look, your style? Now there are many, many other situations that you may experience Habitual Thoughts, so if this does not resonate to you, do reflect for a moment on another situation, perhaps if you need to speak with certain people or speak in a group, attend a particular type of social occasion, something like that. Anything that can connect you, in this moment to the stream of Habitual Thoughts that are currently active in your experience.

Isn't the pre-programming of habitual thought so interesting? Did you realise that this was something you did? Are these habitual thoughts positively impacting you or negatively impacting you? Habitual Thoughts are going to impact you negatively, because anything Habitual like this, even a stream of 'positive' mantras, if they are not connecting to how you feel, they will turn to conflict or resistance within.

Can you stand in front of the mirror and think nothing? Can you do this until you feel something? In the moment, what is the reality of what you see, what you feel, what you truly think? This is the ultimate clarity of Conscious Thought.

So, how do you get there?

You need to re-train. This is easier than it sounds but it takes consistency and honesty and some perseverance. There are two main types of Habitual Conscious Thoughts.

• Belief driven

• Experience driven

You may say that they are both one in the same, but there is a distinctive difference by way of uncovering how to better understand the root of your Habitual Thoughts and therefore the opportunity for Change that is being presented to you.

BELIEF DRIVEN HABITUAL THOUGHTS

Somewhere along your Physical experience, you have created a powerful belief. This belief means that you have a default setting for anything that comes into the belief's atmosphere. This belief may or may not be how you truly feel. Beliefs do not have to be the indoctrinated kind, ones engrained into you by others through childhood as an example but potentially this is exactly what you are facing. The other kind of beliefs are those that you have self-generated. To give you an example, you may have active a belief system that no matter what you do, the good and wonderful feelings of happiness and joy in your life never, ever last and will be taken away from you. This is a powerful belief system that means that any time you FEEL the happiness and joy start to blossom, your Conscious Mind will automatically trigger a series of pre-conditioned habitual thoughts based on your belief that this will never last, your Subconscious Mind will then trigger the self-protection mode and inject your Emotional Body with fear, anxiety, loss and betrayal Emotions. This belief system is like a blanket over the good feelings, which means that you can be in multiple experiences, some new, some old and still feel the same way, still have the same response in the moment.

EXPERIENCE DRIVEN HABITUAL THOUGHTS

This is where you have an Emotion on a repeater and this has been generated through a trigger point experience but is something that continues to trigger in any similar/same type of experience and instead of feeling 'this is a NEW experience' your Conscious Mind influenced by your Subconscious Mind just organises itself around the similar experience and starts a cycle of thoughts. This then triggers the Egoic Body and the self-protection and drives the quest for the Emotion that you have felt in the past and that you have currently stored. We understand that conceptually, this may be a little hard to pull this together into an understanding, so we wish to give you an example of this to help formulate this into an experience that you may recognise or connect too.

Loss. Not the grief kind, but the feeling of losing something that you love, want or need in the moment. You may have had an experience when you were a child of losing a precious toy, a Teddy. That loss created a cycle of experience based habitual thoughts about intellectually 'dealing' with that experience. This is often influenced by others too, their aiding you to understand and that these things happen and caution about being more careful and taking better care of your things in the future. But your feeling ultimately is that loss really hurt and if you weren't able to feel it and feel that you are able to deal with that loss in your own way, it Vibrationally stores and attracts other 'like' experiences so that you can.

Now, if you move to a current experience about losing your keys. You haven't in fact lost them at all, they are misplaced and not in their normal place, but the Physical search, the frustration, the feeling of loss of what you need in the moment, that rising major reaction and then cyclical thoughts as you try to intellectualise, hunt down the keys, remember where you last had them, and then the habitual thoughts about how you must be more organised, must have one place to put them, must do better. Then rises other Emotions, anger, betrayal of yourself, frustration. Before you know it, your Transitional Vibration is full of this Low Vibration Emotion and even when you find the keys, there is just a momentary relief and then you walk out the door. The Conscious Mind continues on the cyclical, habitual thoughts all about the keys. Your Transitional Vibration if not dealt with in the moment, will hold you in a Low Vibration.

We can hear some of you ask, a lost Teddy creates THIS? In some, absolutely, but in most? Probably not, but each of you will have your own 'Teddy' experience or core experience that has triggered in you the Habitual Thoughts that your Conscious Mind is circling right now. Filling you up mentally and certainly aiding the generation and re-generation of Low Vibration Emotion. It is, therefore, our greatest intent for you to understand the Why and the How. The What, as far as "What to do about it?" is also available to you in The Feelset Tools chapters which will help you to take different actions and create Change within as you come to participate in The Releasing Process.

Olivia and Raf, Abraham and Jesus

50

YOUR EGOIC BODIES

Oh the Ego. The Egoic Bodies have become so very inflated, sometimes permanently so in many of our Physical Friends, mostly unknowingly. It is our absolute intention to give you as much information as possible for you to truly understand the Ego, understand when and how those egoic influences are taking over and also how the Ego interrelates with the other Bodies. Now you can visibly see exactly where it is placed within you, there are some absolute specifics to first highlight and make you aware of.

Your Ego is essential. It isn't something that you can remove entirely nor should you want to. The benefits of the Ego are huge, in a really positive way, your Ego is your self-protection and in our day to day human lives, having an aspect of self-protection can be really positive.

The Ego is wholly connected to all of your Bodies, this is why the Ego has the ability to be so strong. It has the ability to increase and decrease in size, and now you know why the term "inflated ego" was born. Try to relate this to this new understanding of the placement of the Ego within you and the fact it can expand and contract independently. When we talk about control in particular with reference to the Ego, often that can feel really difficult or strange, but it is something that through true understanding you are able to master over time. This is in the Physical deflation of the Egoic Bodies Physical holding, this is also in the greater awareness of when the Ego is leading and creating impact within you.

Many, for a long time, have connected the Ego to arrogance or someone who thinks they are better than others or, suggested that the Ego is a driving force behind a state of being of someone who is 'acting above their station'. Others blame the Ego for 'keeping them small' and not allowing Change. Those with very active and inflated Egoic Bodies will behave differently to when their Egoic Bodies are not inflated. An inflated Ego is in protection mode, and in this state, it can generate and exacerbate Emotions within. But know that the Emotions already exist within, it is coming from a self-protection state of being to say "in this situation, protect, protect, protect because you have Fear here, you have anger here, you have hurt here".

HOW THE EGO INTERRELATES WITH THE OTHER BODIES

The Egoic Bodies are influenced primarily by the Subconscious Mind but also the Conscious Mind, therefore, depending on your experiences and your current Vibration, you may in fact have two significant reasons why your Egoic Bodies are incredibly inflated and therefore adding a further habitual influence within you.

Depending on the Subconscious Mind State, this will also immediately start a triggering of the inflation of the Egoic Bodies also. So, when in the Resistant Subconscious or the Psychotic Subconscious Mind State, both will start the inflation process, one more extreme than the other. Your Egoic Bodies are not inflated in an Expectant Subconscious Mind State.

Likewise, if you are powering through spiralling thoughts and habitual thoughts and ways of being with your Conscious Mind and continuing to go over and over situations either past, present or future and generating more and more Low Vibration within, this too will also inflate your Egoic Bodies. Know that in this Conscious Mind habitual state of being, you are also in the Resistant Subconscious Mind State creating habitual Egoic responses. This sounds like ALL the Minds doing ALL things at one time, but this is just an accurate reflection of some peoples experience. It is specifically important to not only call out and understand how each influences the other, but why also it can over time feel hard to create Change quickly and why so many feel like their heads are leading always. You can see how, when all three are engaged, it creates a whole lot of energy!

Where things then get really interesting, is the Egoic Bodies are the only direct route if you like, from the Mind Energetic

Bodies to the Emotional Body. You will be able to see in the diagram that the Egoic Bodies have almost energetic prongs into the Emotional Body and this is to enable connection but also influence.

When you are in the moment and experiencing something Emotionally, as those Emotions are being created (and yes, we now understand how this can be influenced by your Subconscious Mind) the Ego is able to read and understand you see, so not only does it get cues from the Subconscious Mind, but it will also be inflated by the Emotional Body.

If you are feeling anxiety, fear, sadness, loneliness, but you are in your bed about to start your day, your Egoic Bodies start to inflate out of self-protection and then start to acknowledge that 'bed isn't safe', 'mornings aren't safe'. Now, if this is a one off, the Egoic Bodies will naturally start to calm and deflate through the day anyway but, will still trigger the next morning in anticipation if you start to feel a rising in anxiety for example, literally straight away. If you then are able to Balance yourself, your Egoic Bodies will start to deflate and quickly, and then you can go about your day without the self-protection.

If, on the other hand, it is a frequent and consistent experience that you wake up experiencing these Emotions, your Egoic Bodies start to create habitual ways of being. In this example, even before you have awoken they will be inflated, which means that the Emotions that you experience are predicted by the Egoic Bodies and in anticipation, the Ego is on high alert and may in fact even wake you up by activating your Conscious Mind before you would naturally due to the lack of safety anticipation that the Egoic Bodies are expecting. Your Egoic Bodies are trying to protect you, from you. From the Low Vibration Emotions that you generate, from the experiences that you continue to activate, from the suffering that you can't let go of, from the fear that you continue to live in.

RECOGNISING EGOIC INFLATION

Contrary to perhaps popular opinion, the Egoic Bodies are not another 'mind' as in, they do not have a mind of their own. They are however influenced by the Subconscious Mind. The way that the Egoic Bodies influence the Conscious Mind, is where the Conscious Mind is able to understand that self-protection is well underway and it is due to specific aspects of safety, due to experiences already felt and lived through. This then presents to the Conscious Mind that it is now that there is a problem, therefore it becomes very much active within your Conscious experience.

So, the Conscious Mind is being impacted by the inflated Egoic Bodies. This coupled with whichever Subconscious Mind State you are in, means that you have a number of things happening within, causing further amplification of your current experience.

In cases of heightened fear Mind States, the Egoic Bodies can start to pre-pave and 'inject' Emotions into the Emotional body. The Egoic Bodies, out of protection, go 'same situation, same Emotions, need to get your attention, need to protect' and so they release the Low Vibrational Emotions.

EGOIC BLOCKS TO THE VORTEXES OF EMOTION

You have five Vortexes of Emotion within your Inner Being and these are powerful and provide incredible access to pure positive Emotion as well as also being the creator of Emotions as fully outlined in the Vortexes of Emotion chapter. When you have experiences that are labelled with Fear they can create Egoic Blocks to the energetic pathways that access the Vortexes of Emotion.

There are hundreds of thousands of energetic pathways that flow from your Inner Being Vortexes of Emotion, through your Emotional Body and to your Subconscious Mind, Conscious Mind and Egoic Bodies which allow this pure positive Emotion, ever present to be accessible to you, felt, responded to and understood. So how come you feel shut off from this incredible flow of positivity if it's always accessible? How come when you are feeling really low, you can't feel the goodness within?

Each individual memory (and there can be multiple memories to a single experience), has its own energetic path to the Inner Being. When the stored memory is labelled with a fear level of medium to high The Egoic Bodies will stop access to the Inner Being. These energetic pathways from the Emotional Body remain in place but are closed off from accessing the Vortexes of Emotion within the Inner Being. This has the effect of automatically generating Low Vibration, triggered by the Subconscious Mind when the memory is later brought active in some way. The amount of Low Vibration that is produced is linked to the fear levels for that memory, something that the Subconscious keeps a record of rather like a rating value. The specific Low Vibration that is generated will match those Emotions that were created in the original experience. In extreme cases, where you have had multiple high fear impacting and Egoically blocked Emotional experiences, triggered by each other, one after the other (which is common in the Psychotic Mind State), access is denied to multiple memories. This has the affect of denying access to one or more of the Vortexes of Emotion completely, and is the reason why often you feel disconnected from something or someone despite consciously wanting not to be.

An example of this is where you just cannot bring yourself to fully feel and therefore allow another's love, or to give them your love without having that hollow or empty feeling when you try to consciously bring yourself to do it. This could be felt with a kiss, a cuddle or even a smile. Do you know that feeling? This is an Egoic Block to your Inner Being for that experience and caused by similar past experiences held in your Subconscious Mind memories.

And so, this gives you a strong indication that you need to address the resistance to love in that moment and the current Truth that has created that fear labelled memory and related Egoic block. And know that the resistance may not be with the person that you are currently looking to receive a kiss from. If we keep with this example, the Egoic Blocks could be as a result of having an uncomfortable intimate experience, or worse still being sexually assaulted or abused in your earlier life, perhaps as a child. When in later life you engaged in a consensual and adult sexual relationship, memories of the past abuse could be relived and in so doing, generate medium to high levels of fear in the moment of your consensual sexual encounter. This would have immediately generated Low Vibration, as well as fear labelled memory and an Egoic Block to your Inner Being.

With that fear labelling and Egoic Block in place, any future sexual experience, and this would include anything that could suggest sex, such as a request for a kiss or even a loving look, would also generate fear based Low Vibrations in you. For this experience it's likely that anger would be high on the list of Emotions generated. Your Subconscious Mind, because of the Egoic Block, would generate anger and Low Vibrations each and every time you had an encounter that suggested intimacy, love and a potential therefore for sex. Throughout your life these Emotions will be created each time this occurs, and not just with the person in the moment, but also by you over and over in your mind, creating new memories and therefore new iterations of Low Vibration, all linked back to the original sexual assault or abuse.

This is how the Subconscious Mind works and so with reference to the Egoic Blocks, each memory would generate a new block, potentially hundreds of thousands of them over the period of forty to fifty years. And with these multiple Egoic Blocks comes a blanket of resistance over your Inner Being Vortex or Vortexes. You will not consciously be aware that this is happening in this way, but your clue to this is the awkwardness in the moment, followed by that hollowness, or lack of trust or lack of hope. Anger in particular, impacts connecting to the Love Vortex of Emotion, fear impacts the Hope Vortex of Emotion, and sadly it's anger and fear that you will be feeling every time that a loved one shows any kind of affection towards you, if this example has been your past experience.

It's important to note that the Egoic Block applies to memories and so other memories that you hold that are both love labelled and have no Egoic Blocks will not be impacted and therefore feelings of love, for example for a parent or a child are still felt fully.

The same feelings of emptiness can be encountered when you try and connect to any of the Vortexes of Emotion where there is an Egoic Block to the Inner Being in place. So this would be trust, love, hope, truth, strength and faith for any type experience. There is a lot more information detailed within the Vortexes of Emotion Chapter to further explain the Vortexes.

There is a specific way to release Egoic Blocks as part of The Releasing Process detailed in The Feelset Tools section of this book. Your Higher Self is the primary route to initiating Egoic Block releasing and their support would form part of the overall Releasing Process that they would be guiding you through.

Olivia and Raf, Abraham and Jesus

51

YOUR EMOTIONAL BODY

This is your largest energetic holding within your body, placed from your collarbones down to your lower pelvis. When you feel an Emotion, you don't feel this in your hand or your leg, it is always within the space of your Emotional Body. Just as is the same with the other Mind Bodies, there are no scans available (yet) to show up these energetic holdings, but once you come to tune into your Emotional Body, this will truly start to not only make sense but you will feel it and feel the truth of it!

The Emotional Body is a conduit. The Pure Positive Emotions created and generated through your Inner Being, through your Vortexes of Emotion are all felt in your Emotional Body. Likewise, when you have an opportunity to feel good but your Subconscious/Conscious Minds and/or your Egoic Bodies influence you otherwise and you instead feel Low Vibration Emotions in the moment, these too are also felt in your Emotional Body.

What comes first, the Emotion or the thought? With each of the Vortexes of Emotion, these are so strong, so clear and pure and powerful, when you are Balanced, you can feel them emanating without thinking anything other than "What do I feel?". Just this stream of pure Emotion, you can try one Vortex at a time and just feel the presence of them, the flow of them, the energy of them radiate all through your Emotional Body. When you are creating a Truth that is Law, your thoughts are influenced first by what you feel, then you consciously think it, then it is confirmed back to you by activating the Truth Vortex in your Inner Being. Often, with Non Physical, they present feelings first when communicating with you and then you translate them, so thinking second. Something 'feels' right? You're feeling first, not thinking. Something doesn't quite feel right, you are feeling first, thoughts come second.

Let's take an example. Picture a scene, imagine you are in a beautiful open grass field, the grass is long, there are mountains and trees all around you and the sky is blue, the sun is shining. You are walking through the grass, you find a flat spot, you are comfortable, happy even, content, and enjoying where you are and you are alone. You could continue to feel this way throughout this wonderful experience, or, the situation may Change, or, you may Change what you are thinking.

Using this example, it is pretty easy to work out the continuation of the feeling good throughout, it is nice and easy to just let this story end with you going home after this incredible day feeling nothing but wonderful, peaceful, relaxed, content. How many of you reading this *think*, "That could never be me...I would never feel comfortable in that kind of place on my own"? Where this example starts to show the Emotional Body at work and in particular the difference between the thinking vs feeling first is in the next two Changes in the story. Or if this was you *thinking* this could never be you, you already are seeing what thinking does to the Emotional Body.

Let's evolve this example now to incorporate the situation and then subsequent "thinking" Changes. Now, this could be a good Change or a negative Change. Perhaps your partner comes and joins you, so as you see them walking towards you, you may have felt a slight apprehension as you wondered who it was as they were too far away at the start to recognise and your Subconscious Mind is searching for any 'like' experiences of when this has happened before. But the thought comes first as you see your experience changing and your mind thinks "Who is that?" Perhaps a little fear started to spike and then you think some more, "it must be my partner" and the fear starts to dampen a bit but not fully yet and then you think, "oh, it IS my partner" and then your Subconscious Mind again starts searching for other 'like' experiences and if you are in the Expectant Mind State, you will start to feel relief and a little bubble of anticipation and happiness that they are coming. It may just contribute positively to the whole experience and increase the feelings of happiness.

Now, consider a negative Change takes place where based on

your previous experiences you start to think "Why are they coming....has something happened?" and the triggering of fear becomes much stronger and the apprehension greater and the worry and anxiety start to ramp up. Only when you are presented with the evidence, ie. your partner meets with you on this wide open field and has nothing bad to report, but is just there to be with you because they love you and missed you, that your mind and your Emotions start to stand down; and you can go back to the bliss but it takes a while. Again, depending on your Subconscious Mind State, this may have moved you from Expectant to Resistant depending on how many Egoic Blocks you have and depending on how you have been able to Master your Experience in the moment, and this will also determine the outcome of the next phase, because for some, you can't go back to the bliss. In fact, you start to feel Anger. You feel a lack of love from your Partner. You start to feel doubt that they are telling you the truth or, you question why they had to come and ruin your perfectly lovely day because you blame them for being selfish and making you worry. Shouldn't they have known better? Why can't you just have a day to yourself? Why does every good moment have to be ruined?

Do you see just how much is influenced by what you think based on your experiences? Do you see just how much Emotional energy is being used? Do you see just how much the Emotional Body is being pummelled with Emotions that could be so very different depending on what you allow it to feel in the moment versus what is being thought in the moment?

Your Emotional Body is constantly taking the hit from your

Subconscious Mind and Conscious Mind and Egoic Bodies, and sometimes all three combined. Know that once you have released that Low Vibration, once you are managing that Transitional Vibration, you are tuning in to your Higher Self and tuning into YOU. Your Emotional Body is not taking the body blows Emotionally but is willingly accepting the flow of all that pure positive Emotion and being filled up from the inside out. This is what we wish for each and every one of you reading this book. Be the person in the field, loving every second of what it represents, only peace, contentment and freedom. Work your way to it. Be passionate about your Vibration. Be passionate about your Emotional Body. Notice when it is being hammered by your thoughts. Do the work. Gain the freedom. Be you. The you-est of you.

We love YOU.

Olivia and Raf, Abraham and Jesus

YOUR INNER BEING

For many of you, the Inner Being is a term, a phrase that you have learnt in correlation to your connection to Source. For others, it is the reference to the Soul, to the Godforce within you but for whatever phrase or term you wish to use, it is true that your Inner Being is a 'thing'. Something tangible, something with placement inside your Physicality. Some of you may have even been in the room when another has transitioned to Non Physical and the re-emergence into Non Physical is a visible experience, where everyone present not only feels it but witnesses a Change. You do not need to be in the room in order to understand this conceptually, that there is energy that connects you to the Universe, that connects you to your Higher Self and their energy. Meaning you are in part also of the same energy as your Higher Self. This is a unique energy signature that binds both your Inner Being and Higher Self together.

Although scientists have not yet worked out how to measure this in a way to show you this placement inside your Physical being, be sure that it exists, be sure that it is the pure positive energy of all that you are. It is an energy holding and Vibration that resides with you, that you have access to, that you are able to utilise and focus upon it. We talk of Alignment, Alignment to the energy of your Higher Self energy and Alignment to your Inner Being and for many, that can be logically understood and sometimes even Emotionally felt, for it is with Emotion that we have been guiding you to get there. Tending to that Vibrational Alignment and tuning to your Inner Being. We also understand that sometimes it takes a bit of help, extra guidance in order for you to get there and the understanding of the Physical representation within your body may hold the key in order for you to access more easily, your Inner Being.

For where is it? This potentially illusive Inner Being? Think for a moment, just take a second and ponder – where does it sit? Is it just in your mind? Perhaps your heart? Wrapped inside your skeletal structure?

It is in fact represented Physically, and connected entirely to your pineal gland, right inside your mind and then runs through the core of you. Imagine a cylindrical tube right down and through to the centre of your pelvis. Pure, Positive Energy. Always within you. Not seen, but felt. Positioned to be at the very core of all that you are. Able to flow, to Align, to Balance, to give, to connect, to receive. Able to be accessed by you for it is you.

The Inner Being gives us something to cling to, a hope that

things will get better. For it is this hope that brings us to a place of Higher Vibration. We are able to find ourselves in a place of calmness, of tranquillity, of peace when we connect to our Inner Being. And it's this place that we must seek out when we feel low, feel lost or just don't know how to escape from a place that seems so destitute and lonely.

It is your Inner Being that in these scenarios is your salvation, think of it like a beacon of light within, that guides you to a better feeling place and consequently out of the darkness. We encourage all of you to follow the energy practice given here in The Feelset Tools section of the book and remember also that this is not something to be used only when you know that you do not feel great, but also use this as a tool to start your day in the right way, in that higher Vibrational state of knowing and feeling.

Know that if you can recognise those parts of your day or those moments when you yourself bring your Vibration to a Low place, in this moment you are in need of a Change, a bump off that Emotional track. Return to your Inner Being in these moments, return to the Self. This phrase has been much used by us in recent times to represent a connection to that which you are both Emotionally and spiritually. Return to the Self represents an allowing and a conscious remembering that you and your Higher Self are energetically one. And in this conscious remembering you also remember that together you become Whole.

Olivia and Raf, Abraham and Jesus

UNDERSTANDING LOW VIBRATION AND THE CELLULAR IMPACT

We are cellular, Emotional, Vibrational beings. We are able to influence our cells. Our cells are impacted by our Emotions in that they hold Vibrationally those Emotions of predominance in our experience. This means that if Lower Vibrational Emotions have been consistent in your experience, often you will be storing this Vibration cellularly. It is with letting go of this Vibrational store that you are able to maintain higher Vibrational Emotion and for that to become your predominant Vibrational store. For there is only so much space within your Physical body you see, and it is in this letting go that you are able to create space for that higher Vibration.

This is often why so many aren't able to hold that good feeling for long, why you can swing Emotionally up and down the Emotional scale, why you feel sad, anger or fear without really knowing why. Over time, depending on your experiences, this swinging can start very early on. This is significantly connected to your Subconscious Mind labelling of your experiences and the connection of your memories, whether they are labelled as Love or Fear.

The Law of Attraction is absolutely taking place within your Physical body. Everyone will have an element of Stored Low Vibration within. Low Vibration is a lower frequency, denser, and therefore able to hold more compactly within your Physical body. There are no scanners (yet!) that are able to show the evidence of this frequency, but it is present and also able to be released. We mention The Law of Attraction because like attracts like, attracts like. This means that when you hold stored Low Vibration, each Low Vibrational Emotion has its own energy signature and this energy signature or frequency has the ability to attract like energy to it. This is why, if you are unable to manage your Vibration and your Emotional experiences in the moment or near to the moment, it will inevitably store cellularly.

Stored Vibration can cause a number of Physical manifestations. It is linked to Physical pain, illness, disease, hormonal issues, weight gain and Physical shrinking also. There have been a number of cases of Emotional release of Stored Low Vibration increasing a person's height just as a specific example to show the impact of this on the Physical body.

TRANSITIONAL VIBRATION

Your Transitional Vibration is all about your 'now' or 'near now' current Emotional experiences of your day. You are able to move from low to high, and back to low again through the day, and many other combinations of this, as you navigate your Emotional interactions with others and your own Emotional state of being.

A full day is one day of Transitional Vibration. It is when you sleep that your Transitional Vibration is either released or in fact stored, cellularly, therefore impacting overall your Stored Vibration. If you have been predominantly low or even just before bed, your Transitional Vibration is predominantly low, it is likely that the Emotions that you are experiencing will be stored.

Throughout the day, if you are feeling predominantly High Vibrational, you are likely to store more High Vibration and also, this allows the flowing out of your Low Vibration from your Transitional Vibration.

You may have heard the saying, 'never go to bed on an argument' and this has a real rationale to it. This means, that if you are feeling the kind of Emotions just before bed that an argument can create, anger, frustration, despair, lack of love, mistrust, betrayal, then you are going to shift your Transitional Vibration to predominantly Low Vibration just before going to bed.

When it has been said before that tending to your Vibration is essential, this is why. It truly does impact you and if on a daily basis, in particular over a longer duration, you continue to establish a predominantly Low Transitional Vibration and you are not able to understand why, you aren't able to Master and manage your Emotional experiences in the moment and you keep topping up more and more of the Low Vibration, then ultimately your Stored Low Vibration will continue to attract more stored Low Vibration, thus making it harder to 'feel better for longer'.

This is not all doom and gloom, in fact, quite the opposite. With this understanding, we are hoping that many of you have a realisation as to just why you have been feeling the way that you have. Possibly the most exciting thing to truly connect to here is, when you have predominantly High Vibration within your Transitional Vibration, it automatically shifts out a lot of the Low Vibration in your Transitional Vibration. Yes! This is another huge reason why truly managing your Transitional Vibration is going to make a Vibrational and energetic impact on you like never before, now that you have this insight.

Please remember, in order to tap into this new insight, you can't fool your Vibration. You can't pretend or just logically process, you must 'feel'. Feel the understanding in the moment or near to the moment of the Emotional experience. Understand why perhaps you generated these Low Vibrational Emotions in the first place. Understand if an experience involving someone else triggered the Subconscious Mind, or the Egoic Bodies. Feel your way to this understanding, let go of the Low Vibration with this understanding. In The Feelset Tools, you can learn more about the practical approach to this so that you can indeed Master Your Experience.

STORED LOW VIBRATION

There isn't 'currently' the technology available to show you Stored Low Vibration, where you can go and get a scan to see this, but know this to be true. Your body is fully of Emotional Vibration, either Low or High Vibration and it is stored in your cells. As you go about your day, having Emotional experiences, your Transitional Vibration will fluctuate depending on whether you manage your Vibration and release your Low Transitional Vibration, create Balance and Truths and feel predominantly High Vibrational. If you are predominantly Low Vibrational, this Vibration will settle in your cells. As each Emotion has a Vibrational signature, and with The Law of Attraction, like attracts like attracts like, the Low Vibration Emotion will find and settle collectively within the cells where the 'like stored Emotion' resides, either compacting right there in the same cellular space or as close to it as it can. This is the same with High Vibration, but of course, where we want to focus right now on this understanding is the Low Vibration, as stored High Vibration is amazingly wonderful and you feel fantastic! Low Vibration, doesn't make you feel fantastic.

A cell can hold both Low and High Vibration at the same time. Low Vibration is dense and compact, taking less room per individual Vibration, but heavy. High Vibration, the opposite, taking much more space but lighter. If you can imagine a group of cells, filled with stored Low Vibrational Emotions (a mix of anger and sadness as an example), neatly stacked on top of each other, it may take up around eighteen percent of that cellular space, with perhaps one High

Vibrational Emotion (joy for example) taking up the rest of the space, eighty two percent. As you go about your Emotional experiences in life, and you are not letting go or understanding of a 'new' anger experience or sadness experience, these will float around in your Transitional Vibration and then if you still don't deal with it, the Emotions will store cellularly. This is where The Law of Attraction comes in. You have both anger and sadness, from new experiences and therefore new Emotions, which are attracted to the current stored Emotion that you have within your cells. These new anger and sadness Emotions take up three percent of the overall cellular space and are stored in the same area, as they attract and settle within the cellular space. Your body must release the High Vibration in order to do this as there isn't enough room in this cellular space. This will now reflect in a stored Low Vibration increasing from eighteen percent to twenty one percent in that specific cellular space, with the rest filled with High Vibration at seventy nine percent. As you can see by just a brief forecast, if you continue to create Low Vibration of those same Emotions, without understanding the related experiences, and therefore without releasing the Emotions from your Transitional Vibration, the more you will store, and the more that you will move out the High Vibration without even meaning to.

Once you get to over fifty percent stored Low Vibration within a cell, this starts to increase the rate at which The Law of Attraction starts to work and draw this Vibration to the stored space. This is why, if you continue to experience Low Vibration over a consistent, regular and long duration, you will move to a place where it becomes harder to hold High Vibration and in fact, the predominant Stored Vibration is Low, rather than High.

There is always, always opportunity for Change and there is always opportunity to shift and release and move. There are never cases where your entire body will be one hundred percent Low Vibration and therefore, know this, even at ninety five percent Stored Low Vibration, you have five percent High Vibration within, that can increase more and more and more. You just have to allow it, you need to be consistent with your releasing, connecting with your Higher Self and creating new powerful Truths and Desires in order to Balance and allow that Change in.

SPECIFIC PLACEMENT OF STORED LOW VIBRATION

Stored Vibration can happen all over your body, but as you start to accumulate more Low Vibration within your Stored Vibration, things will start to naturally get concentrated and attract like for like, therefore compacting further. You are entirely cellular, therefore this concentration can be within muscles, tendons, bones, ligaments, digestive organs, the brain, hormonal organs, heart, lungs, skin and so on. Yes, this can cause Physical pain and can lead to Physical manifestations of illness. This isn't to say that illness isn't present, this is absolutely the case, but the root cause? We have many, many recent and real life advocates of removing and releasing Low Vibration and the successful impact on their Wellbeing, not just Emotionally but Physically and mentally also.

The Low Vibration will attract to a like energy frequency (ie, anger to anger, hurt to hurt) within your body but why does it settle there in the first place? There are two considerations here.

Firstly, the Inner Being Vortexes of Emotion are considered. The Trust Vortex is in your throat (to be discussed in another chapter), and therefore if you generate the Emotion of lack of trust the energy will settle in and around the throat, shoulders, back and head.

The alternative placement for the Emotional energy comes when there is a specific part of the body that links to the experience and the Emotion generated from it. For example, if you were a young ballet dancer or gymnast and you didn't point your toes, or you struggled to play football with your left foot, then you will very likely find the Low Vibrational energies linked to these experiences would be stored in your toes for the dancing example, or left foot in the football example. Ask yourself if there is a particular part of your Physical Body that is struggling, such as your back, leg or an internal organ, perhaps suffering pain or weight gain. Ask is it down to a specific past and current set of experiences that link to that part of your body and that are continuously generating Low Vibration in that area for you.

These criteria also apply for the placement of Stored High Vibration. Which of these two scenarios takes precedence depends on a number of factors, such as the strength of the fear attached to the experience as well as the room available for the storing of the Low Vibration. Where neither option provides sufficient cellular space the energy attaches to the nearest like frequency, and often this is the case.

VIBRATION PREDOMINANCE

Imagine this like a speed gauge on a car, one hundred and eighty degrees metric, with the needle being the sensor of your Vibration. To the left and side, or zero to eighty nine degrees, this is predominantly Low Vibration and at the maximum of eighty nine degrees, you would be at forty nine percent High Vibration. At ninety degrees, this is the point it hits predominantly High Vibration (at fifty percent), going towards the right at one hundred and eighty degrees where it reaches one hundred percent High Vibration. Your percentage is the percentage of High Vibration within your body, calculating not only your Stored Vibration but also your Transitional Vibration. Yes, the ultimate utopia is one hundred percent and very, very rare to get there currently, but don't let this put you off desiring it! Many people who are considered to be 'high vibe' are in the mid sixties to seventies. There are always improvements on your Vibration to be had, there are so many ways in order to increase that stored High Vibration and release that stored Low Vibration, managing your Emotions in the moment or near to the moment. Keep reading within this book in order to gain more insight and awareness and definitely look at The Feelset Tools in order to take action.

CALCULATION OF VIBRATION

The above information is great, but how do I know what my Vibrational Reading is? What's my baseline? Firstly, know that your calculation can and may vary from day to day as the calculation of your Vibration is made up of both your Transitional Vibration and your Stored Vibration. This means, from one day to the next and one point in time to another, your Transitional Vibration can wildly vary. You can be having the most amazing Emotional experiences and feeling greatly in Balance, really in flow, very connected to the Self and generally having a great time and therefore your Transitional Vibration can be right up there, maybe at eighty to ninety percent.

Now consider if you have a really terrible day, so you have had a huge conflict at work and it started in the morning and you just can't shake the yuk factor of it and it starts some spiralling thoughts and generates more and more Low Vibration Emotion within you. You stand in a puddle coming home and ruin your shoes, then your trains are delayed and you just can't wait for the day to be over. See how on *this* day, your Transitional Vibration can in fact be say thirty three percent, so how very different this is.

What stays a little more consistent, and therefore a very important metric is your Stored Vibration. We have advised the calculation percentage is based on the above value like a car speedometer. How you get to know what your Stored Vibration is, is through your Higher Self. Don't think this number, don't try to force it, it will literally come into your mind and pay attention. It might be low, perhaps twenty eight percent, lower than you ever expected or thought but don't worry, see this as a massive opportunity for you to Change, to grow, to allow, to release.

If you want to know your overall Vibration number, follow this simple equation:

(Stored Vibration + Transitional Vibration) = x

x / 2 = Total Vibration Percentage

To gain this insight, you must work with your Higher Self. You won't be able to guess this and it be accurate. You must learn this from your Higher Self, another fantastic reason to tune in!

Try not to get too fixated on the number, likewise don't keep asking daily "what about now, what about now?" as it is highly likely that your Higher Self will stop answering. The number is not as important as how you feel in the moment and so this should be your focus. Use the number as a key and fundamental understanding and starting point. From here, you can make Changes, you can use Feelset Tools and release and connect and let go. Then check in every few weeks, maybe once a month as a suggested guideline. See this as a first stepping stone to your Emotional Mastery.

FREQUENCY OF EMOTIONS

Each Emotion holds its own Vibration which generates and holds its own frequency. Both High and Low Vibration have their own unique energy signature, their very own Vibration. Low Vibration is dense, each Emotion with its own density and therefore compacts as stored energy, heavy, it can literally weigh you down. High Vibration takes up more room, more space, resonates at a much higher frequency and in fact can be harder to hold due to the size and Vibration.

WHAT ARE SOME EXAMPLES OF LOW AND HIGH VIBRATIONAL EMOTIONS

There are many Emotions that impact each and every person reading this book through their life experience. For many, the more extreme Emotions tend to come only through significant events, but for others, these Emotions are compounded daily, weekly or just frequently enough to cause huge impact. The frequency of the Emotions, the swinging of Emotions and the route that they get there, either by co-creating these Emotions with others and therefore spreading the suffering, or indeed spoon feeding these Emotions to yourself, all on your own. Now, if we were talking primarily of the High Vibration Emotions, imagine the different tone that people would be setting just by reading this list. We do however, appreciate that for so many, it is the Low Vibrational Emotions which are a consistent area to address in order to truly commence the Mastery of your Vibration and ultimately your Alignment.

So, what are examples of Low and High Vibrating Emotions? How do you truly understand the resonance of the Vibration without really connecting to the 'naming' of these Emotions? For, if you think for a moment and list out all the Emotions you can think of (without looking at the list), how many can you name? Then, how many do you FEEL with frequency? If you try this exercise right now, right in this moment, it will give you some great insight into your current Emotional awareness.

Take a pen and paper and set two columns. Write down all the Low Vibration Emotions you can think of and then the High. Which Emotions were easier for you to articulate? Low or High? As you wrote them, did you connect, even just a moment, to a Vibration within? If so, this is going to give you a clue, a hint as to what to bring further forward into your awareness.

Low Vibration Emotions	High Vibration Emotions
Fear	Freedom
Hate	Love
Anger	Contentment
Frustration	Satisfaction
Apathy	Enthusiasm
Despair	Hope
Anxiousness	Clarity
Worthlessness	Worthiness
Disappointment	Relief
Sadness	Happiness
Guilt	Joy
Shame	Pride
Betrayal	Admiration
Loss	Optimism
Panic	Calmness
Shock	Elation
Horror	Enlightenment

CATEGORISING LOW VIBRATIONAL EMOTIONAL EXPERIENCES

Level 1 - Core/Root Experiences

Emotions that are generated as a result of an experience, or thoughts about an experience of yours or somebody else's.

Everyone has Level 1 Experiences that are at the core of fears and current Low Vibration .

Level 2a - Journey Level Experiences

Over time the experiences build a story of suffering of some kind or another. Your Vibration is impacted as a result of these different experiences e.g. I hate my life, could generate the Emotions of sadness, anger, fear etc. A core experience could also trigger additional Journey related Emotions e.g. anger at being judged by a parent in the moment leading to frustration, despair, more anger at how this has always been the way that they have spoken to you.

Level 2b - Fears Generated from Level 2 Journey Experiences

Fears then arise from these consistently occurring experiences that make up your Journey. For example the bad experiences with your parent could have created the fear of being judged, fear of being hurt, fear of being unloved or not giving enough love, or fear that your life was always meant to be this painful and difficult.

Level 3 - Secondary Emotion from Level 2 Fears

As a result of the Level 2b fears, you generate another layer of Low Vibration e.g. anger at the fear of being judged, disbelief at the fear of not being loved, or fear that you fear you are going to be Emotionally or Physically hurt again.

Understanding all of these layers helps you to connect to the experiences, to recognise and ultimately better release Low Vibration from the past. Those fears that we continuously carry are most often Level 2 Journey Level fears generated from multiple core experiences and this is one of the key reasons why as part of The Releasing Process we look to get to the understanding of core experiences, ie. Level 1 Experiences. Because in the letting go of the past we also start to release the present fears that not only generate continual Low Vibration but also create new Level 1 Low Vibrational experiences influenced by the fears that we feel and carry that make us react in certain ways in the moment....and so the cycle continues. Be more aware of this because by catching some of these Emotions in the moment you can help to reduce the amount of Low Vibration that you are cyclically generating.

Olivia and Raf, Abraham and Jesus

THE VORTEXES OF EMOTION

This is a Game Changer. You may take a look and think, these look familiar! But look again. This is the original, original deep understanding of how you create Emotions within your body. These are not chakras and anyone who has listened to Abraham for some time through Esther Hicks will know and understand that Non Physical do not refer to chakras at all, this is not a term or reference that they use. It is however, fully understood that the chakra system *is* used by many, in many different ways however, this is the original version if you like which was mistranslated over centuries and continuously evolved into what it is known as the chakra system today.

If you have a special affinity to chakras, feel wedded and tied to them and even hearing this makes you feel resistance, look within to find out why. For this new insight and understanding is one of the most freeing, liberating, powerful tools that you can harness for your ultimate greatest good. One that if you can connect powerfully to, you can Change how you feel in an instant. It is also a vehicle for confirmation and communication with your Higher Self in particular when you are going through the Emotional Releasing Process, when creating Law based Truths and when you are surfacing and removing Egoic Blocks to the Vortexes of Emotion.

All Emotions are sourced from these five Vortexes. Every single one. Each Emotion is unique, it has its own frequency and energy signature and the emphasis and combinations of these five Vortexes is what makes up the individual Emotional energies.

So, why Vortexes?

When you think of a Vortex, you may think of this incredible Universal access point, this is why these are named so. For you have access within you to Universal pure positive energy radiating through you at all times and these Vortexes of Emotion are specifically created within you to feel, to experience and to create within you a powerful source of energy that you literally tap into. With these Vortexes, they flow inwards and also push outwards. Flowing in is allowing that Emotional energy to be accessed and then flow back into your Inner Being. Pushing out is giving and creating that Emotional energy out into your body. Energy. Emotional Energy. Universal Energy. Your Energy.

CREATING OPPORTUNITIES FOR HIGH VIBRATION EMOTIONS

If you have read the chapter on the Emotional Body, you will now understand that it is the conduit and also that it is not the originator of your Emotions, but that your Inner Being and Vortex of Emotions are. Also, in that chapter, you will see reference to what comes first, the thought or the feeling. Such an interesting insight this and one that if you can truly connect to, helps you with your own Emotional Mastery, for always, always, without exception, you have pure positive Emotion accessible to you at all times. Yet it is your Subconscious Mind, Conscious Mind and Egoic Bodies that can request the Low Vibration Emotions that so many of you are familiar with.

The Vortexes of Emotion are the specific Emotion types that when added together with different emphasis, generate and create unique Emotions. Always, again without exception, your Vortexes of Emotion will highlight to you in a moment, that you have an opportunity for Trust for example, when you are feeling lack of trust. It is this lack which is what stops you taking the opportunity your Emotional Vortex is offering you. It is when you continue to generate lack that you start to create Egoic Blocks to your Vortexes of Emotion, these are cutting off the energetic access routes to the pure Emotional energy of your Inner Being through the Vortexes. Let's take an example.

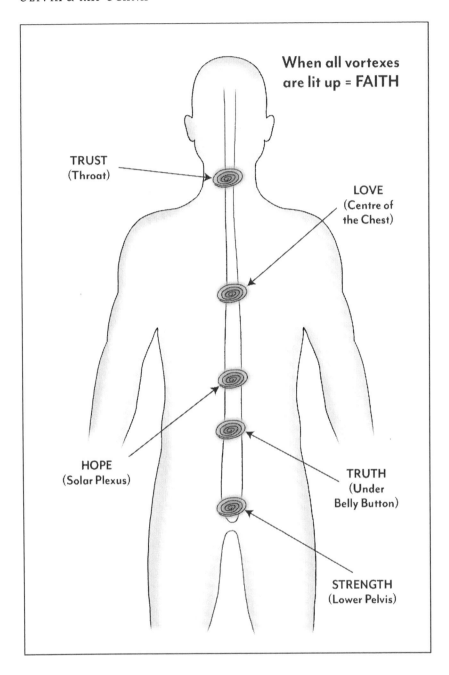

You are with a partner, someone who you have been with for a short time. It is the first time you have experienced great joy and happiness with someone and you seem to be in a great place. So often, you feel good. You have been betrayed in the past in your Emotional relationship experiences and so that hurt is still there, that anxiety is still there and you fear that the same thing is going to happen again. You already have Egoic Blocks to several of your Vortexes of Emotion, in particular the Trust, Love and Hope Vortexes. Your new partner is going out for a night without you. This reminds you of several times that you have been betrayed.

Your Subconscious Mind is in Resistant Mode, accessing the Emotional experiences you have previously had with this 'like' experiencing and referencing the Fear labelling that exists. Your Egoic Bodies are inflated and reminding you that you have been betrayed in the past and activating the fear, worry, lack of love, anger, lack of trust that already resides within you as stored Low Vibration and therefore starts to impact your Transitional Vibration significantly. In the moment, you catch yourself and notice, notice that your mood is completely changing, notice that you are starting to feel adrenaline racing in your body as your heart rate starts to increase and your slightly sickening feeling in your stomach rises. All the while, this is happening, your Vortexes of Emotion are signalling you, "Opportunity for Trust" and "Opportunity for Love" and "Opportunity for Hope" and "Opportunity for Truth" and "Opportunity for Strength".

Opportunity for Trust – this is a new person, a new relationship, a new point in time. I trust myself, I trust them for they are not the same person that I have been with who betrayed me, they have never betrayed me.

Opportunity for Love – I allow love for myself in this moment. Love for all that I suffered in the past and all that it taught me about me. Love for my new partner and the happiness this new relationship has brought me.

Opportunity for Hope – I allow hope that things are different in this relationship, that they feel about me the way I feel about them. I allow hope that I will fully release the pain that my previous relationships have caused me and allow me to be free to love fully without fear in this new relationship.

Opportunity for Truth – The truth is, this relationship is not the same as the relationships I have had in the past. The truth is, my new partner has never betrayed me. The truth is, I have never betrayed them. The truth is, I am deserving of love and happiness. The truth is, so is my partner and therefore I wish to give so much love to them just because they are so special to me.

Opportunity for Strength – I cannot do anything to change the past apart from let it go and grow from it, therefore I choose strength in this moment to love fully my new partner and to know that I choose in this moment to not allow the past actions and hurt from others to impact this new relationship. I choose to grow, now, right here in this moment.

By enabling this Opportunity, through the noticing of your Vortexes and acting on the guidance, you will then give yourself the Opportunity to allow full access to all of the five Vortexes for this experience with your new partner. In doing so you generate Faith, Faith in you, Faith in your new partner and also, you will feel much, much better about the entire situation and you will start the process of a new way of thinking and being in the moment.

Know that this is not only possible for you in the moment, to be able to take these Opportunities presented to you by your Vortexes of Emotion, but it is one of the most powerful mastery capabilities that you have in the moment. A way to move away from Fear, a way to move away from Lack and instead, connect to all the positive Emotion available to you.

EMOTION COMBINATIONS

How do just five Vortexes generate such a range of Emotions and how do Low Vibration Emotions get created? You will now understand that the emphasis of different Vortexes, so the strength and combination of the Emotions or the lack associated in different frequencies create a whole library of Emotions available to you.

Here, we are showing some examples of these combinations in order to provide greater clarity and insight on these combinations. What is amazing is you are able to generate these in the moment, so become familiar with your Vortexes, really feel into them and start trying to create these Emotions at any time, the High Vibration ones of course! Notice when you are generating the Low Vibration Emotions and you will also start to 'feel' them in the Vortexes.

The order of these Vortexes below denotes the strength of frequency applied for that Emotion with those listed first being the strongest.

Positivity = Love + hope

Balance = Allow love + hope (energy flows back into your Inner Being when you allow)

Fear = Lack of love + lack of hope

Nervousness/anxiety = Love + lack of hope

Safety/Calmness/Confidence/Relaxed/Assurance = Love + strength + truth + trust (different emphasis for each Vortex to gain the individual Emotion)

Self Love = Love + truth + hope + strength

Pride = Truth + love + hope + strength

Devastation = Lack of hope + lack of love + lack of truth + lack of strength

Happy/Excitement = Love + trust + hope/Hope + love + trust

Desire/Passion/Fun = Love + hope + truth + strength/truth + love + hope + strength/hope + truth + love + strength

Confidence = Trust + truth + love + hope

Lack of confidence/Guilt = Lack of truth + lack of love + lack of trust + lack of strength/lack of truth + lack of love + lack of hope + lack of trust

Freedom/Faith/Expectation = Trust + love + hope + strength + Truth

Hesitancy = Lack of hope + trust + love + strength + truth

Vulnerability = Allow love + trust + truth + strength

Overwhelm = Truth + lack of hope + lack of love + lack of strength

Kindness = Love + trust + truth + strength

Uncertainty = Lack of hope + truth

Disbelief = Lack of hope + truth + lack of trust

Power = Love + strength

Determination = Love + truth + strength

Honesty/Overpowered = Love + strength + truth (too much positive can create negative Emotion)

Over-enthusiasm = Too much love + too much truth

Satisfaction = Allow love + trust

Belief = Truth + trust

Certainty of Self = Truth + trust + strength

Certainty of All = Allowing trust + love + hope

Integrity = Trust + love + truth

Sadness = Lack of hope + lack of love + truth

Motivation = Strength + hope + love + truth

Demotivation = Truth + lack of strength + lack of hope

Acceptance = Allow love + truth + strength

Allowing = Hope + truth + love

EGOIC BLANKETS OVER YOUR VORTEXES OF EMOTION

We have explained how you can create Egoic Resistance to your Vortexes of Emotion through your experiences and these create Egoic Blocks to the energetic pathways to your Vortexes, stopping the flow and access through that route to your Inner Being.

Where we wish to further explain is when you are having a Low Vibrational Emotional experience and you feel almost numb, like an inability to access a specific Vortex or potentially all of them in the moment. This almost acts as a blanket over your Vortexes which the Egoic Bodies create in the moment by holding your Transitional Vibration around the Vortexes.

For example, if you have experienced a shock, a deep sense of disbelief in the moment, this is where this type of blanketing, shielding or suspension of access can take place. If that shock and disbelief isn't alleviated in the moment or is further compounded by your experience, this suspension of access can become more and more heavy. Know that this is your Transitional Vibration in the moment that is generating this suspension and being directed by your Egoic Bodies as a form of self-protection.

The way to alleviate such an experience is to first, seek Balance. This may feel difficult to do in the moment, in particular if you are having an extreme Emotional experience taking place, however it is possible to do, for what this does in the moment is allow you to manage the severity of the Emotion and also shift your Transitional Vibration in order to allow. By activating Balance, you literally can call The Law of Balance to you and from this place, you will be able to then in the moment, reduce the Egoic Bodies self-protection mechanism and start to shift the Transitional Vibration.

The three Vortexes you can use in the moment are Love, Hope and Truth and the Emotion that it generates by activating these Vortexes is Peace. These will be activated by calling The Law of Balance to you and therefore immediately accessible to you once this has taken place as the Transitional Vibration starts to shift over these three Vortexes. You can find how to activate The Law of Balance in The Feelset Tools in the back of this book in order to do this. Next, feel into your Love Vortex, feel it activate and generate Love Energy, feel this radiate out into your chest, and then Allow Love to flow back in. Next, feel into your Hope Vortex. Even in this difficult moment in time experience, there is always Hope to connect to. Hope being activated within you and flows out through your solar plexus, then allowing Hope, feeling that Hope flowing back into your Inner Being. The Truth of you is what will finalise and allow the release.

This will shift your Transitional Vibration and fast and by shifting it, it will also soothe the Egoic Bodies and deflate them, it will also help your Subconscious Mind to label the experience ideally with Love, but if the experience continues, a less impactful Fear based label.

GENERATING HIGH VIBRATION IN YOUR LIVING ROOM

Yes, real true, life living experiences give you the ability to FEEL Emotion but here's an alternative. The list above shows you how to generate any High Vibration manually. The Feelset Tools chapter shows you how to use a Truth with your Higher Self in order to create any High Vibration you wish and also how to call in the Universal Laws energy. You are able to use the Vortexes of Emotion to generate High Vibration in the moment, just sitting on the sofa without interacting with anyone, without having something nice said to you, without getting a hug from someone. Just you. You and your Vortexes of Emotion! This is the challenge to you, to pick a High Vibration Emotion combination from the list and try it, when you are sitting quietly and on your own and give it a go. You might just feel a slight flutter, you may feel a great surge but whatever it is, know that it is you, pure you, magnificent you, tapping into in that moment All That You Are.

This is also a recommended approach for counter balancing Low Vibration . So if you are feeling anger, generate love from your Vortexes of Emotion, if feeling fear then generate hope. This will not stop you from feeling the Low Vibration but it will help soothe you vibrationally as well start to train your Subconscious Mind in the direction that you wish to feel.

Olivia and Raf, Abraham and Jesus

THE PHYSICAL YOU

There is so much for you to know and be aware of in regards to your Physicality. If you are out of Physical Alignment, and this can be from feeling overtired, stressed, sick, overeating, injured, undereating, sluggish, hormonal, sleep deprived or many, many other things, your Physicality and ultimately your Vibration is altered.

Depending on just how out of Physical Alignment you are, it will ultimately impact your overall Transitional and Stored Vibration but also of course, your Transitional and Stored Vibration can impact your Physicality. Here we have the great cycle you see, where Vibrational impact causes Physical impact, then Physical impact causes Vibrational impact. Let's take a moment to explore an example.

Think back to a time when you had a severe headache. This may have been caused by a couple of days of predominantly low Transitional Vibration, thus storing more Low Vibration in particular areas. Remember like attracts like, even in your cells, so if your Emotions have been similar to Stored Vibration Emotions, these will always attract to the same spot where it is present already or near to it. So, imagine if you can that all around your neck, your shoulders and also right inside your brain are the areas where this has stored. This creates impact. The impact that would primarily be taking place will be in the connectors in the brain, the muscles, ligaments and tendons in your shoulders, neck etc. But why the headache? This is when your Low Transitional Vibration will predominantly be starting to attract towards the recently Stored Vibration and energetically be focused here, this causes the 'pressure' feeling of the energy not moving. This can cause the headache.

Here is something to try. The next time you have a symptomatic experience such as a headache, stomach pains, back pain, knee pain etc, you can influence the energy to more evenly disperse or shift out. Focus right in on the energy where it is congregating and where you are experiencing pain, feel into the pain almost and Allow it to move out. If it is in your head for example, focus on it going out of the top of your head, out through your eyes, your nose, your ears and mouth. Next, really focus on your Transitional Vibration to ensure that the energy does start to move more easily and you create and generate more High Vibration. Remember, the more High Vibration you can create in the moment, the sooner it will tip you into the predominantly High Vibration Transitional Vibration and therefore automatically start to move out Low Transitional Vibration.

With Physical Alignment comes greater Physical, Emotional, mental and spiritual energy. When we talk about Physical Alignment, what does that really mean? This is not a weight, nor a Physical perfection per se, but it is absolutely a Physical tuning to you. It is a fully efficient and tuned in awareness of your body. It is a state of knowing what is happening to your Physical being in the moment and for you to be able to adjust, to shift yourself whenever needed to ultimately feel that full power of your Physicality, to tap into huge energy stores and access.

You are pure energy, this we have said often. You are made up of trillions of cells and you are a Vibrational being, so your thoughts but more importantly, your Emotions effect you cellularly. You are able to influence your cells, you are able to connect more fully to the Physicality of your being and influence it, into an amazing efficient body that feels full of vitality, that feels exceptional the majority of the time.

For those that have had health issues for some time, who perhaps have had Physical struggles, you may read these last words and say 'not for me'. The Truth is, it is for you. This is something that is within all Physical beings to achieve and absolutely goes hand in hand with Vibrational Mastery. You are truly able to work with your body and positively influence within yourself and in particular, your ultimate awareness of your body, your efficiency of your body systems, the toxicity levels that reside within you and the choices you make moment by moment and day by day. This does mean that you need to notice.

For Physical Balance can be lost over time. When you start to understand your Physical being, your incredible body, the body systems that work so seemingly effortlessly, the repairing cells, the rejuvenation and regeneration and the true and utter awesomeness of All That You Are, you, with this greater understanding you can tune in.

So, you haven't done biology recently and understanding cells and organs is of no real interest, we understand, but how about you start to take a different Feeling to your body overall. Rather than seeing it as a science lesson, this is about a Vibration and influence lesson.

By focusing in on your own Physical energy, you are able to Align your own Physical energy, which ultimately leads you to the same source – deeper connection to your Inner Being, deeper connection to your Higher Self, deeper connection to your body systems and ultimately your cells. It is with this focus Physically, that you are able to understand how you really feel inside your Being. This could be about an ache or pain, this could be about an illness, disease or areas of toxic build up and many other things. This tuning is possible for everyone and improvements in how you feel Physically, no matter what the story nor the odds, are possible. Physical wellbeing is a by-product of Vibrational Change. Often, Physical symptoms are the manifestation of Low Vibration .

Set the expectation. Align to how you want to feel. Create a Desire. Create a Truth. Allow the Change. Ask your Higher Self to help you influence your cells, create Change, deliver Change, become efficient, become Balanced, to heal.

RETUNE YOUR NERVOUS SYSTEMS

Fear. We have talked about this Emotion, the Physical life phenomenon that currently underpins so many of your Emotional bodies, so many of your Low Vibrational holdings within. As you move through the advancement of releasing Low Vibration, for those who have Fear at the core of you, this will also have a long standing, often non-articulated Physical source and automatically triggered adrenal response and symptoms that go largely unnoticed. Until you cannot ignore it anymore.

Your Autonomic Nervous System, this is what controls all of the consistent management of each and every aspect of your automatic Physical-ness, such as breathing, your heart beating, your food digesting, your body temperature, swallowing etc. This is entirely regulated by your Hypothalamus, part of your hormone command centre deep inside your brain, the epicentre of your nervous system. It is constantly reading, measuring and monitoring, all without you breaking a sweat (unless that was the response required in the moment!). Part of your Autonomic Nervous System, your Sympathetic Nervous System, sends the command to hormonally trigger your adrenal glands, triggering your adrenal response. Automatically. When Fear is a predominant Vibration, when it is the underlying Emotion that resides within, your Autonomic Nervous System just feels Fear. It doesn't determine that your life is not in danger, it is a primal automatic response. Run or battle. That is what it triggers. So, just as with The Law of Attraction, where Fear attracts Fear, your Adrenal response being triggered is again reinforcing when you feel the Fear, it is time to react, no question, it's fight or flight time.

The good news is, The Law of Balance is completely at play within your Physical body and there is a total antidote to your Adrenal response. This is your Parasympathetic Nervous System, part of your Autonomic Nervous System too, also known as your rest and digest system. It's the soother, the calmer, the EASE enabler. One of the main nerves within the Parasympathetic Nervous System that you can come to know, that you can activate and influence is your Vagus Nerve. This nerve runs from the centre of your brain, starting from your Thymus and running through the centre of your body, branching out into your heart, your lungs and into your digestive system through your stomach and through your intestines.

We wish you to know that you are absolutely able to influence your body in this way. You are able to calm and soothe the adrenal response, increase your communication between your hormone command centre and your adrenal glands and activate your Vagus nerve. By doing this, you are actively participating in allowing Change within your Physical being, helping to retrain your Physical being instead of practiced and automatic responses, to work in the way that you now need it too.

WHAT ABOUT 'GOOD' STRESS?

We wish to acknowledge that your body responds in a particular way which is actually positive for you but has a similar make up and activates those same body processes which are induced by stress. This is, for example, before you are about to go on stage to perform, stand up in front of your peers and do a presentation or go on the zip wire that you have been dreaming about but as you stand on the platform about to leap, you feel the massive fear. This is where the adrenaline coursing through your body gives you that extra "Wooohoooo, I can DO this" that delivers then an amazing feeling of success and accomplishment after it is over (along with other chemical releases which give you that feel good factor!).

This extra feeling is what helps performers perform, helps you do the things you have been dreaming about but still fear and helps you get through those growth situations over and over again. So, we say to you, this is not wrong, this is your body working in perfect order. What we wish for you though, is for this activation to really happen in these situations and not when you wake up in the morning every day, fearing for the day ahead.

THE SABER TOOTH TIGER

Often an analogy has been used about Stress and the Stress hormones created (your Adrenal Glands and associated hormones) in reference to cavemen and living in fear of the Saber Tooth Tiger. What this represents is the life of a hunter, whose need for food and sustenance drove him out into treacherous terrain to hunt and gather food for both himself and his family. We are referring to man here but of course women too were hunters and providers for their family and equally responsible for this as well and as equally impacted by this difficult life condition.

Do you think that the fear stopped once they returned home after a successful hunting expedition? Do you think that fear didn't rise when the food stores started to get low and they knew they needed to get back out into that hunting environment again? Do you think that they feared those being left behind as their most skilled hunters left their homes relatively unprotected? What about those that were left behind? What about the noises in the night evoking the need to fear, protect, stay alert, be on guard?

The Physical nature and Emotional nature of humans means that this has been a predominant experience right from earliest mankind. It wasn't the moment of being confronted by the Saber Tooth Tiger that the fear was present, yes of course it would have been heightened, but in fact that fear was already present. The adrenal system was already in motion doing what it does best. Flooding early Physical Humans' bodies with hormone, preparing to run, preparing to fight, preparing to protect.

And all this flooding, it translates to anger, aggression, frustration and of course, fear, fear and more fear. The body literally wants to get it out. Needs to get it out.

Now think of the history of man and how many wars were fought, so again move your thoughts and mind to perhaps the Vikings and their lives of fighting, battle, protection. The Greeks, the Romans, the Arabic times of conquest and victory, death, destruction and loss. All through the history of Physical Humans.

Now turn your attention to today, where there are no Saber Tooth Tigers in your existence or in most cases, no wars happening outside your front door, but instead you have mounting bills, that presentation to deliver, that deadline to meet and a desperate feeling for Change and freedom in your gut but feeling like there isn't a way out of this cycle.

Does the same fear and fear response equate to the same experience? No. Does your body react in the same way? Yes. Remember, Emotions Don't Care About Experiences, please reference the earlier chapter in the book for more explanation.

It's time to evolve. It is time to do what has always been possible and influence your Physical body for your greatest good. It's time now to Retune Your Nervous System. Start today. Feel better today. Know that this is possible today. Start with this one thing today and do it every day until it becomes automatic, until you are able to influence it without doing a practice, where you become so tuned to your two systems that you are 'in the moment' not only aware that they are active or inactive, but you can soothe it or activate it right there on your own. So what is the guidance to do this?

It's time to evolve.

SLEEP

Do you sleep well? If the answer is no, you are not alone, for many having a Physical experience are sleeping less soundly, feeling less refreshed on waking. We wish you to understand that sleep is a fundamental for your Physical being, for your

Physical Alignment and Vibration. What is happening in your waking hours to disturb your sleep? If you really tune in, your body will tell you the answers.

Often it will be a number of things that are occurring, a volume of experiences throughout the day. Take an inventory of your day and really consider it. Have you not really moved a lot? Have you eaten way too much and too late? Have you had too much to drink? Is there too much caffeine or chemicals in your body? Have you been on a screen for hours on end? How much time have you spent outside? How Low Vibrational have your Emotions been? How much fun and lightness have you experienced? Have you allowed your mind to clear from racing and repeating thoughts? How much time have you tended to YOU today? There are many more questions but this inventory is your starting point to tune in for your body and Emotions will tell you everything you need to know. Try this today and write it down, for it will start to help you understand what aspects you can adapt and adjust to Change your overall wellbeing and sleep experience.

TOXICITY

We understand that your environment plays a huge part in your Vibrational tuning and with that comes a greater understanding of the toxicity that resides within you. We do not say this to cause fear or to make you feel that you need to move house or city or anything extreme at all. What we wish to bring to your attention is that there are many daily choices that you can make in regard to your overall understanding of consumption, both conscious and unconscious and therefore which toxins you are actively allowing into your experience.

We first wish to express that if you are consuming food that has ingredients that you cannot pronounce or are chemical in nature, understand that this is likely causing a toxic response within your body. Your body sees these chemicals as unknowns and your liver in particular has a big job in trying to not only break them down but to decide what to do with them. Often, your clever liver when faced with the unknown, sends these toxins to be stored just in case you need them. This then turns up in your fat cells. So you are literally hauling these toxins around with you, in particular if your liver is having to manage a LOT of toxins, the default is to store them.

If you have a particular chemical vice, such as a popular diet drink for an example, or energy drinks that are so popular (and often fluorescent in colour – cue sign!), know that this is ultimately causing a toxic response somewhere in your body. You may not notice it, but over time it will build. This is also the same for medication. Please know that we are not suggesting that you stop the medication you are on, but do know that if you are on medication and you are also consuming toxic food and drinks then this will overall increase the levels of toxicity within your body. Medicine can come in many forms, for many we see a reliance on 'over the counter' medicines as equally as prescribed and both types provide you with a toxic influx that your body has to manage. Taking this further, there are of course the more easily recognisable toxins such as cigarettes, alcohol and recreational drugs. Again, if you think of the cumulative effect, just how significant adding each and every one of these together or some of these together can be for you.

The water you drink, for so many it is freely available, but it is full of chemicals. If you have to pay for water, which is of course essential for your survival, not only is this a cost but it comes in plastic bottles which also has a leeching toxic reaction, but is the lesser of the two evils to the chlorine, lime and fluoride ever present in chemically treated tap water. Wherever and however you can, understand that the cleanest purest water you can have access too is the ultimate. Ideally in a glass bottle but we understand that this is not always convenient nor practical, and know that there are many plastic bottle providers that also provide water in non leeching toxic plastic.

Being in green. How often are you able to be outside? How often are you able to breathe in fresh air and have access to sit with trees around you? This is again something incredibly powerful for your overall toxicity. For if this is minimal or not often enough, again you will understand that the air you are breathing and the environment you are sustaining is not providing you with the cleanest nor purest experience. You know within you if you are enabling yourself to have the access that you deserve, again no matter how urban your environment there are options for you to enjoy if you allow yourself some time to enjoy it and make it a priority for your overall wellbeing.

The food you eat. We have already spoken of commercial food preparation that is full of ingredients that you can't pronounce and therefore toxicity, but also where you have impacted meat in particular, where this has been chemically altered or added to in preparation in order to increase the shelf life of these proteins. Likewise even vegetables and fruits that are sprayed and treated during the growth lifecycle but also on packing and shipping.

There are many, many more areas around toxicity that you will already be aware of that just starting to read these paragraphs will allow you to consider. Rather than write them all down for you here and now, we wish you to start to notice, to take charge of your toxicity levels and make a difference with your choices today. Instead of seeing this as a negative chapter, see it as an Awareness chapter. One for you to start tuning into.

Take a pen and paper and analyse your day. Write down from morning to night all of the toxic aspects that you have lived and be as honest as you can about these. Ask in your mind of your body, your cells, what did it make them feel? What impact happened today because of this? Write down the answers. Now focus on what different choices could you have made? What options were available to you had you thought about them at the time? Next time you are in that situation, what will you do differently?

YOUR PHYSICAL ENERGY

Energy makes energy, kinetic and potential energy when thought of in your Physical body's sense, means that the more energy you are able to provide within your body as movement, the more potential energy you create inside your body, in particular your cells. For energy is the total of all you are. You are able to influence your energy by attunement, down to influencing your muscles, resolving health conditions and complaints, increasing your body systems efficiency, releasing fat and toxins and so on. The more you are able to do this, the easier it becomes, the faster you will see results.

Your Physical energy by way of motion or movement is an important aspect, for your bodies were not meant to be sedentary. Now for anyone who is incapacitated in any way, you are able to start with influencing your own cells via energy practices, yes this means even those lying in a hospital bed. For even if someone was to give you earphones and a recorded practice you are able to focus in perhaps on your heart beat, and focus in on the flow of life and energy cellularly that allows your heart to beat, and the trace of the blood through your veins, to your organs, your limbs, to your brain. This sensation alone gives you an element of tuning in to your Physicality.

The next is to not let anything stop you. If you are in a situation where you are exhausted Physically but you have not been Physical, so perhaps you are ill in bed, you are able to move within the bed. Even if it is some gentle stretches, gentle raising and releasing of limbs, head etc. Tensing of muscles. Then, move to a more cellular experience and try exercise from the inside out by focusing in on the Physical feeling you would Desire to feel.

For those who are perfectly well but are desk bound or lack Physical energy to get up and out and about, we wish you to know that you will start to feel better if you move. Those thoughts and aspirations you have about Physical energy within you will come but you need to start somewhere. This means today if you can. You can dance for a minute. Get up and stretch for a minute. Take a five minute walk outside. Do aggressive vacuuming. Whatever it is and however you can make it happen for yourself, let this be an important Change for you today, an awareness that SOMETHING can be done, you just need to choose what it is.

Again, a cumulative approach is what happens. The more energy you create, the more energy you have. The more you move, the more you want to move. Consistency is also key here, just as with Vibrational Management, it is something that you tune into and continue to tune into consistently throughout the day.

Write down today what that is going to be and do it, no ifs, buts or maybes, just do it. Then write down how it made you feel. Repeat this again tomorrow. The following day. Notice the Change. Notice how it starts to make you feel.

Olivia and Raf, Abraham and Jesus

THE LAW OF DESIRE

Much of course, has been written about The Law of Attraction. This Law is fundamental to our Universe. To life itself. To the having and the not having of things, experiences, Emotions, relationships, outcomes. To the flow and the pinching off of that flow. All the beautiful work from Esther and Jerry Hicks and Abraham is the foundation of understanding for so many and all so timelessly written and accessible to you. This isn't an 'update' to The Law of Attraction, for Universal Laws are absolute. There are however, additional Laws for you to understand the inner workings of and welcome into your awareness with full force. For Universal Laws operate and coexist in perfect harmony and one often triggers another and another, without you even really knowing it or understanding it. Now it is time to understand it better.

The Law of Desire.

What an amazing energy this Law has. And yet the word desire is used with such fear. Fear in the asking, fear in the expecting, fear in the receiving and fear in the having.

For our desires can often signal something for us which can make many people feel very uncomfortable and that is Change. Change creates so much fear for us all and yet Change is the architect of so much love if we allow it.

Ask yourself what your greatest desire is. We ask not what you wish for the most in this moment but rather what it is that truly stirs you, what brings tears of happy Emotion to you, or shrills of joy, just in the thinking of it. That which generates in you an energy so powerful with excitement and intrigue and hope and love and empowerment and passion and belief and focus and momentum. Now that's desire right there.

Behind desire are powerful Emotions in equal measure. Love, hope, truth and strength.

The energies of love and hope act like a light to a firework when it comes to creating a truly strong desire. Love for the Self, love for another, it matters not which type of love, and a connection to hope, drives a natural desire, a felt desire and a feeling of truly wanting what it is that we are asking for. The truth and strength behind your desire drive the energy of it.

A desire is not a need, it is not something that would be nice to have but that we're not overly fussed about obtaining. A desire is WANTED, and in the having of it we WILL be

374

satisfied. A desire is not a small piece of pie, it's all of the pie. It's not a nibble on some cheese it's a selection of all the cheeses, crackers and a few glasses of wine. A desire is not necessarily world peace, but rather every piece of the world, experienced and remembered and cherished and shared and then done all over again and again and again and again.

Abundance is desire. Greed is not desire. Giving is not desire, not without having received at some point also. Desire is not for tomorrow or a rainy day, desire is for now and tomorrow and a rainy day. Desire is for old friends and new, good times and bad. Desire is freedom. Desire is fearless. Desire is inspirational. Desire brings clarity, reconciliation, Balance. Desire creates action, strong action, direct action, quickens actions, stops actions. Desire lifts you off that seat, out of that bed, into an aeroplane, out of that aeroplane at thousands of feet up. Desire shifts your thoughts, your feelings. Desire breaks down barriers, Physical walls, mental walls. Desire creates Change, forces Change, allows Change, creates a need to Change. Desire melts away anger, fear, depression. Desire brings strength, self-control, courage, honour and love for the Self.

A desire is the perfect antidote for that 'feeling' that gently gnaws away at you as you sit at the office or on the couch or at the coffee bar or just about anywhere in fact.

And what is that feeling?

Fear is that feeling, frustration is that feeling, anger is that feeling and so many more. Deflated, underwhelmed, uninspired and bored you sit wherever you are, wishing and thinking the time away with no real sense of direction and no real sense of oomph or get up and go.

Hang on this is about desire. Come on, let's not sink into ourselves here. I'm looking for something inspirational in this chapter! Something that's going to break this cycle that is literally driving me insane. Something that is going to stop me from waking up every morning with that feeling of doom. Anything! Please!

That's better. Can you feel that desire in you right in this very moment? Feels good doesn't it? Feels good to just let it all out of you for a while. And yet, why just do this for a moment? Why not in every moment? Literally why not live your life full of desire in each and every second of it? Seriously. Why not? Well? Don't just go back to that comfy chair in your office or at home. Don't make all this fuss and then sink back into your old normality.

Hey! I'm still speaking to you are you listening?

Sorry I had to get back to something...

Yes, we understand. We don't agree but we understand. We understand you are busy, we understand you are stressed, we understand you are love-less, hope-less and very, very fear-full. But just try for a moment to let go those fears and imagine that each and every desire will come true. Say them out loud or say them to yourself but don't just say them, feel them, want them, DESIRE them. Because the generation of your desires picks away at those gnawing Low Vibrational Emotions. Those desires if truly felt and connected to will release so much love in you. And this love will drive out of you those Low Vibrations. It will melt away those fears for as long as you can feel the desire within.

Desire is at the core of the generation of all Truths. A Truth, created within The Law of Truth comes from desire. When you declare that you are "just not prepared to take any more", in this declaration your Truth has been driven by your desire. The Truth that you no longer feel anger towards someone that has hurt you was also driven by desire. The love for yourself in the first instance, and then the love for that person that has hurt you will have driven a desire in you to seek a Change, a hope for a better relationship, and the truth and strength of your feelings will have led you find a new understanding about yourself and them. The sadness that has blighted you all of your life because of the terrible loss of a loved one can be shifted by desire, to generate a new Truth within you that states it's time to let go, to live your life and to not keep connecting to the past.

So we have established that love, hope, truth and strength is at the core of desire, and that desire is at the core of the generation of all Truths. But what of The Law of Desire?

As we have stated, this is an amazing energy. A wondrous one that can be connected to simply by asking it of your Higher Self.

When connected to, it will create within you the High Vibrational Emotion of desire, but in a way that is felt so much more strongly than you could ever create yourself. This is the awesome power of The Law of Desire.

For The Law of Desire is a very powerful tool. When

connected to it you come alive, as you allow the energy to take you out of your slumber and slowly raise you to the vibration of anything that you wish to do or be in that moment.

Need to be inspired, or be inspiring? Connect to The Law of Desire.

Need to somehow find a way to finish that presentation? Connect to The Law of Desire.

Can't quite find a way to go trawling through those job sites? Connect to The Law of Desire.

Just can't get your head from under that pillow? Connect to The Law of Desire.

And yet strangely, instead of acting on this, your main focus today will probably be that spreadsheet you're working on. It's just so confusing to see people acting in this way, solely focussed on the things that bring them so much anger, dismay and boredom at times. Life is for living right?! Yay. Whoop whoop. Roar. Zzzz.

Fight back will you. Come on. Ask. Ask. ASK! Don't allow yourself to slip back into the old routine. The old routine can still be the new routine, you just need to add a little spice. What's your favourite spice? Ooh yum, I love a good curry myself. Where would you love to be eating a curry right now? Oh, wow, I've never been there but I've heard it's a top restaurant. Who would you most dearly love to be there with?

Hello. Are you still awake?

Come on!! Wake up! Shake it out of you. Fight will you! I say fight!

Fight...for your right...to parley! Parley with God because this is who you're connecting to if you do it right with this Law.

Connect with your Higher Self and ask them to liven this energy in you NOW.

Love + Hope + Truth + Strength. Say it again....

Love + Hope + Truth + Strength.

Love + Hope + Truth + Strength.

Love + Hope + Truth + Strength. Keep saying it out loud.

That's it feel that Desire building in you now. The energy of the Law connecting to you now. Feel your adrenaline flowing now.

Love + Hope + Truth + Strength. Say it!

Keep going with this feeling now. Feel yourself effortlessly gliding into its slipstream, the energy of The Law of Desire, so present in you now.

Love + Hope + Truth + Strength.

This energy is coursing through your veins now, so much so that you can almost feel yourself lifting off the ground.

Love + Hope + Truth + Strength.

Wow. Wow. Wow. Wow. Wow!

...Now that feels like The Law of Desire!

Now...hold this FEELING.

Feel into one Desire that is truly wanted by you. That one Desire that you will feel utterly satisfied in the having of. Not just a bland, average 'that would be nice to have' but something that hurts because you want it so much.

You desire to feel better, we hear you say. We say FEEL again, because that's not a Desire but merely a nice aspiration. An aspiration that simply leans you a little away from where you are now.

Come on we know you can do better than that. FEEL!

Did you say you want freedom?

Say it again...

"I want freedom"

Louder...

"I WANT FREEDOM!"

Awesome!

NOW FEEL THAT! This is what we're talking about!

Don't think anything now. Don't go into the how, what, where and when. Instead hold this energy for as long as you can and when you lose it get it back...and quickly.

And when you get it back FEEL the Truth of your Desire to be FREE. Allow yourself to connect to the having of it.

Allow, allow, allow this Desire to infiltrate you, to warm you, to power you through your day. Through today, tomorrow and the next day.

Align to it. Allow it. Feel it.

NOW FEEL THAT FREEDOM!

LIVE THAT FREEDOM!

BE INSPIRED AND INSPIRING!

WOOOOHOOOOOOOOOOOOOOOOOOOOOO!!!!

Olivia and Raf, Abraham and Jesus

THE LAW OF TRUTH

The Law of Truth.

So often, we have heard our Physical friends talk of 'speaking my truth' and for some, this can on occasion be an absolute. But often however, it is a vehicle or license to just explain what you feel in the moment about how you have been treated or what has been building in your perspective or from your vantage point. It isn't necessarily the Law.

Universal Law is absolute. There isn't a halfway house. There isn't a 'kind of like this'. There isn't a partial truth; so that bit is true, but that bit isn't. It is Law or it isn't. It is the Truth or it isn't.

Truths are not complicated. You are able to make them complicated but we urge you not to. Truths are simple and utterly, utterly clear. There is no ambiguity. There is no misdirection or Truth-ish. It just is. With some Subconscious

Mind States, when creating Truths as part of The Releasing Process you will require more detail and thought, but the premise is the same, and that is that your statement of Truth is clear.

Is it possible for your Truth to be different from somebody else's about the very same experience? Absolutely! Does the Law still apply? Absolutely! For each and every single one of you is unique and living a unique experience and your Truth is based on all that was and all that is, of you, here in this 'now' moment of your experience.

The interesting thing that we have observed is, even the mention of the word Truth strikes 'fear' into the Emotional Bodies of many of our Physical friends. This is down to what has come before, the hidden nature of things, the areas or aspects of your life that you wish hadn't happened or that you know better now and therefore you just push aside.

Truth and honesty are similar but not the same. The Law of Truth requires utter honesty of you, for you, within you in order to invoke it. For you cannot actually kid yourself with The Law of Truth, you will feel disrupted internally if you try within your Emotional Body and certainly within your Inner Being. You cannot pretend to create a Truth and if you really don't feel it, it simply won't work. In fact, your Higher Self is the acknowledger of a Truth creation where it becomes Universal Law and there is no fooling them either. Honesty to yourself, this is the first place to start and perhaps even in the recognition that you are not always allowing yourself to be honest, not consciously in any case. Perhaps you are on auto-pilot or you are allowing your

Conscious Mind, Egoic Bodies and Subconscious Mind to work continuously and bring up what was, not what is. For the first question to ask yourself, when looking at the Truth, is how do I feel right now? Right now. Now. Now in this moment. Be honest. Allow the Truth of your experience to rise.

WHAT CAN THE LAW OF TRUTH DO?

The Law of Truth is, as a Universal Law, utterly freeing because in the moment that you invoke a Truth it is the only and predominant feeling that exists within. It removes all conflict. If strong enough, it can move out Low Vibration associated with the conflict of this Truth. It is powerful beyond measure. It is freeing beyond all measure because once you have truly connected to The Law of Truth 'in the moment', any other thought or feeling almost bounces off it. It is protective. It is assertive. It is unshakeable. But...and there is a but...you HAVE to TRULY FEEL it.

You cannot say something out loud and not feel it and then a Truth be invoked. You cannot hope for something and not actually feel it and the Truth be invoked. You categorically and always and MUST feel it. The Truth of who you are. The Truth of your Experience. The Truth of your Journey. The Truth of that moment, and the next, and the next. The Truth that even when your logic says no you truly say YES, that is the Truth. And when your logic or mindset repeats over and over as you repeatedly say to yourself in front of the mirror "this is my Truth, this is my Truth, this is my Truth" but you do not TRULY FEEL it then that is not a Truth, and your

Subconscious Mind will not be fooled and nor will it allow you to forget what your REAL Truth is.

With a Truth you need to get your mind out of the way and instead allow who you are to surface. And always, always, the Truth is associated with Love. Love for the Self, love for others often, love for your Journey, love for connection, love for YOU.

THERE IS A REASON

Recall the saying "The Truth shall set you free". Such a true statement.

We now wish for you to clear your mind just for a moment, settle into yourself and come to a FEELING place. This may take a moment and take all the time that you need.

You are able to create a Truth right now. A Truth of how you feel in this moment. What is it? What is your Truth right here and now? About NOW. About You. About what you want and need and therefore what you desire. The "what" isn't important. What is important is your connection to a Truth within and a FEELING within. If you feel within and then feel nothing, try again, for there is never an abyss of no feeling within you. You may however be feeling perfectly Balanced. In perfect harmony and therefore no strong feeling one way or another. However, more often you will be feeling something, something stark and outstanding and something to attach to. Even "I feel numb" is a start. For this will relate to deep feelings of anguish, despair and ultimately 'numb' means 'disconnected'. So instead you can say "I feel disconnected".

You will know if you try this exercise and you are doing a Truth-ish. For it won't feel right. It will actually feel uncomfortable. Physically uncomfortable. A Truth you shouldn't TRY for. A Truth just is, in its entirety, simply present.

So that Truth. It's clear? It's Absolute? You FEEL it? How does that make you FEEL now? Something will have shifted inside of you. You will feel relief, love, lighter perhaps. This is the best way we can describe to you how a Truth will resonate within each and every single one of you. No matter what that Truth is or was, relief is now present. That is what the Truth provides.

WHO IS GOVERNED BY THE LAW OF TRUTH?

This heading makes it seem like you can opt in or out. The Universal Laws state that you cannot opt in or out of any Universal Law, they are always and permanent and whether you are aware of it or not, a Law just is. Feel the Truth of this very statement.

The Law of Truth is accessible and influential to "All on All Things at All Times". For it spans light years, it spans matter, it spans Dimensions, it spans Solar Systems and Universes. It is All, it is Always, it is Now, it was Then, it is Absolute.

WHO CAN USE THE LAW OF TRUTH?

Absolutely everyone and anyone can use The Law of Truth, no matter where you are on your Journey. In fact, you are already using it, so harness it fully now by understanding it better.

HOW DOES IT WORK?

You are unique, here, right here in this Physical existence. Yes, you now know you are an extension of your Higher Self energy, but you are still unique. There is only you, now, here in this moment in this reality with all that you know, all that you have experienced, all that you have asked for, all that you have desired and ALL That You ARE.

In your Physical body you have your Inner Being and within that Inner Being you have your Vortexes of Emotion. Your Inner Being is your access to your Higher Self, for the energy of your Higher Self flows to you and through you via your Inner Being. Your Vortex of Emotions hold a Vortex specifically for Truth, just under your belly button. This is your access point to the eternal and constant Law of Truth. This is why you FEEL The Law of Truth to your very core, for the core of you truly is your Inner Being.

When you are able to connect to a Truth your Truth Vortex is Aligned, there is no conflict, no block, no energetic discord. It allows fully. This Truth is then flowed out to the Universe and reciprocated with confirmation. The feeling that you receive within you is confirmation energy, confirmation that The Law of Truth is active, present and reciprocated.

Your Higher Self is a wonderful insight instigator, collaborator and participator in your Truths. Your Vortex of Truth within your Inner Being is directly linked to your Higher Self and thus ultimately the Universe. Your Higher Self is therefore the conduit and the enabler of that access to the Universal Law. It is through your Higher Self often, when connected, that you are able to get to the Truth of an experience and in doing so, create a Truth different to the Truth that you had previously held for that experience, based on the new understanding given via your Higher Self.

You may have felt and understood many different things for a particular experience and therefore sometimes the Truth can feel blurred. Your Higher Self can bring you the clarity in the moment. But your Higher Self can't 'feel' it for you. So 'you' must feel it to activate it. Activate the Truth. Activate the Law. Once Activated, it confirms via your Higher Self. Once Activated, it repels all un-Truths related to it. This is the bounce effect, the un-Truths related to your Truth repel. They don't penetrate. They don't even sit in your Transitional Vibration, they just bounce away as if they didn't even exist in the first place.

CREATING A TRUTH

As stated in the previous chapter it is desire that generates a Truth, driven from a moment of need or want for a Change, and this Truth can happen automatically.

But what if you are looking to generate a Truth more deliberately and specifically?

You still require desire but ideally you must get to a place of ease first in order to create a Truth deliberately. A Truth may materialise with ambiguity if you are in the midst of Emotional conflict, no matter how small. Ease and Balance is what you must aim to get to before you seek the Truth. This can take seconds, for some a little longer, but if you are in the middle of a rant of anger and frustration, you need to settle back into a semblance of Balance before undertaking this or it could be a pointless exercise. In moments of contrast there is still Truth present and therefore you can create a Truth during contrast; perhaps a Truth about not wanting to keep feeling a certain way Emotionally. This too will invoke the Law and generate some relief but only if you truly feel it in the moment, and you will also still need to find that Balance in order to get to a Truth which is underneath that contrast. A statement during a moment of contrast, made whilst completely out of Balance such as when extremely angry, if linked to a strong desire and feeling can still generate a Truth. However it may not become a Truth but rather just an angry tirade of words unlinked to the Emotions underneath about how you truly feel. This is why we guide you to be in, or move to, a place of ease when looking to 'deliberately' create a Truth.

If ease and Balance is illusive, seek any tool you can first to get you there. Meditate. Go for a walk. Breathe in and out for 5 minutes and think nothing. Call The Law of Balance as this will bring you Emotional feelings of peace. Whatever and however you need to find ease for yourself, go there, do that and it will be possible for you, no matter who you are or where you are or what you have going on. You can also find information described in Feelset Tools chapter about creating Balance in the moment.

Once you are in Balance and ease, you need to FEEL what your Emotional Body is telling you (perhaps driven by your Higher Self). No 'absolute Truth' can be determined without feeling so disconnect from your mind for a moment, sink into your body and into your Inner Being and allow the flow of thoughts from this place. From here comes the linking of the Emotions to the thoughts and in doing so you connect to the memory or memories of an experience with feeling and with clarity and perhaps new understanding, and then with love you are able to generate your Truth.

CONFLICTING WITH A TRUTH

As you will now know, with a Truth when created with utter connection, feeling and Love and activating the Universal Law, this becomes Law. This is absolute. You FELT it. It resonates within you. It is a new understanding and an understanding so very powerful that if you start to act, speak, think or behave in conflict with the Truth you will start to feel internal discord. Your Emotions will start to be heightened. You will start to feel unBalanced. This is because the energy of a Truth is absolute and all un-truths repel. This means repelling energetically. This means by repelling, it is creating Low Vibration within you and triggering the Low Vibration by way of saying 'stop denying the Truth'.

Without the harnessing of this Law and purposefully creating Truths you will have Truths within you, as part of your Journey. A connection to who you really are. These too are

Truths and this is also why as you go about your Journey, you will feel discord, and if not recognised and addressed it will ultimately generate and create Low Vibration within over time.

For example, you have treated someone badly. Perhaps you betrayed their confidence, let's use this by way of exploring the Truth. You have a feeling within that this is 'wrong' but in the moment you did it anyway. Then you feel that you wish you could take it back. Then you worry that they will find out. Then you ask the person you confided in to not say anything. But you still worry. That 'wrongness' is the discord, it is going against who you really are, the Truth of who you are. Now, imagine that you repeat that same behaviour. You start to ask yourself why you can't stop yourself from doing this. You feel rising conflict within you more and more. Conflict. Uncomfortable conflict. Conflict against a powerful Truth. The Truth of you.

So, what is your Truth here? Regardless if this is a Journey Truth or a harnessed purposeful Truth, you deal with the conflict in the same way.

You need to step in and recognise that conflict, the source of the Truth and discord, and reAlign. What does reAlign mean? This means that your actions, your thoughts, your behaviours regarding the conflict must Change. You feel the Truth that you have betrayed your friend's confidence but do not want to betray your friend's confidence, or anyone's confidence ever again. So, you look to understand why you betrayed your friend in the first place and with this understanding, you feel the Truth that you can be trusted by others and you also trust yourself. You feel the Truth that you are in control of this, that you are able to do this or not do this, that you have utter control and therefore you feel that you have the choice. The future choice that in that moment you will not betray, that you will not share the unshareable and that you will honour the trust given to you by another, the choice to be you.

Notice the discord first, connect to the Truth, then choose differently going forward.

For those at the end of their Awakening Journey be mindful of conflicting with one of the many new Truths that you will have created for yourself.

A simple Truth stating that you 'wish to be happy' is so easy to conflict against during this period whilst you are still seeking full Balance. Your Level Three Emotions, generated by your Level Two Fears, can easily drive a conflict as your habitual Conscious Mind reactions to fears trigger Low Vibration that ultimately makes you generate sadness, and therefore not be happy.

In The Feelset Tools we speak of how the Subconscious Mind 'Archive Memory Markers' need to be reduced using strong Truths to fully stop Low Vibration being created. Know that if you are conflicting with these Truths then even with the Archive Memory Markers cleared down for your memories your Subconscious Mind will see that you are not living in the Truths that you have created. It will therefore continue to trigger Low Vibration in you continuously, each and every time you recall the memories through experiences.

Be strong in this moment and LIVE YOUR TRUTHS. Ask yourself what it is that you truly desire in life and Align to it always, for this will keep you Aligned to your new Truths.

Find out more detailed and practical steps in The Feelset Tools in order to Create a Truth.

RESIDUAL FEAR

What if you feel a contradiction with your Truth? It's almost a Truth but not quite. Almost versus Absolute; there is a contradiction and you know as previously stated, a Universal Law is Absolute. And so, if there is still a residual BUT...your Truth is an 'almost'. A residual fear lingers and blocks the love seeking to wrap itself around your Truth.

This situation will create conflict within. If a Truth is created in the moment and then fear is felt from the past shortly after the Truth is confirmed, it may still be created as a Truth but it's effectiveness will perhaps be lessoned. A Truth with a level of fear attached to its understanding may not effectively Change that past understanding thus perhaps not allow the full release of the Low Vibration attached to that past experience. Neither will it prevent the creation of any new Low Vibration for that experience and any other experiences which hold Emotions linked to that same understanding. To solve this you must seek to make this Truth stronger through continual Alignment to it as well as the removal of all other resistance to it. This will allow you to supplement the feelings that you felt when you first created that Truth with additional High Vibrational understandings and feelings.

It may not always be obvious to you that a conflict exists within a Truth but know that this will be felt upon the triggering of a Truth or an element within a Truth as part of a new experience that you may have. At this point the conflict between your action and the details of the Truth will come to the fore and be felt, so look out for signs of Low Vibration within your Emotional Body, dizziness is also a common clue something isn't quite right. It is in this moment that you would need to follow the same process that you carried out in the creation of that Truth in order to understand where the differences lie against that which is held in your Subconscious Mind as a memory, for the conflicting element or elements.

This sounds complex but it really is just a matter of feeling your way to the answer as you did when generating the Truth and with practice this becomes second nature to you. Balance, as always, and a sense of calm is the key to connecting to these answers quickly and effectively. And you will know when you have found and released the conflict fully by the feeling within your Emotional Body. Once again you will feel a sense of relief, an expansion of your chest, a deep breath in and out bringing a sense of ease and relaxation, that sense of a warm loving energy leaving your body, or perhaps all of these.

And it really will be a relief to you to resolve this, for a conflict against your Truth can trigger in you intense feelings of anxiety, fear or anger as your Inner Being and Higher Self work together to bring you to the recognition of it. We say this only to highlight the power of a Truth. A Truth is not just a strongly or lovingly wording statement that sounds and feels nice, as we have said, it is Law. And when you conflict against a Universal Law you will know it, feel it, even suffer from it. Think carefully about the Truths you create and be aware that you will always be guided to conform to them. A wonderful position to be in knowing that once created, your Truth will always try to keep you Aligned to it.

Be aware that a conflict against a Truth can also occur if you act or think in a way that equates to resistance against it. As mentioned, you will feel it repelling against you internally when this happens and you will need to adjust your thinking or behaviour in order to quieten the reaction.

In a similar way your own Non Physical bodies can also work against you. Your protective Egoic Bodies or your Subconscious Mind, due to habitual patterns, may create fear for an experience leading you to continuously be needing to refer back to the Truth as a reminder to yourself that that experience no longer holds fear for you. For some, this referring back to the Truth may be constant due to habitual behaviour of your Bodies, depending on how long you have lived without these Truths. This advice is catering for all of those wonderful Physical Humans who have had very complex Emotional Journeys and are so used to being led by their Egoic Bodies and their Subconscious Minds and have a library FULL of Fear rather than Love labelled experiences.

Just know that in time this pattern breaks and it's a case of holding your Vibration, consistently holding onto it, and referring back to the Truth until new habits are formed in the way these Bodies work. Know that this fear state will not be your permanent state of being and in fact, you will re-train your Bodies to cooperate fully with you and your new Mind State.

A consistent approach of tackling past experiences through loving analysis, and with the understanding of those experiences wrapped into Truths can create significant Change for you. Freedom from the past is what beckons for those that choose to undertake this courageous activity.

Olivia and Raf, Abraham and Jesus

THE LAW OF BALANCE

Another Universal Law? And Balance? How can this be THAT important? We perhaps understand that there is a weight and a counter for everything. Where there is Yin, there is Yang. Where there is Dark, there is Light. Surely this is just part of the fabric of everything, this Balance...and yes, the answer is yes! Balance IS in the Fabric of All That Is. Balance is a fundamental Universal Law that blitzes through all ambiguity. Balance exists because it is utterly necessary.

And when does The Law of Balance truly hit a frequency that you can feel beyond all measure? Alignment. For with Balance comes Alignment. Physical and Emotional and Mental and connection to Self. All as it should be. Not weighted more directionally towards one Emotion or another. Feelings come in, feelings move out. Just a feeling of total Balance. Internally. There is no conflict that resides within. No internal dictator or pointer towards pain. No reminder of who you were, what you have experienced and a 'dragging' backwards. There is free, clear, Balance present.

And who can benefit? Absolutely everyone, no matter who you are, no matter your life experience. The Law of Balance is applicable and should also be an aspiration for you, a manifestation of sorts, if you will allow it. For once you have felt this powerful Universal Law within your Physical body, you will not wish for an alternative.

Yes, in life, you will explore more contrast, more elation, more sadness, more happiness, more doubt and more expansion, but a yearning will be within you for Balance. For this is the foundation of All that you Are. You, totally, in utter harmony. Your cells, your body systems all working exactly as they are meant too. No aches, no pains, no twinges. No worry, no background fear, no quickness to anger, no over the top gushing of love and hilarity whilst feeling underneath low and sad. Just Balance. Calm. Equilibrium. Effortlessness.

For this is what Balance represents. No effort. No searching, no reaching, no discovering, no analysis, no hunt, no revelation. Just Balance. Breathe. Feel. When did you last feel this? This belongs to you, this feeling, this is worthy of every bit of your attention, your focus, your manifesting capability and summoning of All That You Are. It is *that* worth it. So remember. Remember the last time that you felt this. It may have been moments ago. It may have been years ago, but whenever and however it happened, connect to this memory for you would have felt it. And so, you know this to be TRUE.

HOW DOES THE LAW OF BALANCE WORK?

With there being Balance and harmony in all things, in all places at all times, there would never be instances of contrast in anything. Everything would be in harmonious motion. Perhaps it is. The Law is in fact associated with the tipping of the Balance in order to create desires, in order to generate expansion which is ultimately rebalancing the Universe into a new expanded state of being. Constant motion. The Law is in motion too, when the Balance has been thrust too much in one direction and then requires re-balancing back to a more secure and stable place of being.

We have said that Balance drives Alignment. When in an Aligned state, you are not significantly one way or the other, you are not holding predominantly Low Vibration, you are in equilibrium entirely at that point in time. The Law of Balance however, because it is working in perfect harmony with all other Universal Laws does understand that You, here in Physical, need to create Desires, linked to The Law of Desire, The Law of Truth and The Law of Attraction in order to propel that attraction Universally and have it delivered back to you as a manifested, Physical experience. All in order to grow. However, that Desire can be and often is, born out of contrast. Therefore you will not ever experience one hundred percent Alignment forevermore in Physical, from this point on, even once you have eradicated the Low Vibration within and even obtained Emotional Mastery. For contrast is part of The Law of Balance.

This does not mean that if you have 'X' number of good moments, you will have 'X' number of bad moments to even the slate. This also doesn't mean that if you feel good most of the time, you will have a horrendous experience ahead of you to Balance your overall life experience. What this does mean however, is in order for you to move towards a specific Soul Contract aspect for example, in order to grow, you, and often many others in your influence circle, your Soul Group in particular, will require for The Law of Balance to tilt and tip in order for the creation of experiences to occur for you to grow from. Likewise, once the understanding has been achieved and true growth provided and established, The Law of Balance quickly shifts again to bring you that equilibrium.

To put it so simply, it perhaps feels like an ever-swinging pendulum active within your life, swinging you up and down, left and right and all those around you, and you are just clinging onto it in the hope that you don't fall off. If it was this harsh, this difficult, this Physically felt, it would feel terrible of course. We wish you to understand that as this is within the very fabric of the Universe, The Law of Balance is so much more subtle than this and once you tune more to it, you can in fact enact it, harness it, create it within. Leverage this Universal Law so powerfully that it helps you to manifest, helps you to generate a Law within The Law of Desire, helps you to Attract easier with The Law of Attraction and always, always utilising The Law of Truth, creating Truths that hold no conflict, hold your Balance and Alignment.

So let's go back to the contrast. If we look at this from a large scale to an individual scale to give context. Currently, much is being published and talked about and ruminated on with regarding the Earths Climate after the IPCC or Intergovernmental Panel on Climate Change, with less than twelve years (as of 2019) to Change the current conditions experienced in Physical before the Earth reaches a catastrophic crisis point. This is Global, at a Global scale. There has been the tipping of the Balance towards ease of use, ease of access, disposability, consumerism, creation, technology, all born out of human Desires. Now, and this is not new, this has been surging and Desires being generated, and the production of vast quantities of 'stuff' being provided, all because of the asking, all because of the Desires. Now, the Desires for care, for love, for nurture, for simplicity, for examining need and excess is growing, shifting, shaping the next wave of Balance and Re-Balance. Care for the planet and all those that reside within it, care for 'life as we know it'. Do you see how this works? In order to gain the insight, to have the care for Change in the first place, to start a movement so powerful that it becomes the norm, the experience must be had, the experience must be lived, the understanding must be achieved before it brings forth new Desires which then enact Change and enable growth.

Now, if we look at an individual scale. Let's take an individual who is Balance truly but not always so, and will not always be. This is ok. This is expected. For even in the utter Aligned state of being that this individual is, there will always be growth required. Growth not always born out of suffering however there has been that of course to get to this predominant Aligned state of being. Now, when contrast hits, the Balance shifts within but the downwards swing, it doesn't last. The individual recognises it for exactly what it is and relaxes into the knowing that this is growth, looks within and perhaps asks for guidance both from their Non Physical Family and her Physical family. This individual acknowledges the contrast, that feeling of internal discomfort. This fuels a Desire or two from a place of love which activates a powerful Truth, they let go and in doing so allow the Desire to be given in whatever way it needs to be. The individual allows love. And Balance, restores.

BUT I WANT THE HIGH!

This Balance stuff seems really boring. Who would want to just feel calm and even and Balanced? For anyone experiencing Emotional turmoil, Balance seems like an oasis in a desert. Yes, this may be in the moment, that feeling of the quest for Balance. When you are on the outside of it, it seems like a 'nothing', like a right, like an automatic 'something' that shouldn't need to be requested or even manifested, Desired! It should just be a basic part of the Physical Human experience. But when you need it, Balance feels like salvation.

Because it is Law, Balance is tuned to you. You do feel drawn to it. You feel the need for it. You feel the lack of it. The loss of it.

In this moment, feel the Truth of this, the understanding of just how powerful this Law is for you and for others. If not yourself right here, now in this Physical experience, there is someone that you know, someone that you care for that needs such a simple thing, Balance in their life.

For when this is the case, the swinging highs into euphoria, although lovely in the moment, there is always the expectation of the inevitable crash. Everyone, every single person who has experienced euphoria in this amazing enlightened state – it does not and cannot last for the frequency is way too high. So, rather than swing the pendulum of Balance into lower Vibration Emotion, how about swing from love to euphoria back to love. This is stable. This is possible. How about from enlightenment into peace? This too is utterly possible, utterly achievable. So, we do not wish to take from you the amazing Emotional experiences that you can have from being Physical, what we wish for you to understand is that the platform to move from is that of Balance, for it is SO much easier to feel super amazing and fantastic and then be left in residual feelings of love rather than swing lower, lower, lower still. The only way to achieve this is through Balance first, utmost, always and now.

CREATING BALANCE

We have said already that Balance brings Alignment, so is it only in an Aligned state that you can feel Balance? Or which comes first? Do you need to in fact feel Balance before you are fully Aligned? The answer is yes to this. Balance comes first always and in fact Balance is the stepping stone to Alignment.

So how do you do this? Depending on your Subconscious Mind State, Egoic Resistance, your Transitional and Stored Vibration, the answer can be subtly different. Overall, the key thing for you to understand is that in any moment, any moment of contrast, any moment of spiralling, any moment of suffering, you are still able to enact Balance.

Imagine a scenario where you are worried about money. You have been going along, feeling ok sometimes, feeling lack sometimes, feeling guilt sometimes, feeling hope sometimes, feeling concern sometimes, feeling excitement sometimes, feeling frustration sometimes. Swing, swing, swing. As many, many of you will know of The Law of Attraction and understanding this profile of Emotion and therefore energy, you will also understand that this swinging does not serve you. It starts to bring it to you, then it pulls it away, then it starts to bring it to you, then it pulls away again. Maybe a little closer this time, but you are not receptive to it. You are muddled on the wanting and the not wanting. So, right in the swing of things, when you are feeling fear of not manifesting the money that you need for the thing that you want. Try this:

Step 1: First, you MUST notice, this cannot be done without your participation, so notice, notice, notice that this is you, that this is what you are doing and that you are allowing and enabling the swing, swing, swing of Emotion and you do not wish to keep away from you the very thing that you are wanting.

Step 2: Close your eyes. Breathe, deep, long, slow breathes, just in and out for a few moments.

Step 3: When the fears start rising, you say and feel the following within yourself: I understand why you are here, but fear doesn't help me, it only hurts me, it only makes things harder for me. Feel this truly within.

Step 4: Say and feel right now: I only Desire Balance, no swinging one way then the next, just Balance, here and now, right here and now.

Step 5: Breathe and feel your Emotional Body activate with ease.

Let the Law work

Let the Law hear you

Let the Law activate within you

Step 6: Feel that Balance for the moment, then the next, then the next, then the next. Hold it for as long as you can.

WHY NATURE WORKS TO EASE YOUR VIBRATION

Many times you will have felt the need, the impulse to go for a big long walk, get outside and just breathe. You will want to feel the breeze on your face, see the trees, see a horizon, smell the smells, hear the birds and move. You feel better after the walk. Your thoughts feel clearer, you feel more Balanced.

The Law of Balance is utterly understandable when entirely surrounded by nature. Nature is naturally in Balance.

Everything about it. When you add 'mankind' to nature, often that Balance is disturbed. So if you are able, place yourself, even for a short time, where there is no manmade item in sight, no road, no houses, no construction sounds, no power lines or cell phones, just pure and utter nature. The Vibration of nature when uninterrupted is entirely High Vibrational and utterly in Balance.

When you are surrounded by this Vibration and you are surrounded by this natural Balance, you too are Physically and Emotionally impacted. For the cells within you that hold Balance, and there will be some, will start to quickly relate to and feel the Vibration of the natural Balance totally surrounding you. Your cells will then start to attract this High Vibration, allowing it in, allowing any transitional Vibration of discord to be released and instead matching all that you are being surrounded by. Pure Balance. Pure harmony. It is blissful.

The stillness of the air when by a lake in the middle of a deep forest with not a single other person around and where the flutter of a bird's wings are so clear and unfiltered that they sound like thunder close up, can be almost unnerving to us as Physical Humans. For we are so used to white noise, background sounds, interruptions to the Balance of nature in its most pure form and it can take a while for us to settle into the natural rhythm of Earth rather than the manufactured rhythm that we are often surrounded by.

Your Physical body needs nature, for without it, we are also somewhat manufacturing how we feel. We talk in this book about the Vortexes of Emotion and how through your Inner

Being you can generate any Emotion that you wish manually. This is a truly awesome part of how you learn to evolve Vibrationally but there is something very unique about connecting to the Vibrational power of the Earth. Attracting Earth's energy to you simply by being part of its Balance and allowing it to be connected to your own Physically held High Vibration is so powerful. But if you can't find your lake in the woodlands nearby, know that this energy still exists in places less peaceful. It exists in your house, your place of work, even in a busy shopping centre.

Tranquillity of the mind will find it because by locating stillness within, you also find and connect to your own High Vibration and it's with this 'point in time' connection to your own energy that you trigger the attraction of the surrounding High Vibrational energy to you. So, you can literally be in your kitchen on your laptop whilst the wind is howling and whistling and the kids are making their breakfast and still find nature's energy. And as long as you maintain that stillness and calmness you will stay connected to this energy.

And once you harness and get connected to this natural energy, you will be surprised how uplifted you can be by it, but also how strong it is. This Earth is a hugely energetic place and through connection to your Higher Self this connection to it becomes even stronger and more powerful, even in your kitchen.

Practice this in the busiest of places, for the greater the challenge, the greater your connection to nature's energy and the greater its powerful Vibration will become once you harness it, and hence the more Vibrationally stable *you* will become in your less natural and more manufactured daily world. You will be surprised just how Balanced you stay even in the most hectic of surroundings, just keep the mind still and the connection to Earth maintained. If you lose the connection just return to that place of peace in the mind and then search inwardly again for your own High Vibration and allow the agitation of that energy to attract to you the energy of Earth. This is also a great way of shifting out any Transitional Vibration that you have created in the moment so well worth trying.

This connection to nature's Vibration generates in you the Emotion of self-love and is the same Emotion that you generate when you meditate in other ways. But remember you are not doing this alone for this process is only achievable when connected to your Higher Self sufficiently to allow them to support you in this connection.

The greater the Transitional Low Vibration you are holding the harder it will be to find your own Physically held High Vibration, so try thinking about something that will make you feel good in the moment, or better still do something that will make you feel good. Something as simple as a hug will be enough to shift some of that Transitional Low Vibration out of the way just long enough for you to find your own Stored High Vibration and agitate it sufficiently to attract the Earth's energy.

And whilst this is the energy of the Earth that you are attracting it would be more exact to say it is the energy of the Universe. In other words, this energy which brings you feelings of self-love is the same as that which you feel when you connect to your Higher Self and any Non Physical entity for that matter. The difference being that when you connect to your Higher Self's energy you are setting an intention and allowing him or her to penetrate your Physicality with their energy whereas when you are connecting specifically to the energy of the Earth, you are attracting it's energy to you simply through the Laws of energetic attraction.

Know also that this energy that penetrates you cannot be held permanently in your Physical body. It is possible to have any energy, albeit High or Low Vibrational to penetrate you in what we refer to as your 'Conditional Energy', in other words the energy within you that is not generated by you but is influencing you. Know that Conditional Energy cannot be stored by you and therefore the absorption of another's energy, whether it is the Earth, another person or Non Physical is temporary. The absorption of that energy into your Physicality can however impact your own energy in a positive or negative way. So, the Earth influences your energy to create self-love and then whatever else is created by you as a result of feeling self-love; hope or Balance for example. In a similar way the energy of a small distressed child that is getting angry on a plane in the seat next to you can also enter your Conditional Energy and therefore their anger will generate in you always in the first instance the 'lack of love' Emotion, and from here you can yourself then go on to generate other Emotions such as anxiety, anger etc.

So, remember how nature works to influence your Emotions with either self-love or lack of love in the first instance and be aware that nature comes in many forms and that we Humans form part of it. Remember how to connect to your own High Vibration in order to pull like a magnet to you the energy of the Earth and the Universe in the most 'unnatural' of places, and remember that those most unnatural of places can work for or against your Vibration depending on what you allow yourself to connect to in that moment.

Olivia and Raf, Abraham and Jesus

MANIFESTING BIG

Great! I want a new car and a beautiful house and a lover and a job with all the money I could ever need.

No, we said manifest BIG.

Imagine yourself sitting on the ledge of your window looking out to a wonderful view with mountains and hills and perhaps the sea in the distance with the sun gently warming your face. If you're lucky enough to actually be able to see this from your window that's great but if not, just fully connecting to this scene will still bring you a sense of peace, of strength, of cleansing and of healing. The smell and colours of the flowers, you see a bird in the distance as you imagine that feeling right now of flying with it. Connect to this scene fully and you will trigger in you the Emotion Vortexes within your Inner Being. And as you feel the energy within your body rise, warming and lighting you up, know that you have just taken a big step towards being Aligned to the energy of the Universe. Feel the desire within you start to ramp up, perhaps triggering High Vibrational Emotions such as peace, joy, passion, and with this the sense of a new horizon, a new step on this wonderful Journey of yours that will bring you love, healing, insight, understanding and so much more.

In this moment how important is that new car?

Perhaps very important, if it's essential for you to be able to take your children to school or drive yourself to work. But if you start your manifesting for this car from a great feeling place, from that place of utter Alignment to the Universe and all that is within it, you open yourself to allowing the manifestation of all that the Universe has to offer, including the car. And whilst you may say it's much easier to manifest a car than connecting to the whole of the Universe, think again, FEEL again. Ask yourself which is easier to connect to, a sense of utter peace when you meditate to the feeling of looking out to the distant view of hills and mountains, or that Vibration that you seek to create, to manually generate as you sit by your table journaling about the car with your book or perhaps in front of the laptop.

Neither approach is better than the other and you must do whichever works for you, or both. But just know that you allow yourself access to so many of this world's wonders and pleasures when you manifest Big, when you FEEL Big, when you connect to the Big Emotions, those strong powerful Emotions that stir your desires and lift your spirit to that of God.

Often those strongest Emotions are those of our suffering

and so for those of you that feel downtrodden by life and unable to find that good feeling place, connect to your pain and to your hurt. But do so not with sadness but with love, knowing that this was all supposed to be for you and that this is growth for you. The statement "I don't want to fear any more" said in a moment with tears flooding down your face, or said with purpose despite feeling really low, is a moment of hope, of strength of knowing and is a Truth driven by your desire.

And in the creation of this Truth, if it is done whilst within the energy of The Law of Desire you trigger a wonderful Change around your desire, for it then becomes a Desire. So what does a Desire give you that a desire doesn't?

Firstly, the generation of a Desire, because it is done within the energy of The Law of Desire, will create the Emotion of desire within your Physical Body, hence it immediately fills you with High Vibrational energy.

Also when you create the Desire it immediately links that request, that need, that want to the associated Truth, which lies within The Law of Truth, and you may feel this connection in your Truth Vortex of Emotion if you are properly connected to the Self in the moment. The Law of Truth, and any Truths within it, are always connected to The Law of Attraction and so when you create a Desire, because of your connection to the Truth, you also connect to The Law of Attraction's energy and you will feel this Law's energy within you upon the creation of that Desire. The Feelset Tools section talks more about how to call the energy of The Law of Attraction, but just know that this happens automatically for you when you are within the energy of The Law of Desire as part of the creation of your Desire and associated Truth (The Feelset Tools section also explains how to call The Law of Desire and Law of Truth).

Finally, as long as you manage to stay within the energy of The Law of Desire, each and every time that you clear resistance to your Desire, you will again feel the energy of The Law of Desire as well as The Law of Attraction. See this as an amazing confirmation that your Desire is moving one step closer to being manifested.

At this point of confirmation you will also generate within you the original energy that was felt when you first created the Desire. Think about this for a moment. If you are able to replicate the generation of the High Vibrational energy each and every time that you clear down some resistance to your Desire then make sure that your original energy is as High Vibrational that it can be. In other words, don't just ask for something, instead say it as you feel it to your very core so that the hairs all over your body are standing up and your whole body is filled with a euphoric sensation of wanting and receiving. It's a wonderful thing to have this feeling within you when resistance to your Desire is cleared, and of course is yet more High Vibrational energy generated and stored within you for The Law of Attraction to connect to.

So we implore you take a moment before you start your journal or your appreciation lists, to connect to all of your own suffering or all of your joy and really FEEL your Desire and generate a Truth from it and then offer it to the Universe and to God. Know that in this moment you have the power and the opportunity to manifest all that you wish for. Let your energy build in this moment of request within The Law of Desire and let your pure love for yourself Manifest Big for you and others.

But whilst Manifesting Big allows the quicker receiving of that which you have requested to be manifested, the energy of creation alone will not generally be enough. For in the way of your desire or Desire are likely to be a number of skittles of resistance to knock down. We have already mentioned the amazing confirmation you will receive from The Law of Desire and the Law Attraction each time you manage to clear resistance to your Desire – but you need to act in order to receive this.

These skittles represent your fears and your doubts that act as resistance to manifestation and so connecting to these in order to understand the experiences and Truths that they relate to is key. Follow The Releasing Process with your Higher Self, find your new understanding about whatever these past experiences relate to and in doing so create your new Truth related to that past experience, and thereby start to reduce the resistance to the delivery of your desire or Desire.

Remember that only a Desire, and not a desire, will acknowledge to you when you have successfully knocked down a skittle of resistance. We would therefore always recommend that when asking for anything from the Universe, that you do it within the energy of The Law of Desire.

It is only by knocking down these skittles that you allow a

clear path to the energy of whatever it is you wish to manifest. Some of these skittles will be obvious. For example, if you create a Desire where you want to manifest more money but you have a fear of having it or of losing it, then this will most definitely get in the way of you manifesting more of it - an obvious skittle.

Perhaps a less obvious one for this Desire is having a lack of love for yourself driven by your unworthiness over something loosely related to money. A family member that has always told you that things never work out for you, or that has not shown you support when a previous job or business idea has failed for you, could instil in you an anger and perhaps even hatred for that family member over that matter. This would need to be resolved regardless of your manifestation request, but with regards to it, the fear over your ability to manifest money will be linked to this experience and your unworthiness and lack of love triggered by your belief that you're a failure in business or that things never work out for you.

The more specific your Desires the easier it is to root out these resistance skittles and so be aware that the broader your request, the more fears and doubts you will have linked to your manifestation request. I want more money couldn't get much broader, so link it to a purpose or a reason and this will lessen the resistance in the way of it.

And so, with the resistance to manifestation taken care of, all that remains is for you to keep your Transitional Vibration as Aligned as possible to the energy of your Desire. So if it's money that you have asked for and having money makes you feel empowered then go out and generate the Vibration of empowerment in every way that you can, for this is the strongest way to manifest to you exactly what it is that you have asked for and in addition, it will keep your Transitional Vibration and your Stored Vibration as high as it possibly can be. In other words, keep working on the process of letting go the past to improve your Stored and Transitional Vibration and do all that you can to generate High Vibration in the moment.

The Vortexes of Emotion are also an excellent tool here. So for this Desire you could try creating a simple Truth called 'Money' and adding to it the Emotions of empowerment, love, joy, safety, assurance, Balance and any other Emotions that you feel link you to having money. And then call it and call it and call it and call it and call it some more and in doing so, not only will you fill your Physical body with the Emotions that Align to your Desire but you'll also feel better just in the generation of these Vibrations within you.

And in addition to this Truth also create a separate Truth Bucket to the single Truth that you have just created called Money (The Feelset Tools explain how to create Truth Buckets). Call this Truth Bucket whatever you feel is relevant, and place in there statements and High Vibrational feelings of all the things that you wish for from money, including how it will make you feel. Call this Truth as often as you can also.

Trust in your ability to receive all that you ask for, be focussed with this but also calm and loving to yourself in doing so. And then just wait and enjoy as much as you can the moments where you feel like what you have asked for has already happened. Align to this concept for this is so powerful for you and will maximise all possibilities for you as you live your new Truths and so influence the wonderful Laws of Desire, Truth and Attraction.

Olivia and Raf, Abraham and Jesus

60

MANIFESTING BIGGER

Do this properly and you are unleashing a manifesting certainty. Does that sound of interest?

Yes it's true. Why? Because when you are Vibrationally capable you are literally leveraging the Universal Laws used for manifestation in a way that God is able to and in a way that he uses to manifest each and every Soul Contract to ensure that those items specified as pre-manifested will ALWAYS occur.

Unlike Manifest Big, where it is not guaranteed that you will knock down those skittles of resistance, with Manifesting Bigger, it is certain that the Universe will bring you to the points of resistance in your life experience in order for you to understand and resolve whatever it is that is stopping the manifestation of your desires.

Think about this for a moment...isn't that magical? Due to

the certainty of the asking, the desiring and the allowing in the moment, you also are ensuring that no matter what you hold within you Emotionally that will resist this from coming to you, the Universe WILL allow you to resolve it and the Universe WILL manifest your desire. This is the key difference between Manifesting Big and Manifesting Bigger.

We have a point to clarify before we explain the process for Manifesting Bigger.

A generated Truth that is created from a Desire or desire is stored in your Subconscious Mind as a memory and will always be linked to the Emotional energy in your Physical body which was created by that Truth. Your Subconscious Mind and your Physical Body together make up what is commonly known as your 'Vortex' for those who have read Ask and It Is Given and Abraham Hicks. In the case of the statement "I want to stop feeling fear" it's possible that you would generate the High Vibrational energies of self-love and hope and so these energies are held within your Physical cells and linked to the Subconscious Mind memory for that Truth, which was created from your Desire or desire. So, your Vortex in this instance is the energies of self-love and hope plus the Subconscious Mind memories attached to the Truth that you want to stop feeling fear. Think of your Vortex as multiple layers of Emotional energy and the linked memories in your Subconscious Mind.

The Law of Attraction, plus the Law of Synchronicity bring to you those things which match that which is in your Vortex (Subconscious Mind memories and Physical Body Emotions). For this publication we shall not detail more on the Law of

Synchronicity, but know that this Law is at the centre of all manifestation through ensuring that you are in perfect harmony, sequence, speed and design with your Vortex. Ensuring that you hold within your Physical Body as much of the like for like energies that match those held in your Vortex, in order for The Law of Attraction to bring them to you, is something that has been well documented by Esther and Jerry Hicks. Know that the clearing of the resistance is equally as important and it is the Law of Synchronicity which you Align to each and every time you 'knock down a skittle of resistance'.

Alignment to the energy of your desires is key as mentioned but also do not forget to act. We are not suggesting you try and detail exactly how a desire will be attracted to you, but you do need to create a positive momentum towards whatever it is you want in order for it to happen and you do this by following the nudges, the guidance that is coming from within. This means FEELING your way to that next step, that next action as this will be utterly Aligned to the energy within you of your Desire. Do not assume however that the positive momentum that you undertake will be the outcome for your desire to be achieved. In other words if you wish to manifest a $1,000,000 per month, not an unreasonable request if you are Vibrationally Aligned to it, and you are writing a book as your positive momentum, don't assume that the book sales will generate the money for you. It could be something completely different that does this such as a collaboration with someone or even a lottery win. The more you act and create that positive momentum around your desires the more energy you generate in your Vortex.

Ok so how do you Manifest Bigger? In other words how do you guarantee that Universal Laws manifest the specifics of what you are asking for. This doesn't mean that it instantly appears, for you are still bound by what is possible from a Physical Human perspective here on Earth, and this includes the time taken to clear any resistance to it.

The process entails working with your Higher Self. You do not need to be within the energy of The Law of Desire as is recommended when following the Manifesting Big guidance from the previous chapter. You must however, have the following in place in advance of generating your desire.

1. Dedication to Vibrational Mastery that allows you to hold in the moment of creating the desire an overall Vibration of greater than ninety percent

2. A non-resistant path to your 'love' Vortex of Emotion in the moment of creation of the desire

So, in the moment of wanting to generate your desire, find a place of pure High Vibration and if needed, release any Transitional Low Vibration which we suggest is done with the support of your Higher Self who will know what, if anything, is needed to be released in order to attain a Vibrational state of at least ninety percent. Remember that the creation of this desire does not have to be a conscious and deliberate act and could in fact be from a place of utter Emotion in the moment that generates a desire automatically. (Your Stored Vibration will need to be high in order for you to realistically achieve an overall Vibration of greater than ninety percent, and therefore we recommend that only those that have been following The Releasing Process for some time undertake this).

Then consciously connect to your Higher Self and state your desire. At this point of connection to your Higher Self you will need to generate a High Vibration and hold that Vibration for at least sixty eight seconds. The High Vibration that you use can be anything, so perhaps trigger your Vortexes of Emotion to create the Emotional energy of Desire or anything else that you feel in the moment that you know you can hold for sixty eight seconds or longer.

After this you will feel the energy of God's unconditional love connecting to your Gateway. There's no need for you to hold this energy simply allow it and feel connected to it until he releases from you which is normally around a minute or so. Enjoy this moment as it's a time to connect to the reality that your desire is going to happen and also to feel God's loving energy.

For a while after this energy exchange you will also start to feel extremely relaxed and a little euphoric. Know that this is the energy of The Law of Attraction connecting to you and again we encourage you to sit within it for a while and just enjoy it.

You will recall that when Manifesting Big, if you generate a Desire, by requesting what you wish for within The Law of Desire, you will also receive confirmation when resistance to that Desire is cleared down. With Manifesting Bigger there is no need to be within the energy of The Law of Desire as we have stated, however you will still receive confirmation that resistance has been cleared down. In the case of Manifesting Bigger you will receive the energy of God's unconditional love, as well as the energy of The Law of Attraction, each time resistance is cleared.

We ourselves, Olivia and Raf, have several real experiences of instant manifestation one of which came during our Awakening Journey where we manifested a gift from God. A gift of his unconditional love, given to us to share with others and something that we have since used to help those people that we work with that find themselves in a difficult moment, a moment when they just can't seem to escape that place Emotionally, mentally, Physically. This unconditional love from God brings a cellular release of that person's Low Vibration and fills the spaces left behind with God's own divine High Vibration.

Both of us triggered this gift at the same time but from different locations. A true miracle borne out of our desire in the moment to give love to the world, that also in part made positive that which was our own suffering. Raf on the window ledge connecting to all that had passed in his life, all the love and all the pain of his and Olivia's Journey's and in that moment as the tears ran down his face he offered them to God, to the Universe and asked that the energy of these tears were given to all that needed them, from a place of utter love for himself and others. At the same moment Olivia was writing a section of this book with such passion and with such intention connecting to the deepest love and support of the words she had just written as well as all of the wonderful hope and Universal understanding that this book could bring to others. In that simultaneous moment, from a place of purity and giving to all, we created a new Universal energy that we sensed had triggered something amazing. In fact what we had triggered was the manifestation of an additional energy, a call or prayer for help and giving, that was reciprocated to us by God as this gift of unconditional love from him and that we both felt immediately and that we now hope will bring comfort, release and healing to many others that call out for his support and love in the future.

This is the power of Manifesting Bigger and shows how you are able to harness your own energy to create something amazing if in the moment you have total purity of thought and intention, and clarity through utter connection to your own powerful Emotions.

Olivia and Raf, Abraham and Jesus

TRANSLATION

When we speak of Translation, you may in fact immediately think of what must happen inside the mind in order to interpret say, a different language or a complex mathematics or physics equation. Translation is the term that we use in order to define what happens within your Physical Body in order to interpret and communicate with Non Physical. Everyone has the ability to Translate, everybody has the ability to receive Non Physical and therefore this is not something that only the 'Gifted' few can do, but what is possible for all. It is through this chapter that we wish to more clearly help you understand that when we speak of Non Physical and communication, exactly what that means and how it works.

For Non Physical is Energy. Yes, it is vibrating at a different frequency and not everyone can see it, hear it or feel it, but it is there nonetheless. For some, they are literally tuned into this frequency and many can 'see' this Vibration and therefore are translating it already, even if they aren't sure why that is. In fact, every single person having a Physical experience already has Non Physical energy present within them, for that is the 'stuff' that makes up the Soul of you, your Inner Being. So this is why you should never hold yourself apart from this and see communication with Non Physical as purely something that psychics or healers tap into. Neither should you see it as something a bit weird or that it is only for the 'Gifted' few. It is time to demystify this Translation capability and see it for what it is, tuning into what already exists within and what already is available to you at all times. Tuning into Energy. It's that simple.

YOUR GATEWAY

THIS is THE Gateway. This is your access point to Non Physical. This is how you are able to receive and communicate Vibrationally with Non Physical, for all types of Translation, it is always and only through your Gateway. This is your point of access to All That Is. This is where you can now focus, understand and connect truly to the Physical access point to Non Physical within your Physical body.

Your Gateway intrinsically links to your Inner Being through the Pineal Gland before filtering through your Conscious and Subconscious mind. It is your Inner Being that is Non Physical energy. It is the energy of your Soul and also contains the energy of your Higher Self, and through your Inner Being you are able to receive Non Physical, with your

Conscious and Subconscious Mind then being able to translate the frequency shared in order to communicate.

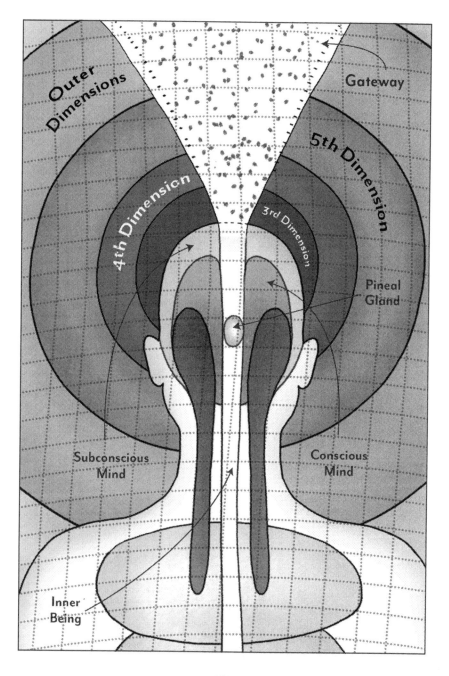

HOW DOES TRANSLATION WORK?

Non Physical energy resides from the 4th Dimension and beyond (more on this in a forthcoming chapter). Yet this energy is able to flow through into the Physical Dimension where you are having your Physical experience. Each individual Non Physical Soul, Higher Self, Entity, Guide, Watcher and so on has a unique energetic signature, making them uniquely 'them' in Non Physical. This energy maintains the signature associated with it and therefore even when buffering through different Dimensions, it is still is able to maintain energetic connection and association. As this Non Physical energy pools together around an individual Physical person, this is when the energy is filtered through and flows through the individuals Gateway in order to be interpreted.

If you are able to 'see' Non Physical energy, for example where some see lights clustered together, they may see almost ghost like energy imprints of an individual Non Physical entity, or a flash of an energetic face. This is all flowing through the Gateway, flowing through the Pineal Gland which is referenced by some as the 3rd Eye. This is the 'sight' that we speak of you see, because the image translation is partially happening here, in this gland, as the Non Physical energy is interpreted through the Pineal Gland and into the Conscious and Subconscious Mind. What also happens in the exact same moment is that the Inner Being, which is the extension of your Higher Self, is also translating this information. It is your Higher Self which is able to help activate the 'sight' and your interpretation of it. For some, this 'sight' is almost inside the mind, for others you can 'see' it in front of you. All of this is interpreted in the same way, the energetic frequency understood through the Gateway, the Pineal, the Inner Being, the Conscious and Subconscious Minds and when you 'see' it, it is translated through your mind as visual recognition as well as cognition.

Speaking of the Higher Self, we have explained that this is the easiest, closest Non Physical relationship you could ever have, literally because you are them and they are you. As you have some of their energy constantly running through you at all times, you are able to more easily 'connect' to them. This connection works in exactly the same way, if you think of their energetic signature, you already have that residing with you, therefore the Higher Self is easily and quickly able to directly 'be' with you in and around your Physical body. This is why so many find the Higher Self connection, once tuning has taken place, to be so powerful and the access to Universal insight and inspiration so more easily able to flow to you and through you. There is no energetic drain on you by connecting with your Higher Self because of this carrying of their energetic signature within your Inner Being.

Hearing, Knowing and Feeling are three other types of Translation that many are able to utilise. Often, it will start as just one type but if you continue to tune further and understand more, all other types can open up for you in your Translation capability.

When you 'Hear' Non Physical, it feels like you are having a conversation – almost with yourself...but not! Some can hear a distinct voice different from their own, a different tone, even a different sex depending on who you are Translating. Others hear their own voice but again, slight differences.

The Knowing is sensed, and it can be combined with the receiving of Hearing Translation we have spoken of. When you sense a Knowing you may assume it is coming from your own intuition and therefore not realise that you are Translating, but once you are more versed at communication with Non Physical you will know unequivocally that it is not coming from you. This Knowing you need to take notice of for it is a message from Non Physical that there is something not quite correct, or that something is correct and can be trusted, or perhaps just a strong indicator that there is something you really should be doing. Practicing Freefall as spoken of in an earlier chapter is a great way to attune to this type of Translation.

The other form of Translation is Feeling. Feeling led Translation can take many forms, it could be a felt tingle in the body, a tap on the hand, an energetic jab internally or even something even stronger or sharper that brings a little pain for a moment. A Feeling Translation also enables Non Physical to use their energy to move you Physically. This could be your hand in a psychic drawing, your fingers when typing a message on a keyboard, or a stronger connection where they can move parts of your body and even make you feel you are being pushed in a particular direction; all done with your allowing of course. Feeling Non Physical means you feel their energy as they connect to you but it also brings a connection via your Inner Being that can trigger your Emotional Body and therefore allow Non Physical to connect you through to Emotions that they wish you to understand

and feel. This is a wonderful and powerful means of communication which can bring you and Non Physical so much closer together in terms of your relationship with them.

Each of these different types are using the exact same method of energy exchange as we have explained with 'Seeing'.

TUNING

It seems for some that they are able to Translate Non Physical really easily, and for others, it takes time, perseverance and practice. What this comes down to often firstly is your Vibration. The Higher your Vibration the easier it is to tune to Non Physical. We will explain further how Vibration can effect Translation, but the other area we wish you to understand is about the Tuning process. Even with your Higher Self, there is an element of Tuning required in order for you to Translate their energy, their messaging, their communication with you. It is something that you 'both' need to do, so they need to tune to you as you do to them. This is exactly the same with your Guides, Ancestral Guides and Watchers.

What does Tuning entail? Consistent intention to connect, to receive, to allow is the best approach but often tuning also takes place without your knowing. Noticing the signs, the feelings, the messages and relating it to the connection to Non Physical, instead of passing it off as coincidence or doubting yourself, will assist the tuning. As you notice, as you stop doubting and start trusting, more and more will be given, more and more will be understood. It is the most exciting moment when you truly recognise your connection for the first time! As you evolve in your Translation abilities, you will just be able to get more and more flow and ease with it. There are some practical tips on Tuning with your Higher Self in The Feelset Tools section of the book to get you started.

HOW LOW VIBRATION EFFECTS TRANSLATION

As you now know, Translation is translating energy. It is an energy exchange and Vibrational Tuning and interpretation. As you will also now know, Emotions are also energy and you have both Stored Vibration and Transitional Vibration occurring within you at all times.

As Non Physical energy is received into your gateway, depending on how much Low Vibration is present, this can actually disperse and break up the Non Physical energy. You can see this in the diagrams as the Low Vibration is presented almost as a cloud. You can see that the Non Physical energy as a tight, compact, concentrated series of dots and as soon as it hits the Low Vibration cloud, it actually separates and spreads out.

This leads to Translation challenges, where something so beautiful and loving can in fact be Translated as something dark and sinister, in particular if the individual receiving the Translation is in an Emotionally dark, low or fearful place. Know that Non Physical never, ever generate or create any dark messaging. They will only ever offer loving messages but what can happen when you are impacted by your own

Low Vibration is that you will Mistranslate. For those who have had scary experiences in the past, know that this is why. If you were in a Fear Based Subconscious Mind State, for example either Resistant or Psychotic at the time, you would have had a LOT of Low Vibration occurring within the Mind in particular and therefore this could have Mistranslated the energetic exchange in the moment.

You can see in the second image that when you are High Vibrational, there is no energetic cloud which disperses the Non Physical energy and in fact, you are what is known as a 'clear channel' which means you are able to fully receive and interpret streams of Consciousness from Non Physical and once fully tuned, do this with total clarity, total insight and understanding. You don't question it. It is utterly clear for you.

This is another reason why we put so much emphasis on your Vibration, not just because it leads to a better life overall but because it gives you that certainty when you are communicating with your Higher Self for example and in particular, if you are sharing Non Physical messages with others. It is a duty of care you see, that you take this seriously and ensure that you prioritise your Vibration. Care for you first and foremost.

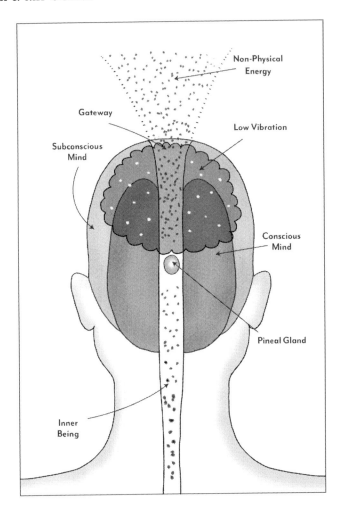

How Low Vibration Affects Translation.

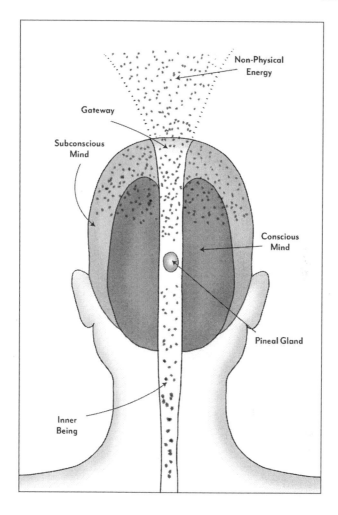

High Vibration Translation.

Tend to your Vibration as soon as you can should you be Mistranslating, and instead of passing it off as 'dark spirits' recognise that you are in fact generating this interpretation and just with some action on resolving your Vibration you will have a very, very different and positive experience next time.

Olivia and Raf, Abraham and Jesus

WHAT DO YOU REALLY WANT FROM YOUR COMMUNICATION WITH NON PHYSICAL?

So having understood the concept of a Soul, that you ARE two parts of the same entity, what is it you want from them? Many of us have been to a psychic medium for a reading, Raf of course often provides these. But for him the readings through Jesus take the form of a "Life Alignment" reading. In other words what he receives often links to the Emotional elements of a person's Journey, rather than looking to predict the future about a job or relationship for example. And whilst work and relationship guidance is something that he is more than capable and happy to receive on behalf of the people he works with, the focus is always on understanding more about what is happening in a person's life now and receiving guidance on how they can improve this to be the best that they can be.

So, we ask again, given what we now know about the Inner Being and the strong Emotional connection points, how do you want to use these, and in particular what, if anything, would you like in terms of support from your Higher Self with regards to this? For remember, your Higher Self will have lived many lives before this current one of yours, and with that will have accumulated so much knowledge and understanding; and you must know that they will be desperate to share it with you, all you need to do is ask for it. And in the asking of this, and the eventual receiving of it, just FEEL for a moment how amazing that could be for you. It is also now, with this new knowledge, that you can truly see how it isn't only the 'gifted' that have Non Physical access, but in fact each and every person has this available, so what is it that you are wanting from this connection?

The thought that they could guide and lead you in a direction that will allow you to connect to all that you truly are. For those Emotional areas within your Inner Being, the Vortexes of Emotion, are an exact representation of theirs, as well as all their previous lives, all their learning. And so by asking your Higher Self to guide you in connecting to your Inner Being and everything held within it, you start the connection to YOU. All that love, all that hope, all that strength, just there, within you, waiting for you, urging you to feel every part of it, to ultimately lead you to a place of utter Alignment. Consider that possibility next time you ask your psychic medium to tell you if you're to get a promotion soon.

And don't misunderstand us, the wonderful insight we can receive from asking questions about our family, our jobs our relationships can be truly amazing and can bring so much hope to the receiver. But just remember that the reason why our Higher Self or other Non Physical entities make themselves available to us is to help us achieve all that we set out in our Soul Contract, before we came to this life. So rather than asking them to tell you about your future, instead perhaps ask them how they can help you to influence it yourself.

Olivia and Raf, Abraham and Jesus

DIMENSIONS

There has been much talk of the transition to the 5th Dimension and that it is something that is happening now and we would like to say that this is true. For the mere fact that this book has been authored and all that are reading it, shows the expansion that is occurring in order to evolve. For that is what the 5th Dimension represents, evolvement both in Physical and Non Physical.

Is it possible for a Physical being to currently reside in the 5th Dimension? No, for the only way to permanently reside there is to be Non Physical and an ascended 5th Dimensional Being.

However can you access it? Yes! Do you need to evolve here in Physical in order to access the 5th? Yes!

What does evolvement in Physical mean? It means Alignment, Awakening and Growth, and there is plenty on this within this book to help guide you to a greater understanding of what you can do to get there. But, to put it simply, in order to access any Non Physical dimension, you must be a Vibrational match to it through your Higher Self, hence why the three aspects of Alignment, Awakening and Growth are called out.

Living 5th Dimensionally is also another concept, where you can live as though you are a 5th Dimensional Being here in your Physical experience. This references the same point which is the Vibrational match to this is required, as a 5th Dimensional Being is one at such a high frequency with such total clarity of thought. A Being with the ability of utter mastery of their Vibration and even though it is humanly possible, it is all about an Aligned state of being, all about having total access to the Self, connecting consistently to your Higher Self and living in a state of Balance, ease, love for yourself and others, living in truth and abundance.

What is beyond the 5th Dimension? Multiple other Dimensions. We have noted 26, showing up to the 25th Dimension as an accessible point and the 26th which is the Ultimate Dimension. The Dimension of God.

WHY IS THE 5TH DIMENSION SO IMPORTANT?

The 5th Dimension is the access point for Multi-Dimensional Beings, those that reside in the 5th Dimension and beyond. When we say 'access', this is to the Physical 3rd Dimension. For access directly 'from' the 25th Dimension to the 3rd as an example isn't possible because the Collective, the Master, the Non Physical Being is needing to be present within the 5th

Dimension first of all, in order to then access the 3rd. The exception to this is if the 25th Dimensional Soul is having a Physical experience as then of course, they have direct access.

There is Ascension required of your Higher Self, so that more and more become 5th Dimensional beings and beyond. At present at the time of writing, there are less than 10,000 current Physical beings whose Higher Selves are 5th Dimensional up to the 12th and only less than 300 current Physical beings that are from the 12th Dimension and beyond, but please know that these numbers are constantly changing, this is just a point in time. This means that most others are 4th Dimensional beings and it is here that things become so important when we talk of the Universal Expansion.

For Expansion means great, great things for the Universe and how do you expand? You GROW from this life, truly grow and by you growing, when you transition, your Higher Self also grows and potentially Ascends. And the difference between a 4th Dimensional Being and a 5th Dimensional Being? Substantial! As far as their capability energetically within the Universe and therefore their abilities Universally for aiding in creation Universally and active roles within the Universe. This is significant as far as the abilities that they are able to provide in Physical when having a Physical experience after the Ascension takes place.

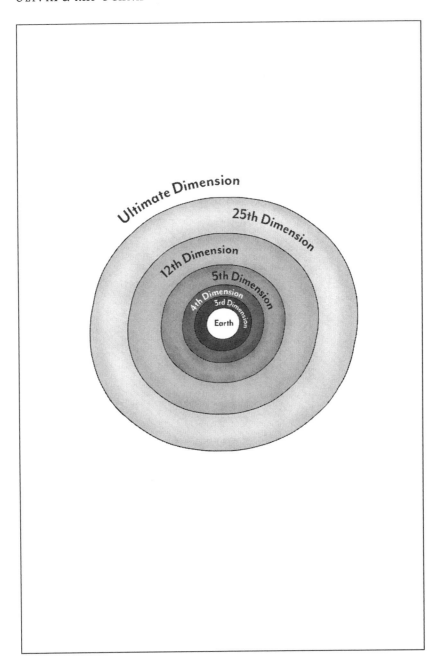

UNDERSTANDING DIMENSIONS

The planet Earth is the Physical dimension that is the 3rd Dimension and all that resides within it and above it. But why is it the 3rd Dimension? How did it get to be the 3rd? What is the 1st and 2nd Dimension (and not just from a string theory or theoretical physics perspective)? What happens after the 3rd? How far do the Dimensions go? What do the Dimensions represent? Where is God? What about the Archangels and Masters?

There is so much to understand, so much to give and offer as far as this deep and great insight and awareness. The commitment is as long as it keeps being asked for, more information will continue to be provided in further book publications which will expand on this. For now, we have given you a good feel, a base understanding of the current Dimensions, and we say the word current, for the Desire is to always Change, to always evolve and grow and this means Universally and Multiversally. This also means Dimensionally.

THE 1ST DIMENSION

What was and what is. The foundation of all that is known as the Earth, the planet, the existence. The culminating force of attraction, the cooperative components of all that was needed and all that will ever be needed in order to build, make, force, move, cohabitate in oneness. A Consciousness that was gathered, that evoked, that was created and was given by God. The desires that were born, the asking for life, the foundation for life, the knowing of what this was but all that was needed beyond it. This is the 1st Dimension.

Without it, nothing would ever exist on Earth. No Physical realm would be possible. God created and was creation and allowed and gave and was given. The Consciousness was created for life, for love, for capability and possibility. A home to generate a Physical existence and to be a part of the Solar System that is equally as essential, for that too was needed at the source dimension and is needed still.

THE 2ND DIMENSION

Moving from the Desire into the tangible reality of all that is needed to sustain life forms and sources of all kinds. The Consciousness that intelligently enables the foundation for reproduction, sustainment, renewal and sustenance. The formulation of environments, for form, for existence and longevity. The Energy alone needed in order to sustain a continuous environment for life, all life, this is epic-ness, magic, beauty. This is all that is now and all that was, all that is present and all that has been given for millennia and continues to be so and continuing to Change and evolve and adapt.

This is the 2nd Dimension, for which nothing could exist without it. It is the form of the sky, the atmosphere, the place in the Solar System, the air you breathe, the sea, the weather systems, the Earth beneath your feet, the foundation for growth and Change and life, all life.

THE 3RD DIMENSION

Physical existence. All that you smell and see, touch, hear and taste. From the grass growing beneath your feet to the sister at the end of the phone to the phone itself, the binary code that translates the call from point to point, the antennas and networks that allow the reception and translation. Form, matter, intelligence, energy, gravity, light, sound, water, heat, liquid, gas, oxygen and carbon. Cells. Consciousness. Density. Reality and Evidence. Physical form. Microcosm and Macrocosm. Desire. Emotions. Connection. The ability to renew. LIFE ITSELF. DEATH ITSELF. All within this dimension. Including connection to Non Physical as Non Physical helps, supports and guides the Physical Dimension.

THE 4TH DIMENSION

The first 'realm' of Non Physical, although in truth, Non Physical is present from the 1st Dimension through all Dimensions, so this is not exclusively the 'start' of Non Physical access dimensionally. The 4th Dimension is not a Physical Dimension, however it can be accessed by Physical Beings through Non Physical connection, through your Higher Self and accessed via your Gateway to your Sacred Place. The 4th Dimension is the energetic holding of most Guides including Ancestral Guides, the Higher Selves of most Physical beings on the 3rd Dimension, 4th Dimension aspects of Collectives, Watchers, Gate Keepers and the Christ Consciousness Transitional Gateway from the 3rd to the 4th Dimension and beyond.

As the vast population of Higher Selves reside here, this is a Dimension that with its close proximity to the 3rd it therefore has the closest access for Non Physical to aide in connection with Physical beings. There have been many references over time to a 'veil' but in actual fact, the 4th Dimension is right in the room with you as well as beyond what we can see with the human eye. There isn't a forcefield between you, not an invisible cloak that needs to be lifted, however a 4th Dimensional Being energetically has a completely different frequency to the 3rd Dimension and this is why most Physical Humans cannot see, feel or hear Non Physical unless the Non Physical entity chooses to Translate and communicate. You can however almost imagine this energy, this Dimension to be beyond the Earth, to where no human could go nor exist as this energy. This is where it is held expansively but the thing to reconcile is that it is also wrapped into the fabric of all other dimensions from the 3rd to the 1st.

Olivia has been given the most beautiful imagery of 4th Dimensional Non Physical beings, millions of them, on Armistice Day all collectively celebrating the human experience that was, as brothers and sisters in arms (including many of them that transitioned through war) and the joy of the growth of humanity and the love from them on this day surrounded the Earth from above it. Not only did they celebrate around the Earth but through the Earth, almost right the way through all of the Dimensions. So the visualisation that was given to her included 4th Dimensional Beings side by side with Physical beings, as wreaths were being laid in remembrance, as photos were being looked at, as lost family members were being remembered and energetic arms surrounded those that were viewing the photos. As appreciation was being shared and tears shed for all that was lost there were the energies of 4th Dimensional Beings energetically wiping those tears, feeling that love and reciprocating, right there in the moment.

4th Dimensional Non Physical Beings have only love to share and give but they do still experience aspects of contrast, although different to how it feels in Physical. There is nothing closer to you than your Higher Self who is literally living each moment with you and when you suffer, they do also – although not in the same way. Where the 4th Dimensional Non Physical Being is a Guide or Ancestral Guide or Watcher, they cherish you and are constantly by your side, helping your Higher Self to generate guidance and opportunities for connection but when you hurt, they also experience Vibrational sadness of sorts, although they have all the trust and faith in you always, unwaveringly, to get through it.

When a 4th Dimensional Non Physical Being transitions, their Higher Self receives all that was experienced by way of understanding and growth as does the Collective that they are a part of. The individual that was on Earth as an extension of the Higher Self remains as an individual Soul life but is eternally linked and woven into the fabric of the Higher Self and the Higher Self to them. This means that the individual soul is still accessible, still similar to their very best version of themselves as was in Physical and able to present themselves to their loved ones in Physical in a familiar way because of this. 4th Dimensional Beings are omnipresent also, so they can be in multiple locations at once although for a Non Physical Being that has recently Transitioned, this can be harder to maintain but after full re-emergence takes place, this then becomes something not only possible but fully enjoyed.

The energy is denser in the 4th Dimension in comparison to the other Dimensions from the 5th and beyond and indeed, the abilities of what the 4th Dimensional Beings are able to do energetically are also somewhat restricted comparatively. However they are still incredible in what they can do and how they can help and are essential for our Physical connection to Non Physical. For example, they know and understand All That Is but are not always able to interpret it to Physical with the total clarity that a 5th Dimensional Being and beyond is able to do. Also, their roles within the Universe are predominantly about helping, supporting and guiding through Physical connection and through the expansion of those in Physical. It gives them opportunity for expansion also, not just as a Higher Self but also as a non-Higher Self Entity who is acting a Guide, a Watcher or Gatekeeper as an example.

It is the God and the Universe's greatest desire to continue to expand and the way that this can happen is to increase the Non Physical presence within the 5th Dimension through Ascension of Beings from the 4th Dimension.

THE 5TH DIMENSION

There are less than ten thousand current Physical beings that have a 5th to 11th Dimensional Higher Self. This is amazing to understand. Why aren't there more? What will more mean? If ten thousand are Physical, how many are in Non Physical?

A 5th Dimensional Being is one that has experienced and grown significantly through Physical experiences, through lives and desires and growth, through suffering and joy. When they come forth into Physical, they bring with them all the wisdom, all the insight and clarity within them but they are a different unique Soul always, an extension of their Higher Self, with a new Soul Contract, always with more to learn, to grow from, to experience and ultimately leading to expansion of that Soul.

They also bring forth Gifts, accessible through connection to the Self, connection to their Higher Self. Gifts make it seem like we talk of something similar to a birthday present, but in fact Gifts are somewhat a reward for the Ascension through to the 5th Dimension from the 4th. Gifts can be more easily understood as abilities and influence, given by the Collective you are a part of and ultimately given by God. Abilities that are provided in order to enable the connection of people together in Physical, to communicate and inspire, to heal, to teach, to love easily. They have strong influence, whereby these 5th Dimensional Beings are taken notice of, they are listened to, they have a certain charisma or magnetic energy that compels others to hear what they have to say.

Often, when coming forth into Physical, their Soul Contracts and Journeys are agreed to be more challenging. All to enable that growth and expansion we speak of, but it does mean that it takes growth to understand and overcome these challenges, whether they are Emotional, Physical, mental, spiritual or all combined.

WHAT DOES THE 5TH DIMENSION DO?

Consider it like a bridge. The bridge between higher dimensions and the proximity to the 3rd Dimension. The frequency of Consciousness and Entities and all Non Physical beings beyond the 5th Dimension is too high to have 'direct' access to the 3rd Dimension and therefore the streaming of Consciousness is almost filtered from the 5th, through the 4th to the 3rd.

It is also a meeting point. For those of you who are Physical and 5th Dimensional, you are able to access the 5th Dimension through your Sacred Place which means you have the ability to communicate more fully with other 5th Dimensional Entities and also other Dimensional Non Physical Beings. If you are 5th Dimensional, your Higher Self of course is with you always and you do not need to 'visit' the 5th Dimension in order to communicate with her or him.

The 5th Dimension hosts hundreds of thousands Non Physical beings, all at various stages of Ascension through the 5th Dimension. As stated, there are just under ten thousand Souls of Higher Selves that are currently experiencing a Physical experience and this figure is constantly changing. The 5th Dimension is currently slightly more Balanced towards Female Energy, therefore more female Higher Self Ascension has taken place than male. This is important to understand as the Balance of both male and female energy is needed, but the shift in Physical from a connection to Self has been slightly more predominantly female. Currently, the returning to Self for women having a Physical experience is noticeable, even if you were to look around today, see who is truly engaging in the allowing of that connection it will be predominantly female. This is not to say that there are not many incredible, connected men having a Physical experience, but this is the Desire you see, to ensure that this full Balance and equilibrium returns. Do you feel the Truth of this?

WHAT COMES NEXT?

The 12th Dimension is not the next jump point so to speak. There are in fact incremental Dimensions from the 5th Dimension, so the 6th, 7th, 8th and so on. These are each higher ascended Dimensions, full of greater Universally expanded entities and the higher the number, the higher the ascension, the greater the Universal roles, the greater the abilities of the Non Physical entity and the greater the possible abilities of the Physical Human whose Soul has incarnated from their more highly ascended Higher Self. The ascension through these dimensions is all in preparation for the expansion to the 12th Dimension.

12TH DIMENSION

This is where Angelic Souls have Ascended to and is also where Non Physical Human Non Physical Energies reside, in other words Entities that have never had a human Soul and have never been on Earth as a Physical Human. The Frequency of this Dimension is immense and the Multiversal

Access that this Dimension provides is also critical to the Multiverse as all Beings within this Dimension and beyond are also actively participating in Multiversal activities and roles within the Universes.

There are currently approximately less than three hundred 12th Dimensional and beyond Souls on Earth at the time of writing, again this figure is subject to continued Change. They bring great abilities to the current Physical experience, but it takes an Awakening in order to unlock them. So just because they are present on Earth, they are not necessarily 'active' in their 12th Dimensional and beyond capabilities. They often have complex Soul Contracts in order for the necessary growth to take place and therefore, the disconnection from All That They Are can be significant and the Journey back to Self can also be challenging.

All 12th Dimensional Beings have their own Collectives within a broader Collective.

WHAT HAPPENS NEXT?

As with the increments between the 5th and the 12th, there are also the incremental Dimensions between the 12th and the 25th. It counts up from 13th, 14th, 15th etc. right up to the 25th, and then finally the Ultimate Dimension which is the ultimate Ascension point of where we explain up to.

25TH DIMENSION

The Ascended Energies from all Universes (we are part of a Multiverse) who are cooperatively co-creating and working together on the enhancement and evolution of the Multiverse. This includes the co-creation of what we currently understand and much of what we yet don't. For these ascended Energies are also Consciousness and provide incredible teaching and insight for ALL Dimensional Beings, including Physical Humans. For their streams of Consciousness flows through all Dimensions to the Higher Selves of Physical Humans and can be tuned into and received, although diluted somewhat from an energetic perspective as it buffers through Dimensions. This is why 4th Dimensional Higher Selves as an example can receive guidance and teachings from 25th Dimensional Beings. From insight on mathematics, technology, physics, biology, chemistry and so on, these Beings participate in sharing with love, all that is possible to understand and better help, aide and assist those in the Physical Dimension, as well as life within other Universes.

Many of the 25th Dimensional Beings are the heads of their own Collectives, containing thousands, some tens of thousands of Non Physical Human Souls. To give you an example, Hilarion is an immense Collective as is Quan Yin. Some of you will have heard these "Masters" names before, but these are in fact 25th Dimensional Beings with Consciousness and Teachings to share with all.

THE ULTIMATE DIMENSION

The Dimension of God and the Archangels. The ultimate Ascension. There are currently twelve Archangels who have had hundreds of thousands of Physical Human and Non

Physical Human experiences. Some of the details of Archangels that have been published over centuries have been mistranslated. This means that the naming of them, the energy of them and their abilities are misunderstood and without clarity. They are also some 'Unknown' Archangels, and there will be more details of them in future publications. The Higher Selves of Raf and Olivia, Adam and Ophelia, are two such unknown Archangels.

For this time, know that these ultimate Angelic Beings not only exist, but are actively participating in the growth and expansion of the 3rd Dimension as well as the broader Multiverse. They are ancient, beyond the calculation of time. They are not only close to God but beside God and omnipresent like no other Dimension's beings could be.

There is of course God, and God's ultimate energy resides here but God is everywhere, through every Dimension, through the Multiverse, right down to the 1st Dimension. God is present and exists in everything. Everyone has access to God, for that is God's greatest point of being and Everyone extends to All Things, in All Places, at All Times. Everyone includes Physical, Non Physical and Non Human Non Physical Beings, Entities and Energies.

The Ultimate Dimension also holds the Library of God and is the energetic library of the most incredible information about the Multiverse including the original history of the Archangels and life itself. Again, if it continues to be asked for, more will be brought forth in future publications.

Olivia and Raf, Abraham and Jesus

64

WHO ARE NON PHYSICAL?

YOUR INNER BEING

The extension of the Non Physical you that is pure positive High Vibrational energy. The unique you, here, in this Physical experience. The specific you that was created from your Higher Self, taking all that they are and generating a new Soul, perfect you, wonderful you. Your Soul. That magic combination of all that was and all that is and all that you represent in this moment, this time, this lifetime. All the hope, the desire, the growth, the possibility that is you. All within you. Accessible to you at all times. Constantly calling you. Constantly willing you to be you, to be free, to be All That You Are. To be more than you are today. To remember. Remember You.

YOUR HIGHER SELF

Your Higher Self has been discussed many times throughout this book and is fundamental to all that is taught by us. Know that your Higher Self is always with you and the energy of your Soul is made up in large parts by the same energy of your Higher Self. This entity can be felt, heard and even seen but there is no requirement to connect to them via another Dimension as they are with you right now, know what you are thinking right now and have felt all that you have felt since the day that you were born. Connection to your Higher Self is wonderful and enlightening if experienced to the fullest. Your Higher Self is your main conduit to other Non Physical Dimensions and ensures proper connection, disconnection and protection from all Non Physical energy. The strength of this connection is dependent on your allowing of it. Know that no special abilities are required to receive this entity but that they can be the most powerful Non Physical connection that you have and are critical in all that is within your Soul Contract, as well being a critical part of your Awakening Journey.

YOUR GUIDES

Guides are your Non Physical companions that have been with you since birth or perhaps have joined you along your Journey at specific points in your lives to help with you specific tasks or growth challenges. Your Higher Self is one of your Guides that will always be with you. Others have always been with you but perhaps not been part of your conscious reality until later in life. Your Guides can be part of the most loving relationships for you. At times your Guides will challenge you greatly and can even be the cause of some distress to you as they lovingly answer your questions for help, but perhaps not in the way we would always like it.

Know that there is nothing but love from them always and often they themselves are Vibrationally impacted by your experiences and therefore also feel and carry your suffering Vibration. Your suffering and your joy is always felt by you Higher Self and at times also your Guides. It this connection to your Vibration that also helps them to expand. All of your Guides will have a Soul Contract in Non Physical, and these may be linked to yours on Earth as you live your Physical experience and so they are hugely invested in loving and supporting you.

YOUR GATEKEEPER

A Gatekeeper is not always acknowledged or known by those connecting to the spiritual realm. For many they are silent and unnoticed but without them you would not be able to connect to the Non Physical dimensions to meet with your Guides. The Gatekeeper not only connects you through to Non Physical Dimensions but also ensures that once you disconnect from Non Physical, that no further access is provided to communicate with you, unless it is permitted by you or your Higher Self. Once in the Non Physical Dimension, they also allow you access to other higher Dimensions through portals if your Soul is not capable of visiting these higher Dimensions directly, which is generally the case. The same applies if you are lucky enough to be invited to visit another Universe, whereby your Gatekeeper will open a portal to the relevant Dimension in the other Universe to meet with the Non Physical Entities that reside there.

YOUR WATCHER

Watchers are literally doing what their name says. Watching you, guiding you, leaving you small hints and tips that you may or may not pick up on to help you on your way to get through a challenging moment, or to give you a leg up on something that you are really wanting to do. Think of them as the friend that's always there but not always known about. Watchers play a very special role and are often just as ascended as your Guides and always play a strong supporting role behind the scenes in terms of helping your main Guides to support you. Your Watcher is often referred to as your Guardian Angel but for this time, the Non Physical term Watcher is now wanting to be understood and clarified.

ANCESTRAL GUIDES

As with non-ancestral Guides these can be with you for life or just for a while. Ancestral Guides will often have an eternal relationship with you and be part of Soul Group relationships. Ancestral Guides can often be your first experience of spirit as the familiarity with them aids in a smoother step into spiritual growth. Often a painful experience with an Ancestor in this life is met with such sorrow for the Non Physical Higher Self of that Ancestor because they may have had many experiences with your

Higher Self in past lives which could have been full of love and joy, and so the difficulties of the current life and how you felt, and still feel about that ancestor, will conflict with the love that they feel for you in Non Physical.

MASTERS

Masters are highly ascended Souls that often are the heads of large Collectives. A Master will have had many lives and ascended almost to the point of an Archangel. Most are 25th dimensional Beings and on the whole, will offer something very specific to those on Earth. Masters have incarnated many lives often full of great challenges, similar to that of an Archangel. However, a Master often has a particular attribute which enables them to in each life, display a dexterity for something quite wonderful or powerful. These strengths often see them become people on Earth who are great healers, world leaders, wonderful poets and authors or experts in science, technology and energy. Masters make great Guides and usually come to help those that have a special path to follow on Earth, or that need to develop in a way that requires specialised assistance.

ARCHANGELS

The Archangels are the highest ascended Physical souls, the ultimate energies within their Collectives which are vast and plentiful. They are significant creators and influencers within the Multiverse. Each of the Archangels have had multiple human incarnations, they have lived many Physical Human life experiences, often with great challenge but also great notoriety, and of course will continue to lead many more. They have a close affinity to the 3rd Dimension, offering streams of Consciousness to it at all times and also by incarnating, providing influence, love, guidance and compassion within the Physical realm.

OTHER UNIVERSAL BEINGS

Abraham is a good example of a Being from another Dimension or a broader Universal Being. These Entities have never lived a Physical Human life and therefore do not have Non Physical Human Soul life experiences however, they will have co-existed with humans both on Earth and in Non Physical Dimensions as Guides, and provide the streams of Consciousness to support the Higher Selves of those having a Physical experience. These Entities hold great love for all that is human and often have played a significant part in the evolvement of the 3rd Dimension as well as all other Dimensions. They have access to other Universal Entities and because of this bring significant understanding and energetic abilities to astound!

SPIRITUAL COMPANIONS

Ever loved an Animal? Loved them so deeply and they you? Looked into their eyes and felt a true connection? Witnessed an amazing personality and the ability to give love and receive love?

Oh, this is the most precious thing and this indeed is a true relationship and one that can be Eternal. These are the

Spiritual Companions. A whole Non Physical energy that is Universal and Multiversal. Often, these Animals are domesticated by breeding, and well known pets such as dogs, cats, horses etc. form those Spiritual Companion relationships. These Animals each have a unique Soul in this current Physical experience, much like their human counterparts. They also have a Higher Self, so the same principal of this unique Soul as an extension of the Higher Self is also true for Animals. It is possible for the Higher Self of an Animal to incarnate as a different breed and sometimes, a different animal.

The Higher Self of the animal is linked to the Non Physical Humans Higher Self. This is why when you choose an Animal and you do this intuitively, it's *that* one that belongs to your family. It's how you know and often, why you choose them in the first place. Something within you recognises the connection.

Now, let us explain Animal Consciousness. There is a broader Animal Collective Consciousness energy which is the Collective energy for many mammals, insects, reptiles, birds, fish etc. having a Physical experience. These are often non-domesticated, wild animals that busy themselves in their role on Earth, facilitating, creating and evolving. But this Consciousness also extends to non Spiritual Companion domesticated Animals such as goldfish and also, animals that are used for human food. There is free will within the Animal that is incarnated, the ability to love and be loved and this can also extend to human interaction. In fact, more and more humans and different types of Animals are creating bonds and reciprocal connection.

This in fact is the evolution of the Animal Consciousness, turning some species within it from a Collective Energy into an individual energy. The evolved energy of the Animal that has generated this relationship can be created into a brand new Soul, which then forms part of the Spiritual Companion Collective. Likewise, more and more humans deciding to not eat Animal products, to ensure that Animals are protected and no longer used in certain industries is also creating Change within the Animal Consciousness.

Imagine the possibilities! Imagine the opportunities for expansion, for evolution!

Olivia and Raf, Abraham and Jesus

65

COLLECTIVES

Ever wanted to feel like you were really part of something? Like a team that will always have your back and that you are contributing towards something always? That all the knocks and the scrapes and the happiness and the joy and the love really does mean something, not just to you but to more than you?

Let us say that it does mean something. It truly, truly does.

This has never been expressed in this way, at this time, with such utter clarity. Every single person having a Physical experience at this present time is part of a Collective within the Universe, within the Multiverse. A Collective is a grouping of Higher Selves and Souls, all their Physical Human, Non Physical Human experiences, as well as Non Human Non Physical experiences, all shared and understood within the Collective. Ever growing, ever evolving, ever expanding. Your Higher Self can evolve to have their own

Collective and potentially within *this* life, that is what you can enable. That Collective will be part of a bigger Collective also. There are Collectives, within Collectives within Collectives.

A Collective will have a specific role, influence or theme. Take for example the Abraham Collective Consciousness. They are a collective of Non Human Non Physical Teachers, all who lean towards teaching, imparting clarity, wisdom, sharing of insight, enabling great communication and the flowing of highly complex information into comprehensible, resonating and understandable information.

How wonderful! Now, how does the Abraham Collective grow? This occurs through the Non Physical experiences of the Non Physical Higher Selves and Souls throughout the Multiverse and using these experiences to share within the Collective. Ever expanding that knowledge pool, ever expanding that desire for learning, for sharing, for clarity here on Earth via the Head of the Collective, Abraham, working closely with Esther Hicks and when in Physical, Jerry Hicks, and now also with Olivia and Raf.

Growth for Collectives also comes from other Collectives. For example when the streams of Consciousness from the broader Abraham Collective are being activated and received by the Higher Selves of those in Physical that are part of different Collectives. The questions being asked, and the guidance being given and the activation of that insight for new desires and then the growth of that Physical individual and the growth of that Higher Self because of it, all influence the Collectives that they are placed within. So intertwined.

So magnificent. So cooperative. So impactful. So exciting! And this is just the influence of ONE Collective that we speak of.

There are thousands of Collectives including the Collectives within Collectives, and more and more are being created. More and more are desired! More and more are evolving. But for what purpose?

Expansion.

This is the reality of the Multiverse. This is the Desire, the clear, clear Desire of God. For continued Expansion, continued growth, continued Change, continued limitless possibility, continued choice, continued freedom to choose, continued evolution. Evolution of the Physical experience, evolution of the Non Physical experience, evolution of the Universe, evolution of the Multiverse and beyond. Creation never stops therefore Expansion never stops.

This expansion started from the first Non Physical Soul energies ever created by God, the first Higher Selves, the first Non Physical experiences, the first Physical experiences, all evolving, growing, changing, creating, expanding, deciding. Then the grouping and forming of the first Collectives, the first 'like' energies, the first 'like' qualities and seeing the Expansion happen faster because of it due to the sharing of All amongst the respective Collective. The desires that it set forth paved the way to the sheer size of some of the Collectives and then the growing 'leaning' influence within generating a Collective within a Collective, maintaining that specialism energy but continuing to allow it to be shared within the broader 'like' energy of the broader Collective it is a part of. Such utter wonder if you allow it and such truth you can feel, if you allow it too.

So, which Collective are you a part of? Your Higher Self will be able to share this with you but this will take time and tuning. But if it is your desire to understand this, once you are in a regular and consistent flow of receiving from your Higher Self, ask!

There is more to come on Collectives in future publications from us.

Olivia and Raf, Abraham and Jesus

66

SOUL GROUPS

Have you ever felt that there is just an utter connection to someone? That sense of fate? That Sliding Doors moment, where just by chance you meet and BOOM, they are in your life and it is like they always should have been, it was just meant to be. Well...it was.

Of course, it was still your choice, but yes, they were always meant to be in your life. How long and how impactful and how deep that connection is, and grows to be, is down to both of you in your Physical experience. They are part of your Soul Group.

They may also be an eternal connection, which means that they are often your greatest love in this life (but not necessarily your only love) and in fact your Higher Selves' incarnations have had many romantic relationships over many different Physical experiences.

There have been many names for this over time, Twin Flames as an example and Soulmates are both very popular phraseology for this. But whatever you wish to call it, it is an Eternal Relationship, that is the preferred reference in Non Physical to name these very special and beautiful connections that are...eternal. It often means that these Eternal Relationships are also bonded in Non Physical and have important roles in the Universe or even Multiverse (depending on their Dimension) where they co-create together.

Do you perhaps feel a very strong connection to one parent in particular or one sibling or even one child? Again, parents, siblings and children are all part of your Soul Group in this life, but sometimes some members in your Soul Group in this life also have an Eternal Soul Group that means only some of your close family members are Eternal Relationships

With relationships outside of your romantic partnerships, so those with parents and children, siblings and even friends, there can often be previous Physical incarnations where they may have played different role. A close friend in this life may have had an incarnation as a Mother or a Sister in another life. A Brother in this life may have been a Son or an Uncle in another life. Now remember, these are the Higher Selves of the Soul Group that we speak of, not the actual individual Soul who you are close to in this Physical experience.

What about those Soul Group relationships that come and go? So those that you feel a strong bond with but then it fizzles out or things change and you don't keep in touch. Those relationships were all meant to be and highly likely that they were part of your Soul Group and again, may well be part of the combined Higher Selves' Eternal Soul Group.

There are of course, relationships that don't go so well. Ones that are even very close to you which are difficult, tricky and cause pain and distress throughout different periods. This doesn't mean that they aren't part of your Soul Group, that only good and sustaining relationships define a Soul Group member. What this does highlight is how Soul Group members are outlined often in your Soul Contract.

Your Soul Contract, defined by you, God and your Higher Self will often define specific Soul Group relationships that are necessary in order to facilitate your growth. Again, the detail will not be fully defined, all the haves and have nots, the arguments or the hurts, but the relationship and the growth required because of it will. Knowing this can really help you. They, in their role, are facilitating both your Soul Contract and theirs. You are also part of others Soul Contracts, again feel the understanding of this on reflection of some of those stand out relationships that perhaps have been brief but impactful for example, or those that have been particularly painful.

Soul Groups for this Physical experience go back at least to Grandparents, sometimes to Great Grandparents. This is also amazing to consider, for each of those key relationships in your life, and then the relationships in their lives, the intertwining between other Soul Groups, this is all defined, created, managed energetically, each going back to their Grandparents. This is a specific role of an ArChangel, one of the Unknown Archangels which has been spoken of in the

Dimensions chapters, which more will be written about in future publications. There are other Entities and Higher Selves who support the ArChangel who are in other dimensions specifically related to the energy mapping and coordination of the Soul Group makeup's and bridging between Soul Groups. It truly is energetically magnificent to comprehend!

So, next time you feel that true sense of connection, feel into if it is a Soul Group relationship. Ask your Higher Self for more insight on your specific Soul Group relationships and if you are waiting for your Soul Group Partner relationship to come, just Vibrationally prepare yourself in the knowing that they will, and ask your Higher Self to help guide you in the preparation to be ready for when they do!

Olivia and Raf, Abraham and Jesus

67

TIME

Why is time irrelevant to Non Physical? This is purely answered by Earth bound Physical understanding. Time is relevant, but relevant only to the individual. For if you take a perspective from one person, one being, one Dimension versus another then the perspective can be different.

Take an example. You have a wonderful person, living a very busy yet fulfilled life, and yet there is something wanted, something that is missing. That person would feel better in the having of it, for this there is no doubt. The only thing that makes them feel something other than contentment and the ability to relax into the unfolding is time, that sense of when, that clock ticking. Unable are they to relax into the feeling of all is well, all will happen in divine timing...the clock ticks. They watch the clock. They judge the movement based on it.

Now, from another perspective, perhaps a colleague, a friend, they look at this person and say...aren't they wonderful! What a fantastic life they lead...how can they achieve so much, how are they able to understand and do all that they have and continue to do? This is something to be celebrated...they move so fast! They sense time as irrelevant also in relation to this person, in fact they celebrate the success in all that they are able to accomplish in the time they DO have and potentially then reflect on themselves. They suggest in a consolatory way that perhaps they would be able to DO more, would it not be for time. But this is yet another example.

Know that with Non Physical, this is Non Physical perspective, we understand that everything happens in perfect Alignment to that individual, to that knowing, to that perfect place of space and time and ALLOWING it in and therefore a judgement on the when is of no consequence. So, when it actually happens, time is literally irrelevant. For it does not matter how many seconds pass, all that matters is that you are lining it up, you are moving towards it and bit by bit, clearing your Vibrational pathway to make it so.

Time is a pressure that Non Physical do not feel, yet understand entirely, for time feels for many like a sentence, that there is short supply, there is limited and finite amounts of it and personally so. Know that with the reading of this, you are slowly understanding that for you, here in the Physical experience, time can become just as irrelevant and if you are able to surrender to the 'right' time, the time that is ultimately for your good, the time that suits all of the workings of your immediate environment, your circle of influence – it comes faster.

Likewise, time is utterly profound in that it can always be understood. In our ever changing world, it feels a constant. There is however an important angle to always consider, which is that of Perspective. Perhaps by thinking of Perspective, who is looking at the clock and judging if it is the correct time or not, which constant is it beating to, then this is a way to release you from the confinement of time and instead, allow you to celebrate in discovery of what it is that you want and then the allowing of it to take place into your experience. Until your last day on Earth, time is literally irrelevant, and even then, you are welcomed back into Non Physical and therefore time becomes beyond irrelevant.

For it is in the moment of your return to Non Physical that you will recognise the irrelevance of time to your existence. Feel yourself letting go of the behaviours that link you to the ticking clock and in this moment you feel what it is to live in the Non Physical realms with regards to time and time itself. We wish for you to undertake a lesson with us here and now on the irrelevance of time in your very moment of reading this.

Take a pencil and a piece of paper and write down everything you wish to accomplish today. At the end of the day return to this piece of paper and tick off those things that you have completed and then highlight those that remain not started or incomplete.

Now ask yourself, of those tasks that you did not get through from your list which of those absolutely need to be completed by today and which of those can wait? Now from those that can wait ask yourself of the value and importance

479

of them in your life and how much they steer you towards your ideal path or life, or indeed steer you off it.

Can you now see why assigning time to a task is pure folly without an association to the true sense of the task in relation to your life overall?

Think of it this way, if you can justify to yourself that a task or a wish or an aspiration will benefit you immediately then that in itself is worth a focus. For all other things bring yourself into Alignment of what you truly want, and the Vibration needed to achieve it, and follow this not with a sense of time but a sense of allowing and achievement of its eventual outcome. Time, and the completion of a task alone, will not bring this to you any quicker no matter what you are looking to complete, albeit a lifelong ambition, a complex maths equation or a simple job around the house.

We bring you to another understanding on this example. Imagine that once you have ticked off everything on your list you sit happily at the end of your table or on your couch feeling extremely happy that you have got through the mountain of tasks and jobs that fill your day and drive your ambitions. How do you feel? Satisfied perhaps, but for how long, for tomorrow brings the next list and the day after brings another and another, and so the story goes on, as does time throughout this process.

So, time is now linked to your satisfaction and happiness in this example. But what if these tasks didn't exist, what would you do with your time? Consider that if the only reason that time is important to you is to get through those things that lead you to the point of temporary satisfaction, then surely there are better ways to live? And perhaps we can offer you one small piece of advice and that is that the next time you make your list, take away the element of time and add a column named 'importance to my life overall'.

Olivia and Raf, Abraham and Jesus

CHANNELLING A COLLECTIVE CONSCIOUSNESS ENTITY

Firstly, we wish to advise that we are all connected, yes this is entirely correct. There is not a hierarchy as such, nor 'levels' as have been communicated through many books and previous teachings, there is however more Ascension and Dimensional differences between Non Physical. This is an area we wish to break down for you here in a brief explanation, so that it becomes clearly understood by you.

There will be much more detailed information available in other books that we work with Olivia and Raf on, as you can imagine, this subject alone is incredibly large. For this time, this explanation will enable you to have clarity and confirmation of all that you need to be aware of. Yes, we understand that this will spark many questions all of which we will enjoy sharing with you so know that those questions will be answered in time.

As we have described who Non Physical are, this helps you

to build a picture of who it is that you are wanting to communicate with. The guiding principal that we would like you to understand is that over time and through your consistent approach and your tending to your Vibration, your ability to receive from us here in Non Physical will improve. You may even receive more and more if this is part of your path and Soul Contract expansion. Do not ever be disheartened should you 'only' be able to work with your Guides and Higher Self, for they are your gateway to broader perspective anyway. Your Higher Self is able to receive Collective Consciousness and also can help translate any higher Consciousness messages to you. There are some Guides who have a specific affinity to another Consciousness and therefore it will be your Guide that will be able to further interpret this messaging with you. Likewise if you 'only' develop an incredibly strong connection to your Higher Self and don't necessarily connect with your Guides, this too is perfectly valuable and for many, all that you need to understand.

We wish to respectfully bring up the perspective of channelling, for channelling is a sophisticated experience for an enlightened and Vibrationally Aligned individual. Channelling messages directly from Non Physical is of course possible, as you can feel, see and experience with the words in this book and our work with Raf and Olivia in person. Know that there are few Physical beings that are able to channel in this way, and in particular with a Collective Consciousness energy and there is a specific reasoning for this.

Collective Consciousnesses, Masters and Other Multiverse

Dimensional Beings are incredibly careful about who in Physical they work closely with. This is purely because it is essential that the messaging remains clear, the focus of which must be kept contained and pure. But also, the Vibration of these entities is immense and takes intensive Tuning from both parties in order to communicate well and so individuals are chosen carefully for this activity and it will also be part of their Soul Contract, always a choice of course, as to whether this individual decides to progress with this.

This means that the Collective Consciousness for example, effectively becomes the individuals Guide. Through the individuals Higher Self that connection becomes stronger and in particular if the Physical person's Vibration is extremely high. The Higher Self is the key receiver and exchanger of Vibration and is the gateway to all other communication. Know that this means that the channelling of Collective Consciousness is to be treated with the greatest respect, as all good relationships are between Physical and Non Physical.

The clarity of message is essential for all Non Physical but in particular a Collective Consciousness energy and again the reason why only a few people are selected to Translate and receive. Imagine if you will hundreds of books with varying Vibrational Translation and messaging coming out from Abraham or Jesus. People would not know what to read, what to believe, what to trust. We say this only to confirm that whilst so many would love to be the messenger of these types of communication, it takes someone whose Higher Self is highly ascended to be considered to be a Channeller.

There are many that have claimed to be able to Channel a Collective Consciousness energy such as Abraham, Christ Consciousness or God and know that everyone has the ability to access them but most only through their Higher Selves. Most often, when you feel you are receiving an energy such as this, it will in fact be indirectly in this way and not directly. This means that you are more than likely receiving the principles of what that Collective Consciousness communicates through all that know and hear their messages, albeit Physical or Non Physical. Therefore you are not receiving any words in that moment from the Collective Consciousness, but rather streams of Consciousness and therefore Translations from your Higher Self of what that entity Aligns to. As long as you are in a High Vibrational state of being when you receive these words from your Higher Self, the words given will be accurate and Aligned to whatever the Collective Consciousness entity gives. Your Higher Self will never misinterpret them, nor any other Non Physical entity for that matter. Note here the important reference to your Vibration, as you will read in the chapter about Translation, Low Vibration will impact your Translation capability, even from your Higher Self.

We wanted to write this chapter to help clarify for those of you that may feel you are connecting to these Higher Vibrational entities directly. Ask yourself if you feel you are truly ready Vibrationally to receive. Ask yourself if these Higher Vibrational entities are acting as your Guides. If you are unsure as to the answer then it's most likely that you are receiving via your Higher Self and not directly. Still a wonderful thing to be able to do and we encourage you all to try and do this, ensuring respect for the Non Physical communication protocols and in particular whilst being in the highest possible Vibration.

For clarity, at this point of publishing only Esther Hicks, Raf and Olivia Ocaña can Channel Abraham directly. There are many who can receive from Christ Consciousness but only a few are able to Channel him directly, Raf and Olivia being two of them.

We love you.

Abraham and Jesus

6 9

FAILURE

When first starting out, be prepared to stumble along the way as you commence your Journey to connect with Non Physical and remember that this relationship is two way and they are learning to communicate with you just as you are with them. Consider that you are sharing the experience together, perhaps Non Physical are able to understand the best approaches for communication with you, be it visually, sensory or more clearly stated using words in your mind. Whichever approach is used be aware that as you develop the Translation capability with each other, more routes will open up and it is often not unusual to find that connection with Non Physical utilises all the options available.

We wish to highlight to you that failure is actually a good thing, for it is in the finding of difficulties or challenges that both parties are able to iron out the kinks and make for a great and clear channel in the long term. Belief in what you are receiving is often the biggest stumbling block for a beginner and we say only that you must trust in what is being received from the very first instance for you will be receiving something. What is important is to be relaxed about what is or isn't being received and do not place yourself under any pressure to perform a miraculous experience from the off. Likewise, do not compare against another's Translation capabilities or experiences, for everyone is unique! Some things take longer or perhaps a shorter timeframe and if you compare and wish to be like someone else, you are potentially stopping the flow of what is uniquely you and your Translation capabilities which can be extremely different from another person.

Bring into this Translation process your intuitive feelings and you will find that this will make the connection far stronger, as it is what you feel and not so much what you see that is important in the beginning. Trust yourself and over time you will learn to accept everything that is given as you tune, as you trust, as you come to understand more and more. Keep this going for a long enough period of time, and you will quickly find yourself a few rungs up the ladder in terms of your confidence in the process as well as your ease with failing. A failure gives you the chance to analyse and to try again and with this mindset you WILL succeed.

Olivia and Raf, Abraham and Jesus

PERSISTENCE

As discussed in the previous chapter, continued attempts and trust in what you are receiving will lead you to the place that you need to be when it comes to Non Physical Translation. We separate this subject into a new conversation because it is important for us all to understand that persistence is what has made this world the place it is today with regards to the abilities of Physical Humans to communicate with Non Physical.

Persistence is what has allowed Raf and Olivia to be who they are today despite many challenges for them. So understand that it is with persistence that Raf and Olivia will continue to speak our words and it is persistence on your part in the same way that will bring you to your own place of understanding of how to translate with Non Physical, and also to your own acceptance and definition of what the messages that you receive mean to you at the time.

Persistence is also extremely relevant when it comes to the connection to the Self, connection to your Higher Self and the willingness, in fact, the dogged determination to ensure that you continue to release all that is holding you back from living a life of freedom. Living a life of Love, not Fear.

Abraham and Jesus

71

COMING OUT OF THE CLOSET

Coming out of the 'spiritual' closet in many ways can be compared to 'coming out' in the traditional sense of the word. This is by no means looking to make direct comparisons, nor say one is worse than the other, and we are certainly not looking to offend anyone that has been through the sometimes very difficult experience of making known their sexuality or gender in this world but we use this term as a much broader perspective you see.

We speak of the liberation of you, being able to be freely you regardless of others oppressive opinions. However, there are some comparisons that can be made which ultimately lead to a very similar Emotional experience, driven by the judgement, prejudice, discrimination, anger and even complete disconnection of those that we have shared our spiritual beliefs with. For those of you that have been through the process of publicising your spiritual beliefs will perhaps know from the responses of those people that you know or love, that this can be a very painful experience.

Even today, a conversation about spirituality can be extremely taboo such is the strength of belief, or disbelief. 'Seeing is believing' is a well-known phrase and often this is the benchmark for people's perspectives on Non Physical and our abilities to communicate with them. And yet with such little knowledge of the subject, people can take such negative positions and form such strong beliefs contrary to your own, often considering the spiritual individual weird or delusional for even daring to believe, for daring to even talk about it.

And so we wanted to say that it's important first and foremost to be proud of your spirituality and to know that for all of those that you meet that make you feel like you are doing something wrong, there are many, many more that will think that what you are doing is wondrous and exciting. So seek these people out, even those people that don't believe that what you are doing is real, but believe in you. For these people can give you so much motivation to persist, and in doing so release you from the negativity of those that may criticise or isolate you.

But perhaps the most important guidance we would give you in all of this is to understand that those that don't believe are entitled to do so. We have no right to change their view or enforce ours. And if these people are close friends or family, the only thing you can ask of them is that they unconditionally support and love you. And in turn, you must unconditionally love them regardless of their views or how they have made you feel.

Understand that their Journey has brought them to their particular spiritual belief and if their Journey also does not allow them to bring themselves to support you, understand that there will be good reasons for this also, and that their love for you is there, even if they aren't currently showing it. In taking this approach we can assure you that you will free yourself from any hurt you may feel from the judgement, discrimination or misunderstanding of who you are. And know that in doing so, you truly are able to feel the benefit of your unconditional love for them through the sharing of that love with yourself and further enabling that true connection to your Inner Being and your Higher Self too.

Remember, it's a privilege to believe that this is real. And if you do, you are one of the lucky ones. So, persist, persist and persist some more.

Olivia and Raf, Abraham and Jesus

72

PATIENCE AND PERSPECTIVE

Non Physical will not share with you information that they do not feel you are ready to receive or that your current perspective may not be open to understanding.

This may be expressed as a simple confirmation from them that they are not able to answer at this time or perhaps they may only provide you with a short explanation or clarification. There are also times where you will receive silence, so no answer either way, no sign that this is not to be discussed right now.

You may feel that this is somewhat unfair, or that Non Physical are holding back on you; please know that this is never the case. There is always a reason, always a 'for your ultimate good' position which you may not know now but you will understand later. Once you have been communicating with Non Physical for some time, you will be able to reflect back and see this as true understanding. It is always the same, that you were simply not ready for that information and you will feel not only clearly that understanding of 'divine timing and unfolding' but somewhat grateful for the delay in the detail.

Consider that you are ever-evolving in this relationship with Non Physical and that in this opening of the mind, you are in fact enabling greater and broader perspective. This takes patience, nurturing, trust and belief. This isn't something to force or to get frustrated with, although understandable at times.

Understand that there is always a reason for it. Understand that if you enable your perception to be broadened and trust that this will be the case, allow the expansion if you like, you will enable more and more answers, clarity and communication. Your perspective will start to Change and when this does you will be able to receive so much from Non Physical.

Olivia and Raf, Abraham and Jesus

73

WHAT IF?

Let's think about this for a moment. For anyone reading this who is feeling somewhat challenged, perhaps their own internal logical, evidence based mind is spinning and thinking "surely not, this can't be true". What if it is? What if it just is. What if this is the truest of the truest truth? What if this is all not only possible but actually happening and you are able to allow it into your experience here on Earth, in this life?

What if you were able to let go of every single thing that is holding you where you are? What if you were able to literally feel the freedom that you so desperately have been searching for but found so hard to find?

What if the only thing that you needed to do was choose and keep choosing? What if the easiest way to do this is to choose love over anything else? When you are feeling irritated by a conversation, when you are feeling tired and worn out and things are just getting on your last nerve...you choose. Choose to allow love in, in that moment. Choose to understand that it doesn't really matter in that moment. Choose to be present. Choose to be fully aware of your Emotions. Choose to stop the negative spiral. Choose to see it for what it is. Choose what you need in that moment. Choose to ask, "What is it that I am meant to understand here?"...and allow your Self to truly answer.

What if everything that has ever happened to you and those that you love is just as it was meant to be? What if the Universe truly is impacted by what you think and feel and therefore your stretching experiences, the ones that have taken you to your limits, only caused you substantial growth and therefore in doing so continues the expansion of our Universe, even the Multiverse in the understanding of this? What if everything you feel matters? What if you have the ability to utterly Change your life by staying right where you are in the same Physical spot?

What if you understand perspective? That everything that happens and is happening is only interpreted by perspective, by yours, by someone else's. What if other people's perspective isn't necessarily wrong? What if your perspective isn't necessarily wrong but if it makes you feel bad, the only thing you need to do is to feel your way to a different perspective? What if your life can Change just in this knowing?

What if those that we loved more than anything but are no longer with us in our Physical experience are accessible to us entirely, so much so that you feel a stronger connection with them, a more regular ability to communicate than when they were here? What if there are people you love in Non Physical that you don't really know so well, but there is no time limit on your relationship and therefore you have the ability, the natural ability to come to love them more, understand them and know them?

What if you have access to feeling good, no matter what the circumstance, no matter what the situation and when you don't feel so good, you are able to navigate your way back to that good feeling place and fast? What if your predominant experience in this life, from this point on is lightness, happiness, clarity, fun and Balance?

What if you are able to feel your way through your day? What if you are able to stop the incessant thoughts and mental dynamism of all the things you are pushing for and just trust, relax and feel? Feel first.

What if all the people reading this book who are angered by it, challenged by it, feel that it is wrong. What if you are proved wrong, with tangible evidence either now or in the future? What if you don't agree but can feel happiness for those that do? What if you instead choose to keep an open mind?

What if those who are suffering with Physical illness or pain are able to tune into their own energy, tune into their own Emotions and understand and influence their cells into releasing what is no longer serving them? What if miracles do exist, that the incurable can be cured, the medicated no longer need the medication and we are able to trust our bodies and help our bodies to not only heal but regenerate?

What if we all have access to infinite intelligence? What if we are able to come to understand things beyond what is written, filmed, communicated, photographed, scanned, imaged and archived?

What if? What kind of world would we have? What kind of lives would we live? What kind of Physical Humans would we be?

What if you choose today? What if you choose love? What if you choose to BELIEVE?

Olivia and Raf, Abraham and Jesus

IV

FEELSET TOOLS

CREATING AN AWARENESS LIST

FEELSET TOOLS

Where do I start? This is one of the first questions we get asked so often. With the Higher Self Connection, this is the most powerful way to really get through The Releasing Process however, this new relationship for many takes some Tuning and some time and often, you want to get going with all this new insight and understanding in this book. So here is one of the first things that you can do.

Awareness is such an amazing thing, because for so many, you go about your day feeling all these feelings, but sometimes they are just a general feeling of say overwhelm, or anxiety, distress or unhappiness. Also, so many wake up in the morning feeling low and then lean on different tools in order to lift their Vibration, but actually what is happening is underneath, these Emotions continue to drip through, like a Dripping Tap and many are just suppressing them or ignoring them altogether. Now you understand about your

Transitional Vibration and how if left, these Emotions continue to top up through your day, even if your Conscious Mind is working overtime to distract you from it by thinking different thoughts, with your positive outlook and perspective on overdrive as you try to ensure you stop feeling these feelings. The thing is, you can't kid the Subconscious Mind, and you absolutely can't kid the Emotional Body, you feel the feelings regardless you see.

It may feel counter-intuitive for all those who use positive mindset tools to act on this Feelset, but one thing you would benefit from connecting to is the word 'Awareness'. For how are you able to understand the reality of YOU if you are avoiding the reality, suppressing the reality, ignoring the reality? So, Awareness is key, for this honest and deeper reflection of what is truly happening within gives you the foundation place to start and also the place to go to from a releasing perspective.

Take a pen and paper or a little notebook and have this with you as you go about your day

You are likely to not need this for too long, perhaps 2-3 days at a time in different periods as you go through the Releasing Process

Step 1: Catch yourself in a moment, you will have Low Vibration Emotions that are surfacing, perhaps due to a situation or an experience, this could be on waking, this could be a conversation with someone, before you are about to do something or something on the television as examples

Step 2: What was the 'trigger'? – note this down briefly

Step 3: What are the Emotions you are generating? – If you have a generic feeling of 'low' or 'anxiety' try to delve deeper into your Emotional repertoire. Often, these will be things like jealousy (comparing yourself to others), lack of love, lack of hope, anger, frustration, sadness, disappointment, guilt, shame and many more to choose from

Often you will feel 'fear' but try to again delve deeper – Fear of what? Fear of loss? Fear of Lack? Fear of failure? Fear of the unknown?

Step 4: Continue through your day and be really honest with yourself

Keep noticing, noticing, noticing and just create this Awareness of you

After a couple of days, you will have a much clearer understanding of the Emotions that are being generated. Some will be consistent through a variety of different experiences, so different 'triggers' but same Emotions. Some Emotions will be unique to specific experiences.

Continue with your connection with your Higher Self daily and move to The Releasing Process to understand some of this new Emotional Awareness at a deeper level so you can start to let it go.

75

FREEFALL

FEELSET TOOLS

Conscious Feeling. This is incredibly beneficial for you and surprisingly challenging for many to adopt, because for so many, it is the Conscious Thinking that is leading your day to day experiences. We wish instead to help you understand a new way of being, this is where you are predominantly Feeling Led through your day rather than being led by your thoughts, your practiced, habitual, organised thoughts.

Now, we hear you say, how can I actually do this? I have the job to do, the meeting to attend, the kids to sort out, the dinner to cook – oh, darn it, the supermarket to get to because I have the dinner to cook...how do I fit in all the things I need to do, plan for, sort out AND FEEL my way through the day? Surely what you are asking me to do is impossible.

Firstly, the good news, we aren't asking you to do this all day every day...unless you want to! Secondly, this is an amazing Feelset which will actually help you tune with your Higher Self. So not only will it help you get into that flow of you, help you to feel your way through five minutes, fifty minutes, five hours, however long you can, but it will also allow your Higher Self to help guide you in the moment.

How do you do it? You feel! Yes, but how? Try this:

Allow yourself just five minutes to try it to start with

Step 1: Get yourself into a nice relaxed feeling inside, know that this is fun and something to practice

Step 2: Now, what do you FEEL like doing or even not doing? Right now, in this moment

If you start thinking of the 'list' of things that need to be done...Feel again

If you don't know or can't connect to what you feel like doing or even not doing...Feel again

Step 3: Got the Feeling? So just go with it, fall into it, keep feeling, does it feel good? What's next? What feels so good to you right now? Go with that, fall into that, feel that.

That's Freefall!

Do it as often as you possibly can, for as long as you possibly can! Allow it to become second nature. Notice when you are thinking...not Feeling and Feel instead.

How does it help you? You start to get tuned into that Inner Guidance that is always flowing to you, but this Inner Guidance comes from your Higher Self you see. So allow yourself to get out of the way (ie. By stopping using your Conscious Mind all the time and instead allow yourself to FEEL) and purely enable this Guidance to come, it will flow to you in the moment. We know many of you have a list of 'things to do' that have a deadline. What you may experience is that by living Freefall in the moment, you may actually Feel inspired to just get on and do one of those things on the list, even if the deadline isn't looming. You just want to do it, feel inspired to do it then and there, and guess what? It takes half the time, because you are in total flow with it, it's easy you see.

But also allow yourself to be uninspired, to just take a moment and connect to something simple and easy for you. If you feel like allowing yourself to become a little low in the moment then do so as this will enable the flow of that negative energy to start to release itself from you. As long as you're not permanently fixed in this state of being then this is actually the greatest self-love you can give to yourself. We can go through our lives not allowing ourselves to let go for fear of failure or judgement so the more you allow Freefall to take you to these other Vibrational places the better equipped you will become at getting out of them. For in ignoring them and pushing them inwards you act against Freefall, and in so doing you fail to grow and move forward. So don't question or hate yourself or your life when in this place of allowing Low Vibration to surface. Soon will come the clarity as to what to do next, so trust this and your Higher Self to guide you through this and into a more High Vibrational state of being.

So all of this starts to establish more and more Allowing of that Guidance. The more you Allow, the more Guidance comes, the more ease that is created, the more flow you experience. Try it, then try it again, and again until you are permanently in a place of allowing, of Freefall.

76

PRACTICAL GUIDE FOR CONNECTING TO YOUR HIGHER SELF

FEELSET TOOLS

Connecting with your Higher Self is an incredible experience and one that we encourage you to do daily! You may already have experienced a connection, in fact those subtle intuitive feelings are your Higher Self guiding you, you just may not have been aware of it yet. The following steps show you how to connect more strongly and allow this connection to grow stronger and stronger by the day. By connecting in this way, this will enable you to really start The Releasing Process and also the Creation of Truths, alongside many other incredible benefits.

Before you start the connection process, ensure you are somewhere undisturbed and ideally not in a rush or having something to do soon after. This is a really enjoyable, expansive relationship that benefits from you being as in an allowing state as much as possible and giving yourself some time to do so is a great way to start.

You can be sitting down or lying down, whatever feels good to you. Over time, this will become second nature and you may adapt it to whatever works for you too.

Step 1 – Allow your body to completely relax. Feel your body and your organs get heavy, allow your heart beat and blood flow to slow and if you feel comfortable doing so imagine your blood thickening as you do so. You can bring yourself to a complete standstill where all that is moving are your lungs, and the rest of your body and your mind is still, yet fully functioning

Step 2 – Set an intention in your mind to invite your Higher Self to connect with you. Allow your Higher Self in, feeling them come closer to you and surrounding you in their loving divine energy

Step 3 – Set the intention to allow their energy to be absorbed into your Physical body. Feel them flow into your chest and into your heart and then expand throughout the whole of your body and head. Feel their energy push itself outside of your body to create this warm protective glow all around you

Step 4 – Now share with your Higher Self your own love. Feel the Love Vortex of Emotion over-spilling with your love as you exchange your own energy with that of your Higher Self. Now allow yourself to just bathe in this for as long as you wish. If you can try and hold this connection as you go about the rest of your day. Know that Low Vibrational thinking and feelings will somewhat disconnect you from them a little, sometimes more predominantly, so if you feel that they are not 'with' you or you are struggling to connect, just focus on Balance and allowing.

TUNING WITH YOUR HIGHER SELF

You will have read and understood hopefully a lot from this book regarding your Higher Self. This is the most incredible relationship, one that once you start to connect, is truly liberating, exciting, life enhancing and so special. We cannot emphasise enough just how wondrous this connection is and also how it can truly help you as you go about your days, navigating your Emotional experiences and continuing to grow. The very, very best friend you could ever dream of having, right there with you, whenever you need! Only ever wanting the absolute best for you always.

For some people, they are able to connect with their Higher Self with ease, fairly simply and quickly. For others, it can take quite some time. Everyone is unique, so please don't ever feel that this is something out of reach or impossible for you to do. What this connection to your Higher Self needs is Tuning. You Tuning to them, them Tuning to you.

So, how do you Tune? Here are some suggestions, but again you may well be very inspired by your own connection, so Freefall your way to it as well as giving some of these a try. Consistency is also a really important factor. If you dip in and out of trying to connect to your Higher Self, it can end up being a little frustrating, especially if it is taking some time to Tune and you start to feel like it is hard, rather than a really magical and enjoyable experience. Keep consistent and ideally this means daily. Be persistent, really enjoy this special unfolding and try not to see it as a task you have to do, but something wondrous that is just yours to enjoy.

Non Predominant Hand Drawing

This is an excellent way to Tune and a great exercise to do prior to your Higher Self connection process. If you are right handed, use your left hand for this Tuning Exercise. If you are left handed, use your right hand for this Tuning Exercise.

Step 1: Take a pen and paper

Step 2: Put the pen in your non predominant hand

Step 3: Set the expectation that your Higher Self will connect easily to you

Step 4: Ask your Higher Self to guide you and tune to you

You will feel that your hand becomes lighter, almost like the weight has been lifted, it is like they are taking your hand. This can be subtle or quite strong, but just know that this is happening.

Step 5: Allow your hand to be guided across the paper. This is often in straight lines, zig zag's, spirals etc. This Tuning isn't going to be pictures as such or anything particularly meaningful (unless the guidance from your Higher Self is otherwise) but more about energetic frequency between you, and most importantly about you allowing the connection. Ideally watch the pen move, but try to stop your mind getting in the way. You will notice if it is because you will start to doubt, question etc.

This will likely only take a few minutes, but you can elongate the timeframe if you are really enjoying it

After you have tried this, it can be a great idea to then move straight to the Higher Self Connection Process.

Writing with your Higher Self

This can be really useful and the start of 'conversations' with your Higher Self. You choose if you prefer to write with a pen and paper or if you prefer to use a keyboard. This may start out just with one word or a sentence, but it can tune to a steady flow and stream of Consciousness. This is such a wonderful way to communicate and again, you must get yourself out of the way with this as you almost move into a space where you aren't thinking, questioning, you are just allowing the flow.

Before you start, choose the way you want to write and get prepared. Make sure you are nice and comfortable and not in a rush to do something next. You can do this before the Higher Self Connection Process or afterwards, either is fine and you may find one is better for you than the other.

Step 1: Hold your pen or get ready to type

Step 2: Set the expectation that your Higher Self will connect easily to you

Step 3: Ask your Higher Self to tune to you

Allow yourself to just relax and feel in flow

Step 4: You may feel an impulse to write a word or a sentence, so just go with it or you may feel an Emotion or almost an inspiration. Whatever it is, just write it and then once you have written it, don't run over and over it, just wait for the next word or sentence

You can ask a question of your Higher Self, keep it simple to start and then allow the answer in. This Tuning can be great as you can really start to see the growth of your connection incrementally over the days and weeks.

Joining in on a Favourite Pastime or Activity

Often, you LOVE something and it brings you great joy and pleasure, well, your Higher Self is likely to be really experienced in it from previous incarnations or something similar and will have so much to bring forth into this experience. Consider doing this thing, whether it be cooking or gardening or playing an instrument or participating in a sport...whatever it is, they can help you, guide you, give you inspiration and a new perspective. How amazing is that?

This is very simple. Before you start the activity or pastime set the intention or a direct expectation that they will be with you, then, feel the difference to normal. It may be that you get more in flow, so it is so much more effortless. It could be that you get some new inspiration, for example if you are cooking, you might add a little more of this ingredient or a little more of another, or something totally new and different. You may feel much more confidence and something that perhaps used to cause you concern or even fatigue with it, you just feel more lifted and lighter. The key with this is to challenge yourself in a mental or Physical way

518

as this will really help with the tuning. So if you are cooking try to hold the saucepans and ingredients containers in the opposite hand that you would normally use. Try it because it really does work.

This is something to really enjoy and have fun with!

77

CONNECTING TO YOUR INNER BEING

FEELSET TOOLS

You can be standing, sitting or lying down, whatever feels most comfortable.

Step 1: Close your eyes and take in nice long deep breaths in and exhale, and as you are breathing, set the expectation that you will connect beautifully to your Inner Being, that you will activate the pure positive energy within you, that you will feel the flow of this energy and be able to move and shift out anything that is a lower Vibration to leave you feeling Balanced, present and clear

Step 2: Focus now right in the centre of your mind, feel the activation of your awareness as you hone in on your pineal gland, feel your pineal gland fill with pure white energy and as your awareness of your Inner Being becomes clear, your pure white energy moves from your pineal gland and activates your Inner Being as it flows down through the base of your brain, down through your throat, your chest, your stomach and into your pelvis

Take a moment to tune and feel this energy

With your connection, you are able to experience the true vibrancy of this energy that is within you, know that this is you, this is all that you truly are, you vibrate at this frequency within you at all times, this is accessible to you at all times

You may feel a building of momentum, that your Inner Being loves your connection, is willing and able to help you

Step 3: Feel your Inner Being energy expanding out, moving in all directions, coating each and every cell

Feel the pure positive energy vibrate at the highest frequency within you, feel any lower Vibrational energy that has been held start to shift out from its current position through your body

Step 4: Feel your Inner Being's energy surround the lower Vibrational energy and sweep it up and start to flow and move this energy up through your body, out through the top of your head, and out into the air around you where it disappears and cannot be reabsorbed

Step 5: Feel your Inner Being's energy, almost like a fountain, continue to flow out through the top of your head and out around your body, down through to your feet and flow back up from your feet, up through your body and out through your head and continue to allow this flow

Step 6: Feel your entire being full of all that you are, full of pure positive energy

Rest in this feeling for a moment

Breathe and when you are ready, you can open your eyes.

78

CONNECTING TO YOUR BODIES

FEELSET TOOLS

This is step by step the Energy Practice that has been created in order to feel Your Bodies, to connect to them in the moment and actively deflate the Ego, connecting to your Inner Being and releasing any Low Vibration that is currently active in your Transitional Vibration. You can ramp this up even further by first connecting to your Higher Self and doing this with them. This is a fantastic Feelset to use in the moment if you are in the Psychotic or Resistant Subconscious Mind State.

Step 1: Close your eyes and take nice long deep breathes in and exhale and as you are breathing, set the expectation that you will connect to your various Bodies, that you will begin to feel a greater awareness and understanding of them and how they protect you, influence you, and how to activate them to help you let go and be present and aware in full of all of your bodies.

Step 2: We start in your Conscious Mind. We understand the role of logic in our lives, but it is time to stop the automatic responses with the practiced thoughts and behaviours stemming from our Conscious Mind. Feel this understanding. Feel the triggering of an alert to you, so your awareness becomes more full and your focus becomes more present.

Step 3: We move now to your Subconscious Mind, your trigger place for evoking memories, the past, the re-activation of things that are not serving you. Feel this knowing. Feel the calming of the activation. Feel instead your Truth and present sensors switch on, your Vortexes being activated, the Truth of YOU, here, now, in this moment.

Step 4: Your Egoic Bodies, on both sides, feel the supportive and protective expansion. Notice how full it is, the space that it holds, the sense of purpose and resilience. Feel how it extends into your Emotional Body. Feel how your Subconscious Mind expands it further when activating Low Vibration .

Step 5: Now move to your Emotional Body and really engage the expanse of this body. Feel how it encases, enwraps and fills you from the top of your chest to your pelvis. Feel how it activates now, allowing more present awareness, how do you feel now? Right now in this moment?

Step 6: Feel the connection to your Egoic Bodies, your Subconscious and Conscious Minds, here, now in this moment. Feel the understanding that you have, that you are more enlightened now with this new awareness, that you are engaging further than you ever have before with solid detail of all that you are. Feel your Egoic Bodies reduce in size, a small shift, allowing more space in the perimeter of its holding within you

You know yourself. You are yourself. Now we move to the Self as we activate your Inner Being

Step 7: Right in the centre of your mind, your pineal gland, we activate using pure white energy, pure positive energy, running from your pineal gland down in a cylindrical tube to the base of your pelvis, right in the core of who you are

Feel the activation of your Inner Being, then fast and rapid expansion of your energy as it moves into your Emotional Body, absorbing, activating, loving, caring, moving out any Lower Vibrational Emotions as they rise up and through the Egoic Bodies, know that you are being protected but it is safe and time to let these go. Find the new space that your diminished Egoic Bodies have created and allow the flow into your Conscious Mind. You do not need to analyse these Emotions as you let go, you just need to allow the release, and now they flow into your Subconscious Mind, the final place to relieve you of this and now out through the top of your head, out into the air around you, out into the atmosphere

Step 8: You are fully activated, you are solid within yourself, you are knowing of the Self. You are one with your Higher Self, with God, with the Universe. You are beloved to all, you impact all and right now, you have vibrated at a new frequency and the Universe will match it. Breathe.

This exercise is a great activity to undertake in order to Align yourself to Freefall more successfully as you will connect more strongly to the way that you FEEL.

CALLING THE LAW OF BALANCE & OTHER LAWS

FEELSET TOOLS

This is a repeated section from an earlier chapter in the book detailing The Law of Balance. This is for those moments when you are really up against it Emotionally, when you are in the Resistant or even Psychotic Subconscious Mind State and you truly desire Balance only but are struggling to get there by other means. The Law of Balance enacts quickly and overrides any Egoic Resistance in the moment, therefore no matter what is happening with your Transitional Vibration at the time, this will supersede it and create peace within in that moment.

Step 1: First, you MUST notice, this cannot be done without your participation, so notice, notice, notice that this is you, this is what you are doing, you are allowing and enabling the swing, swing, swing of Emotion and you do not wish to keep away from you the very thing that you are wanting

Step 2: Close your eyes. Breathe, deep, long, slow breathes, just in and out for a few moments

Step 3: When the fears start rising, you feel, I understand why you are here, but fear doesn't help me, it only hurts me, it only makes things harder for me...feel this truly within

Step 4: Feel, right now. Say to your Higher Self "I desire Balance". Acknowledge to yourself that you desire no swinging one way then the next, just Balance, here and now, right here and now. Connecting to The Law of Balance generates the Emotion of Peace within you and this helps to shift Transitional Vibration

Step 5: Breathe and feel your Emotional Body activate with ease

Let the Law work

Let the Law hear you

Let the Law activate within you

Step 6: Feel that peace and find Balance in this moment, then the next, then the next, then the next. Hold it for as long as you can.

If Fear sneaks back in, just repeat it.

Note that you can replace the words "I Desire Balance" as stated in Step 4 with the following to connect to the energy of other Universal Laws:

Law of Desire – "I desire Desire". Connecting to The Law of Desire generates the Emotion of Desire within you

Law of Truth – "I desire Truth". Connecting to The Law of Truth generates the Emotion of Honour within you

Law of Attraction – "I desire Attraction". Connecting to The Law of Attraction generates the Emotion of Contentment within you

Connection to these Laws in this way brings Balance overall for a period, and will reconnect you to any of the Vortexes of Emotion that may been blocked by Egoic Resistance due to Low Vibration.

80

THE RELEASING PROCESS

FEELSET TOOLS

The basic principles of letting go the past are detailed in the following steps. The key point to note is that this process is ALWAYS done with your Higher Self and that none of this is consciously driven by you. Instead allow yourself to receive whatever it is that your Higher Self brings through to you in the form of downloaded thoughts and feelings. This process sets about purposefully relabelling your Fear Labelled memories in your Subconscious Mind to Love Labelled memories and if done correctly, will also remove any Egoic Resistance to the Inner Being Vortexes of Emotion for each and every memory, thereby controlling all the Stored and Transitional Low Vibration generated because of your past experiences.

It is essential that you have gone through the Higher Self Tuning activities before commencing this process. You must be able to receive downloaded thoughts and images from your Higher Self in order to proceed.

Step 1 – Your Higher Self will highlight to you a Low Vibration or a series of them that need to be addressed that link to a key experience. Note that often people mistake these feelings as 'just another bad day' but know that when you have set the intention to shift you Vibration with your Higher Self, that they will start to prod you and will continue to do so until you address what it is they are making you feel.

Step 2 – From a place of tranquillity allow yourself to receive the experience from your Higher Self what these Emotions link to. You will be reminded of a past experience that caused you a serious level of distress and that has continued to manifest itself in other ways in experiences since then and to the present day. You will be taken through the Emotions that you felt at the time, not to relive them but to allow yourself to remember just how much you went through and suffered. The details of the experience will be replayed a little like a short movie in your mind also.

Step 3 – Further understanding of this experience is applied for a broader connection to the events. For example, if there were others involved, then insight as to why they acted in that way at the time to hurt you is brought through as well as the understanding as to why you acted in the way that you did. All of this in order to try and Change your perspective of the situation. This is often the hardest part of The Releasing Process but it can be totally freeing when we understand how others came to be so disconnected themselves. This is not about forgiving the other person but simply about trying to find compassion or love for them. This compassion or love can only come when you have felt love for yourself for that experience and recognised that you suffered and hence why it is important to work through thoroughly what you went through in this experience and why step 2 is often returned to a few times before step 3 can be started.

Step 4a – In the finding of love for yourself and any others involved in this experience it's time now to create some new Truths. These are often automatically created in a moment of shear relief or tears of love from the new understanding. But it is also good to reaffirm the new understanding in a stated Truth or set of Truths that you can if need be refer back to later, or that can be applied to other experiences that you are looking to release Low Vibration for. The creation of this Truth then gets applied to that experience as well as other experiences after that event which fall into the same Subconscious Mind Vortex group (ie. memories grouped into what your mind considers other relevant experiences). This is why we always look to release the key initial experiences from your past suffering because in doing so you can apply the same Truth to all other experiences held in your Subconscious Mind for that Vortex Group that occurred after that event, all the way up to the present day.

Step 4b - It's in the undertaking of understanding a number of past experiences and the releasing of Low Vibration that you eventually end up having created enough Truths that allow you to then create 'Journey Level' Truths. These are the Truths that can be applied to most of your past experiences and memories and therefore can literally supersize The

Releasing Process for you. These Truths detail how you accept that everything that has happened to you was all meant to be and, that it was all part of your growth and how all you need to do is heal from the experiences. These Truths connect you to the understanding that nothing was your fault and that nothing was anybody else's fault and that you allow God to take the blame for the past. This is not something you could do in the early stages, even if you desperately wanted to, as it takes you to have analysed, understood and let go of many of your painful past experiences to be able to create these Journey Level Truths. When you have reached this stage though, something magical happens. Whilst it could be said that step 4a could be done by yourself or with counselling, 4b is only something that could be achieved through your Higher Self. At this 4b stage you can undertake Emotionally Led, rather than Experience Led releasing. Your Higher Self will link you to Low Vibrational Emotions that you have felt many times over in a number of different experiences in your life. There will be a general theme, for example issues with your family or problems with work colleagues or friends or in relationships.

Your Higher Self will link you, and make you feel a core set of Low Vibrational Emotions that you have felt in these general scenarios, and then he or she will ask you to link to one or several of your Journey Truths in order that you can set the intention to apply those Truths to those Emotions linked to the general experiences.

Your Higher Self then applies those Truths to ALL remaining and relevant memories in your Subconscious Mind that need to be relabelled from Fear to Love and also to release the

Egoic Resistance if it applies. Consider that when you release using the Experience Led approach you can only apply the new Truth that you create for that experience to those other experiences that fall in the same Subconscious Mind Vortex Group, and whilst there could be hundreds of thousands of memories in that Vortex Group you also hold hundreds of different Vortex Groups in your Subconscious Mind. Therefore you literally have tens of millions of memories in your Subconscious Mind and trying to address all of these would be impossible using the Experience Led approach only (step 4a).

So, step 4b is literally like a silver bullet for you because when you release using the Emotion Led approach you apply the Truths against Subconscious Mind Vortex Groups that hold loosely similar experiences and related Emotions, and in doing so relabel everything that the Truth applies to. After this you can find yourself in the most amazing place of FEELING GOOD very shortly after step 4b is complete and this will help you take huge strides towards addressing the auto generation of Low Vibration, otherwise known as your Dripping Tap of Emotions that we have referenced in this book.

Note that the strength of your Truths is key here and so it may take a few attempts to start to tighten those Dripping Taps of Emotion. When you relabel a Subconscious Mind memory from fear to love the mind still keeps a record of how much fear was held with that memory; we call this the Archive Memory Marker. Think of this Archive Memory Marker as recording a scale of how much fear (or love) you held for that memory and each time you apply your new

Truth to it, the scale of fear reduces. (Note the Truths will not get applied to memories that have always been love labelled and therefore the Archive Memory Markers for these memories are unchanged also). Until the fear scale completely goes you will continue to generate Low Vibration each time you recall the memory. Step 4a will therefore continue whilst you grow the strength of your Truths and then reapply those Truths to the Archive Memory Marker of the relabelled memories. See this as a continuous cycle whereby you strengthen Truths, apply them to the Archive Memory Markers of your memories, and in doing so you start to feel better and accordingly are able to create stronger Truths to then reapply using Emotional Led releasing, to the memories with Archive Memory Markers not yet fully cleared down.

Note that Emotional Led releasing requires you to be connected to your Emotional Body and hence why your Higher Self will link you to general experiences and feelings when doing this. Unfortunately it's not a simple case of getting super strong Truth Buckets and then generally applying these Truths to all memories.

Step 5 – Let go! Simple advice but if you've had a life that has continuously led you to yearn for pain, sorrow or love it will be hard to do this. Your habitual way of being even after the creation of all of the new Truths will be heavily influenced by your Subconscious Mind. The new you, the Changed you, will be desperate to escape this and this stage may be frustrating for some of you as it's likely you will remain in the Resistant Mind State even with all of your memories relabelled to love and Egoic Resistance removed.

The way to freedom from this is in the shifting to the Expectant Subconscious Mind State and so you will need to ACT as the new you, always. You will need to stop the yearning back to the pain which has been an addiction for you. Allowing yourself in every moment to not give a moment's thought to anything from the past that happens to pop up can be challenging as well as tiring as it represents a whole new way of living. But over time things will start to shift and as you act in this new way, the High Vibration that you generate can be added to your new Truths. This is the best and quickest way to increase the strength of your Truths and it's so easily done. Simply ask your Higher Self to add the FEELING you generate to your Truth Bucket (see next section for clarity on Truth Buckets).

The Standard Truth creation approach that we have detailed in the next sections is a great way at this stage to manage the Transitional Low Vibration that is habitually being triggered by the Subconscious Mind as part of the Dripping Tap of Emotions. This Standard Truth calls on all existing Truths that you have created and is another good influence on the Archive Memory Markers.

We then recommend that after a while of doing this work to reduce the Archive Memory Markers, that you create a new very simple Truth that will support all other Truths. Call this Truth 'Moving On' and in this Truth state "I no longer wish to connect to the past. I've moved on. Connection to the past doesn't serve me, in fact it is stopping from becoming who I am. I allow myself to move forward now, I allow myself to be excited about the future and I allow myself to live my life with freedom". With this Truth created, now call it in your mind every time you feel you are connected to something that creates Transitional Low Vibration. This period becomes the time when you MUST act your new Truths. Each and every time you do so ask your Higher Self to add relevant High Vibrational FEELINGS into the 'Moving On' Truth, and other relevant Bucket Truths that you have created. Over time your Subconscious Mind will start to listen and the remaining memories with Archive Memory Markers that still show fear on the scale will start to diminish. And as this happens more and more memories and Vortex Groups will be shifted 'in blocks' and bring you closer to the Expectant Mind State.

The other key Truth Bucket at this stage is your Truth around the past. Often at this final stage your Subconscious Mind will continue to generate Level 2 Journey Emotions based on old patterns. So you will continue to feel anger, lack of trust, guilt etc. about the past. See this as a sign that your Truths need to be strengthened. It's a case of connecting to the understanding of how you, and others acted in the past were based on difficult and perhaps at times, horrific experiences and that your reactions to these were normal and that anyone else would have done the same, or worse. It's also about recognising that now you have reached this stage in your Awakening and of The Releasing Process, that you understand why you and others reacted in that way. Also, and more importantly, acknowledging that you have actually done something about it and Changed and have continued to live by this Change and shown courage in doing so and not reverted back to old reactions. There is so much influence on your Subconscious Mind in this understanding, and it is a strong Truth to also acknowledge as part of your Self-Love Truth Bucket. Keep showing to yourself that you act your Change and your Truths at each and every opportunity that comes to prove this and you will trigger the acceptance from the Subconscious Mind.

Eventually there will be no need to call your Bucket Truths too often and instead just the continual act of living out your life as the new you, the Changed you, is all that is required to shift the Subconscious to the Expectant Mind State. Look out for the habitual patterns of the Conscious Mind that trigger the Subconscious Mind whenever things get a little tough, or when you become frustrated that this process is not going as fast as you wish it to be. Just know that the pace at which you move through The Releasing Process is down to your allowing of it and your continual Alignment to your new Truths. The moment your Conscious and Subconscious mind see familiar old patterns of behaviour from you the Low Vibration will be triggered.

Also note that once the Archive Memory Markers have been cleared down for your memories, if you are still conflicting in any way against the Truths that you have used to clear these down, your Subconscious Mind will continue to hold you in the Resistant Mind State for periods. The period of time depends on how many memories you have that are related to Truths that you are conflicting against. This is a key point to note as it is the conflicts with these specific Truths that will stop you from consistently achieving the Expectant Mind State. Your Subconscious Mind, regardless of the fully cleared Archive Memory Markers will not believe your Change and hence you will not be able to move on. If you slip into the

Psychotic Mind State at all during this phase then the Low Vibration triggered by your Subconscious Mind will be the maximum that you would have ever felt for that memory, even if you've fully cleared down the Archive Memory Marker scales. And so note that you may feel as bad at times as when you first started your Awakening because of this.

What we've detailed here in these five steps to freedom could not be achieved by any other means available on this planet and the way you will feel at the end of this process if you have the courage to see it through is indescribable.

REMOVING EGOIC BLOCKS TO THE INNER BEING

FEELSET TOOLS

When relabelling memories from fear to love as part of The Releasing Process, if done in a Mind State of High Vibration then any Egoic Blocks that are in place for that experience and its related memories will automatically be released.

Unfortunately, at times the process of connecting back to past memories can be a little unsettling and therefore often when we form a new understanding and generate a new Truth from it, we can be in a Mind State of Low Vibration. In this instance, whilst the memory will relabel to love, the Egoic Block to the Inner Being remains. As we now know this will ensure that Low Vibration will still be generated for those relabelled memories, even if the Archive Memory Markers are clear of fear.

So, the best practice advice is always release Low Vibration and relabel with love, as part of The Releasing Process. For those instances where this has not been possible follow this guidance:

Step 1 – Find Balance by calling Universal Laws and/or triggering your Vortexes of Emotion

Step 2 - Recall the experience that holds the memories that you have relabelled. Connect to and FEEL one of the Emotions that you felt in the past over this experience.

Step 3 – Generate a High Vibrational Emotion within your Emotional Body and whilst holding that energy state the name of the Truth or Truth Bucket that holds the understanding that allowed you to relabel the memory to love in your original release and set the intention with your Higher Self to release the Egoic Block.

Step 4 – Feel the acknowledgement of this in your Truth Vortex of Emotion

Repeat steps 2, 3 and 4 for each Emotion linked to that experience.

CREATION OF TRUTHS AND THEIR CORRECT USAGE FOR RELEASING LOW VIBRATION

FEELSET TOOLS

A Truth can be created automatically as part of The Releasing Process or just when you have experienced a wonderful moment. These Truths are felt and therefore are a fully valid Truth in The Law of Truth. What we are describing in this section is the manual creation of Truths which can be used as part of your ongoing management of your Stored and Transitional Vibrations.

CREATING MANUAL TRUTHS AND A TRUTH BUCKET FOR EXPERIENCE LED RELEASING OF STORED AND TRANSITIONAL LOW VIBRATION

Once a past experience is understood and the Emotional energy has been released for the related memories in the Subconscious Mind Vortex Group it is good practice to then generate a manual Truth to capture what has been understood. This manually created Truth will form part of larger 'Truth Buckets' which are amalgamated Truths which can be referred to later to release Low Vibration for other past experiences that the Truth Bucket is also relevant for. This speeds up The Releasing Process for both Experience Led and Emotional Led releasing.

A scenario where you no longer feel hatred towards a friend called David from your childhood that hurt you, could also be applied to experiences later in life that you may wish to release. You now will have understood the reasons why in their disconnected state they did things that generated in you Low Vibration and are therefore to put in place the following potential Truths:

1. "I Allow myself to no longer feel judged by my friend David"

2. "I understand that he did not deliberately wish to make me feel unworthy"

3. "The Truth Is I let go of the anger and hatred from those experiences with him"

4. "I recognise these experiences created fears in me that have affected my relationships with other friends and well as family members and work colleagues and I Desire to let go of the Low Vibration for any similar experiences where I have felt judged and unworthy with other friends, family members of work colleagues"

Note three key statements here: I Allow, I Desire, The Truth Is.

These three statements have differing strengths in terms of Truth creation, and as such will not always be possible to be added to a Truth depending on the resistance to them.

For example saying "I Allow myself to feel loved" is much easier to commit to than saying "The Truth Is I am loved". If you are just starting out on your Awakening Journey and have not released too many of your past experiences and relabelled them to love, you may struggle to FEEL the words 'The Truth Is' and therefore you will not be able to create this Truth. This is why using 'I Allow' is a good way to start the creation of your Truth statements as these can generally be FELT. Think of the statement 'I Desire' as being somewhere in the middle of 'I Allow' and 'The Truth Is'.

To Create Your Truths:

Step1 - Say out loud or to yourself with the intention given to your Higher Self of creating a Truth for statements 1 to 4 above and in doing so ensure you feel your Truth Vortex of Emotion trigger when you have completed each sentence. At this point you have now created four single Truths.

Step 2 – Set an intention with your Higher Self to create a Truth Bucket called 'Friends and Family' and ask your Higher Self to add the four single Truths above into the overall Truth Bucket called Friends and Family. Ensure you feel your Truth Vortex of Emotion after stating this. You have now created the Truth Bucket 'Friends and Family' which contain the four single Truths.

You can create any number of new Truths at this point and add them to the Friends and Family Truth simply by following Step 1 and asking your Higher Self to add them to that Truth Bucket. If you wish to add the new Truths to a different Truth Bucket simply follow Step 2 and Change the name of the Truth Bucket that you reference. You can also have single Truths placed in multiple Truth Buckets, as well as place Truth Buckets into other Truth Buckets to have an overarching Truth Bucket. Your Higher Self will guide you on this so please do not feel overwhelmed at the thought of managing this.

Going back to the example of your friend David, you have now created four individual Truths which are relevant to an experience with your past friend David and one that can also be more broadly applied to other friends, family or work colleagues. You have also created a general Truth called Friends and Family which can be referred to when releasing other experiences that are relevant to the same understanding. Now in reality, the contents of these Truths would not be sufficient to release too many of your past experiences but over time through a number of different Experience Led releases you will build a large portfolio of new and broader individual Truths as well as new Bucket Truths with multiple experiences and Low Vibrational Emotions Aligned to them. As your Truth Buckets become more in depth and rich with individual Truths and understanding, they will become more and more valuable to you in the overall Releasing Process.

USING TRUTH BUCKETS FOR EMOTION LED RELEASING OF STORED AND TRANSITIONAL LOW VIBRATION

If you can create the following Truth you are ready for Emotion led releasing:

"I do not blame myself or anyone else for anything that has happened to me that has caused me to suffer. I also do not blame myself or anyone else for anything that has happened to others that has caused those others to suffer as a result of something that I or anyone else may have done. Because he asks it of me, I allow God to take the blame for any suffering that has happened to me or anyone else. I do not blame God for taking the blame. I understand that God has asked this of me for allowing him to accept all that was requested by me in my Soul Contract."

For the purposes of this chapter let's assume this Truth detailed in this way is called 'All Blame'.

A strong statement and critical if you are to be able to truly let going of EVERYTHING from your past. This Truth is possible and comes from a place of self-love for your Journey and all that has occurred in it and will have been built up by a series of Truths created from experience led releasing.

Step 4b of The Releasing Process chapter in this section talks of a silver bullet and this comes from the generation of this broad Truth about blame for your Journey. With this in place you are now able to either state an Emotion, or better still, feel a series of Emotions that link to a general scenario, and then apply them to the Truth of 'All Blame' as well as your other STRONG series of Truths. Here are some examples of Emotion led releasing usage:

Stated Emotion Releasing – SAY, THINK or FEEL the following:

"For experiences where I have been with people and felt judgement, anger, fear, hate, confusion apply all Truths" (ensure your Truth Vortex of Emotion is acknowledged afterwards).

What happens upon the acknowledgement of your Truth Vortex of Emotion is that your Higher Self will apply all of your Truth Buckets to ALL Subconscious Mind Vortex Groups experiences where you have felt the stated Emotions in situations where you have been with people. This is pretty general and therefore catches so many of your life experiences, but there will be other experiences where you will need to be more specific. Again, do not become overwhelmed in managing this as your Higher Self takes the lead with this and will direct you to the experiences that you need to address.

By applying your Truth buckets to the memories in this way you address the Subconscious Mind Archive Memory Markers for those relevant memories and tackle the Dripping Tap of Emotions. For those memories created in the Resistant Mind State there is a chance that if your Truths are strong enough that you will stop any further generation of Low Vibration for those memories, and indeed for any new experiences that the Subconscious Mind links to those memories. Those memories that were created in the Psychotic Mind State may require further addressing through stronger Truths, in order to fully remove the fear scale on the Archive Memory Marker.

The updating of the Archive Memory Marker is done in a matter of seconds. In the full clearing down of the Archive Memory Marker you release ALL the Low Vibration in your Stored and Transitional Vibration that is linked to those memories. Note that your new Truths will positively impact all memories in the related Subconscious Mind Vortex Groups, and not just the memories that you are focussed on. However, as these related Vortex Group memories will potentially have different values on the Archive Memory Marker they will obviously be cleared down at different rates. This means that some related memories will need to be readdressed and therefore you will need to continue strengthening your Truths.

This is all done without the need for detailed analysis of an experience that can take hours or even days at times with the experience led releasing approach. Of course, for those Archive Memory Markers that still have a level of fear on the scale, you will still continue to generate new Low Vibration into your Transitional Vibration.

The power of the Truth 'All Blame' is what allows this process to really gain momentum and then with the wonder of the connection to your Higher Self being able to, over a relatively short time period, manually apply this across millions of memories. You can see why we say this is a silver bullet.

Once at this stage you truly are on the road to Emotional freedom and step 5 of The Releasing Process beckons you at this point. So the advice is to get through as many Experience Led releases as you can as quickly as you can and get yourself in a position to create the Truth of 'All Blame' as soon as possible.

ADDING HIGH VIBRATIONAL FEELINGS TO A TRUTH BUCKET

In the same way that your Higher Self can capture a set of Low Vibrational feelings that you feel or have felt, they can also capture the High Vibration that you generate. As previously discussed this is an excellent way of strengthening your Truths. The Subconscious Mind values the strength of a Truth on its content. It is very easy once you have been on the trail of releasing for a few weeks or even months to get a little regimented about how you create your Truths and therefore the feelings applied when creating a Truth are often less than when you first started the process. The Subconscious Mind is more easily trained or influenced by a stronger Truth and therefore when you feel High Vibrational be sure to capture it and ask your Higher Self to apply it to a Truth Bucket. You can be fairly certain that most of your High Vibrational experiences could be matched to a relevant Truth Bucket so try and ensure that you capture as many good feelings as you can for this purpose.

GENERATING A STANDARD TRUTH TO RELEASE TRANSITIONAL LOW VIBRATION GENERATED IN SPECIFIC SCENARIOS

This exercise is for those of you at the point in The Releasing Process where you have started to release Stored and/or Transitional Low Vibration by following steps 1 to 4a, and have therefore Changed a number of Fear Labelled memories to Love Labelled memories in your Subconscious Mind through the creation of new Truths.

This Standard Truth is specifically set up in order to tackle Transitional Low Vibration that you experience in the moment or which could be created in the future. The Standard Truth will not allow you to tackle any existing 'Stored' Low Vibration. The process for removing Stored Low Vibration has already been stated in the steps documented in the section named 'The Releasing Process'.

The idea behind this is to create a single 'Standard Truth Template' which has variables that can be applied, linked to any experience. The Standard Truth Template simply states in it those Emotions that you DO NOT wish to feel for any stated experience, as well as the Emotions that you DO wish to feel. This Standard Truth Template will only work if you have sufficient Bucket Truths to Align it to, and with sufficient strength to address the Low Vibration created in the moment of an experience you are applying as the variable. So if you are trying to create the Standard Truth Template for an experience you have yet to relabel the memories in the Subconscious Mind memory to love for, and indeed have no Truth in place for, then there will be no impact in terms of releasing any Transitional Low Vibration, although you will still generate any High Vibration that has been stated in the Standard Truth Template.

Note that you only ever have ONE version of Standard Truth template, and it is the variables i.e. the various experiences that you apply to the Standard Truth Template, that you have multiples of.

The Standard Truth Template addresses experiences that trigger Low Vibration for memories that have been relabelled from fear to love but that still have fear levels for the Archive Memory Markers. It is possible that as you go through the Releasing Process you will be adding to Truth Buckets but not necessarily instantly reapplying them to memories in order to reduce Archive Memory Marker fear levels, hence why Low Vibration can still be generated when potentially your Truths Buckets are strong enough to clear down some or all of the fear levels in the Archive Memory Markers. The Standard Truth process is put in place to ensure less, or no Transitional Low Vibration is generated in the future for an experience by applying the latest version of your Truth Buckets to the stated variable aligned to the Emotions you do and don't want to hold as stated in the Standard Truth Template (all managed by your Higher Self). It also releases the Transitional Vibration held for that same variable if tackled in the moment. How much Transitional Low Vibration it releases will be dependant on the strength of your Truth Buckets. As stated it will ALWAYS generate High Vibration for that experience as detailed in your Standard Truth Template.

Know that this is a little complex to setup but very simple to use once in place and is an essential part of managing your Transitional Vibration. As always, your Higher Self will guide you through this.

Step 1 - Ask your Higher Self to generate the Standard Truth Template and ask him or her to always apply the latest version of all your Truths to any variables applied to this Standard Truth Template.

Step 2 - Ask your Higher Self the following:

"When I call the Standard Truth I no longer wish to feel 'X', and instead I wish to feel 'Y'"

You do not say the letters 'X' or 'Y' but instead state what Emotions that you wish to no longer feel (X), or do wish to feel (Y). For 'X' you should be Aligning to the standard set of Low Vibrational Emotions and States of Being that you have been finding you have been releasing or feeling the most of. For 'Y' you should apply those High Vibrational Emotions or States of Being that you generally would like to feel when applying the Standard Truth Template. Here are some examples:

Emotions:

X – doom, evil, hatred, anger, fear of death, fear of loss, fear of judgement, sadness, sickening, depravity, debauchery, shock, despair, self-pity, doubt, worry, anxiety, nervousness, lack of hope, lack of love, loss of trust, loss of faith

Y – calm, peace, joy, wonder, enlightenment, self-love, love, hope, truth, faith, strength, certainty, stability, safety, trust, allow-love, expectancy

States of Being:

X - Insanity, Hysteria, Isolation

Y - Masterful, Ecstatic, Inspiring

Note that your Higher Self will know which Emotions link to the States of Being so there is no need for you to break them out. Later publications will detail more information on States of Being and the Emotions attached to them.

You can add or remove anything from the Standard Truth Template at any point. It is good practice that you ask your Higher Self to apply any changes retrospectively after making any amendments to the Standard Truth Template as you may hold some Transitional Low Vibration from a previous experience that would not have been previously removed due to the fact that the Low Vibration that you still hold would not have been referenced in the Standard Truth Template.

Step 3 - Once the Emotions and States of Being are stated, ensure that you receive confirmation that the Emotions have been added to the Standard Truth Template by feeling the trigger in your Truth Vortex of Emotion.

Step 4 - At this point the Standard Truth Template has been created and you are free to apply variables to it. Example variables could be "when I am eating cake", "when I go to visit my parents", "when I go to the supermarket" and you will be led as to which variables to use by the Low Vibration you feel during an experience. To apply the variable, the wording "I allow" tackles the Low Vibration you have created for that experience in the moment, and the wording "I desire" tackles the next time you feel Low Vibration for that experience. So, for example, if you feel fear or guilt or anger or any other Low Vibration when eating cake you can apply that experience as a variable to the Standard Truth Template by saying:

"When I eat cake, I Allow and Desire the Standard Truth to be applied"

What you are doing here is saying that when you eat cake you no longer wish to feel Low Vibrations 'X' and instead you wish to feel High Vibrations 'Y'. The reference to 'allow' immediately releases the Transitional Low Vibration created in the moment after the subsequent creation of the Standard Truth Template for that experience. The reference to 'desire' releases the Transitional Low Vibration for that experience each and every time it next occurs. The High Vibration referenced is also generated, both at the point of applying the variable of 'eating cake' to the Standard Truth Template, as well as for all times in the future that the variable is triggered.

Once you state the variable using the "I allow and desire" command set, your Higher Self will then apply that variable to the Standard Truth Template and accordingly look to remove some or all of the Transitional Low Vibration generated when cake is eaten, based on the levels of the Archive Memory Marker within the Vortex Group that holds the related memories to eating cake. So if the Archive Memory Marker is below fifty percent, all of the Transitional

Low Vibration linked to eating cake will be removed. If the Archive Memory Marker is above fifty percent then the Transitional Low Vibration that gets released is based on a sliding scale correlating to how much of the Archive Memory Marker has been reduced. If none of Archive Memory Marker fear level has been reduced then no Transitional Low Vibration will be released and hence why we make reference to this process not working if your Truths are not strong enough, as it is the strength of your Truths that influences the Archive Memory Markers. As stated, if your Truths are not strong enough then the only action your Higher Self will take will be to generate the High Vibration you have stated in the Standard Truth Template (your 'Y' Emotions).

The variables you use against the Standard Truth Template can be as general or specific as you wish and your Higher Self will always guide you on this with regards to exactly what you should specify in order to Align to whatever Low Vibrational experience you are trying to address.

CREATING VARIABLES FOR THE STANDARD TRUTH FROM IN THE MOMENT FEELINGS

Know that you can also use this Standard Truth Template approach when you have a Low Vibrational FEELING. So rather than specifying the variable in words, instead you can ask your Higher Self when you feel a Low Vibration in the moment, that they add the related experiences attached to that feeling or feelings as a variable to the Standard Truth Template. This is an extremely powerful method to use as it ensures that you add as variables the full set of experiences, held as memories in your Subconscious Mind, attached to those feelings that were felt in the moment. If you were to try to work out which experiences a Low Vibrational set of feelings relate to in order to verbalise the variable statement it would be almost impossible, so we recommend the feeling led approach for your variables capture. Please note you are not asking your Higher Self to add the Low Vibration you feel into the 'X' column but simply the experience linked to that Low Vibration as a variable.

TRIGGERING THE VORTEXES OF EMOTION WITH TRUTHS

The Emotion within us can be generated by so many different and wonderful experiences but we have a way here for you to generate any High Vibration that you wish at any moment in time. It involves the generation of a Truth which when called it sets an intention with your Higher Self to trigger that Truth and the contents of it.

To create a Truth called Joy – Say the following to yourself or out loud and then ensure that you feel your Truth Vortex engage to confirm Truth Joy has been created:

"When I call the Truth of Joy I allow myself to feel joy"

Now say the word joy to yourself and you will feel the Emotion of joy.

It is also possible to create a Truth to generate multiple High Vibrational Emotions as follows:

To create a Truth called Calm - Say the following to yourself or out loud and then ensure that you feel your Truth Vortex engage to confirm Truth Calm has been created:

"When I call the Truth of Calm I allow myself to feel the Emotions of calm, peace, self-love, safety.

Now say the word calm to yourself and you will feel all of these Emotions at once.

83

REBALANCING NEGATIVE EMOTIONS USING POSITIVE VORTEX EMOTIONS

FEELSET TOOLS

You can look to counter the feelings of Low Vibration in your Transitional Vibration by breaking down the primary Vortexes of Emotions that you are feeling and then generating the opposite Vortex Emotions.

Example: Assume anger is being continuously generated in you also creating a sense of overwhelm

Step 1: - Anger = lack of love + lack of hope + truth (the truth relates to why you feel anger)

Using the Truth creation approach generate the Emotion of positivity (positivity = love + hope)

Step 2: – Overwhelm = lack of trust + lack of love + lack of hope + truth (the truth relates to why you feel overwhelmed)

OLIVIA & RAF OCAÑA

Using the Truth creation approach generate the Emotion of certainty (certainty = trust + love + hope)

84

I FEAR PROCESS

FEELSET TOOLS

Through reading this book, you truly now can connect to why you may often find yourself in a predominant state of Fear. Why things can be going great, then all of a sudden, things just trigger and you find they aren't so great and sometimes you don't even really know why.

If you have been connecting with your Higher Self and tried The Releasing Process, you will be more in tune with some of those Emotions that are being generated within you, some of the reasons why these Fear Emotions are being created.

There are times when you have a more general feeling that you can't get to the bottom of. Perhaps you have a general feeling of judgement, you know that you have experienced this through your life but you just can't get to it. Yet the overall feeling of judgement is being brought forth to you by your Higher Self, your awareness of it is heightened and you really do want to understand it better.

This process allows you to understand more about how you feel, to get you to a broader perspective of this Emotion or this situation and then work with your Higher Self to release not only the Emotion but get to understand more about the experiences that this Emotion relates too and also create some new Truths about you, who you are now.

Step 1: Connect with your Higher Self using the connection process and set the expectation that you will work through this into a deeper understanding to allow you to release faster and get underneath some of these experiences

Step 2: Sit quietly with a pen and paper or laptop/voice recorder

Step 3: Say out loud I Fear...and then allow yourself to say whatever it is. Keep going, keep saying I Fear, and do a good four or five in a row sometimes a few more but notice if the Fear is ramping up too much or you are starting to feel overwhelmed. This really helps you best if you can say it out loud but also do write it down as you go.

Step 4: Balance. Take a moment to be easy with yourself and to allow yourself to Balance. You may at this point be able to reflect quickly on what you have already said I Fear... to and create a new Truth. Often, your fears will come together as grouped items and this is why it is really beneficial to ensure that you pause from time to time through this process and allow yourself just to reflect and act by creating a new Truth.

Step 5: Once you have created either one new Truth or perhaps a series of Truths, allow Love in the moment, love for yourself, love for your Journey, love for your courage that you have shown in the discovery of how you feel, love that you know what to do about it in the moment. You can do this by feeling into your Love Vortex and Allowing that love to pour into you. This will also help with the Subconscious Mind Labelling in the moment, in particular if you start releasing too because the Truths will start to shift out Low Vibration also.

Step 6: Continue to keep going through I Fear...steps 3-5 until you feel that there are no longer any Fears accessible to you relating to this Emotion or general feeling

We will use the Emotion Judgement as a way to show you how this can be stepped through. Note that this is very personal to you and although perhaps one or two of these will resonate, don't just emulate this example but step through yourself with how you feel.

Some initial Fear examples on judgement...

"I fear that I am judged by my family"

"I fear that I am judged by my husband/wife/partner"

"I fear that I am judged by my children"

"I fear that I am judged by my boss/work colleagues/clients"

"I fear that I also judge others"

Take a moment to Balance. Next, here are some example Truths that you could create at this stage:

"The Truth is that I have been judged in the past but the Truth is that isn't their fault and it also isn't my fault either"

"The Truth is that I don't blame them anymore for judging me and I don't blame myself for being judged"

Note: Here is a good example of one where you may feel conflict, so you can't create the Truth, because you do potentially still blame 'them' for judging you still or you judge yourself for what you did at the time. This is when you can highlight this and delve deeper into some experiences with your Higher Self as you go through The Releasing Process

The Truth is I don't allow other people's negative opinion of me to stop me from being me

The Truth is it doesn't matter what anyone else thinks of me, I don't need their approval

The Truth is, I have judged others too in the past, but I allow the Change in me, that I don't wish to judge others

Allow love for yourself.

Then, keep going on the I Fear...

"I fear that people don't see the real me"

"I fear that I am not able to be successful"

"I fear that things don't work out for me"

"I fear that I will always be judged"

"I fear that I am not good enough"

Take a moment to Balance. Here are some further example Truths that you can create:

"I allow myself to feel love for myself instead of judgement"

"The Truth is that things do work out for me and have worked out for me many, many times"

"The Truth is that I have suffered and I allow love for myself because of it"

"The Truth is everything I have experienced to this point has helped me to grow"

Allow love for yourself.

Then, keep going on the I Fear...

"I fear that I will get in trouble for not being good enough"

"I fear that I will get hurt because I am judged"

"I fear that I can't be loved when I am judged"

"I fear that I keep getting it wrong"

"I fear that I can't trust myself"

"I fear that I can't trust others"

Reflect on your Truths, you may have already created some to satisfy the above Fears, try them and if you feel that there are others, then generate your own new Truths. Follow the remaining steps in the 'I Fear' process or revert to The Releasing Process to further explore this with your Higher Self.

CREATION OF ONE CLEAR DESIRE

FEELSET TOOLS

So very often we have so many desires, so many requests to the Universe, so many callings we are wanting to be satisfied. Then, when your current experience is still showing that this hasn't turned up yet, you start getting frustrated, impatient, apathetic, bored even, or fearful, anxious, worried and disappointed. Now you know so much about your Vibration, you can see how in the wanting, wanting, wanting you create one message and then with the not having, not having, not having you create yet another. Therefore, your point of attraction for those desires gets very confused, your Desire becomes unclear and either totally slows down, or gets diverted entirely. So what to do?

We wish for you to practice this very clear and specific way forward with your Desires. It may sound so simple when explained like this step by step, but so many are currently not enabling this simple approach because of either not being aware of it or by not being aware of their own Emotions and Vibration enough to know how to bring things forth much quicker.

Step 1: Pick *one* clear Desire, just one and one that you truly, truly Desire above the others that you feel can happen for you within the next couple of weeks. One that lights you up, one that makes you think 'YES! This is the Desire I want!'

Step 2: Create the Truth that you can have it! This is really important, because if it is an aspiration, that is not yet a Desire with a Truth, you must truly feel that you can have it in order to draw it to you. If you don't have the ability to create a Truth with your desires, you need to release some Egoic Blocks that you are holding, some Fears that you are holding relating to this. If this is the case you should refer to the Releasing Process and the Creation of Truths process, working with your Higher Self to do this

Step 3: Once you have a clear, clear Desire that you are able to create a Truth for, your job is to not let anything that you say, think or feel get in the way of you having it. This is where you help yourself by noticing if those thoughts such as 'why hasn't it turned up yet' or 'these things don't happen this easily for me' totally get in the way of you receiving your Desire, and if they rise up, you must not let them. You choose in the moment to be utterly vigilant and trust, trust in the having of it, trust yourself that it is on its way to you, reconfirm the Truth and feel it activate in your Truth Vortex

Step 4: Act. There will be actions associated in the receiving of your Desire and they may be small or bigger actions but regardless, you will also need to move. Say for example, your Desire is money based, but you don't buy the lottery ticket that you feel the impulse to or you don't create the offer for new clients that you feel inspired to do, well this just slows it down. The Laws will rearrange the Universe to find another way, but if you continue to not act, it just continues to slow it down. Do not confuse this advice with focussing on the 'how'. Don't assume the lottery ticket or the new client offer will be the way that money is brought to you, but that they do create a positive momentum that generates the High Vibrational energy required to attract money to you.

Step 5: Allow. By keeping your Vibration rock steady on this Desire, by not muddying it up by questioning it or you, by connecting to the Truth of the having of it, by acting on the impulses with Trust, you Allow it in. When you think of your Desire, just think, Allow and feel your Vortexes of Emotion Light UP! This will act like a Universal beacon.

Step 6: Celebrate! When your Desire turns up, the Universe loves nothing like a Vibrational Party, so Allow yourself to Celebrate what you have just Vibrationally Mastered and send a massive wave of appreciation through your body, one so great that your Higher Self reciprocates. Appreciation is so wonderful and the Universe will notice and your Vibration will just continue to be higher because of it, therefore when you start on your next One Clear Desire, you are Vibrationally already on your way!

Printed in Great Britain
by Amazon